Modernist Heresies

Modernist Heresies

British Literary History, 1883–1924

DAMON FRANKE

The Ohio State University Press
Columbus

Library of Congress Cataloging-in-Publication Data
Franke, Damon, 1968–
Modernist heresies : British literary history, 1883–1924 / Damon Franke.
    p. cm.
Includes bibliographical references and index.
ISBN-13: 978-0-8142-1074-1 (cloth : alk. paper)
ISBN-13: 978-0-8142-9151-1 (CD-ROM)
1. Modernism (Literature)—Great Britain. 2. English literature—20th century—History and criticism. 3. English literature—19th century—History and criticism. 4. Religion and literature—Great Britain—History—20th century. 5. Religion and literature—Great Britain—History—19th century. 6. Great Britain—Intellectual life—20th century. 7. Great Britain—Intellectual life—19th century. 8. Heretics, Christian—Great Britain—History. 9. Heresies, Christian, in literature. 10. Paganism in literature. I. Title.
PR478.M6F73 2008
820.9'112—dc22
                2007041909
This book is available in the following editions:
Cloth (ISBN 978-0-8142-1074-1)
CD-ROM (ISBN 978-0-8142-9151-1)

Cover design by DesignSmith.
Type set in Adobe Minion.
Printed by Thomson-Shore, Inc.

The paper used in this publication meets the minimum requirements of the American National Standard for Information Sciences—Permanence of Paper for Printed Library Materials. ANSI Z39.48–1992.

9 8 7 6 5 4 3 2 1

E quelli a me: "Qui son li eresïarche
con lor seguaci, d'ogne setta, e molto
più che non credi son le tombe carche."
—Dante, *The Inferno*

"These are the arch-heretics of all cults,
with all their followers," he replied. "Far more
than you would think lie stuffed into these vaults."
—Translated by John Ciardi

Contents

Illustrations

FIGURES

TABLE

Preface

WHAT FOLLOWS IS an intellectual history of the origins of British modernism. The nature of modernism constantly shifts, within its own purview, and within criticism, and this interdisciplinary study embraces such dynamic elusiveness. Aesthetic complexities abound, history is continuous and ruptured at once, and religious concerns, in their very nature, tend to mystify certainty. At the same time, this book is an attempt at a synthesis of the discursive history of modernism, and as such it addresses the modernists in the terms of their own ambitions. For in the late Victorian, Edwardian, and High Modernist times, intellectuals faced the dying belief in a totalizing synthesis of the world. Many fought against a plunge into incoherence and fragmentation in their attempts at universalizing theories or in their invention of substitute aesthetic devices. From the 1880s through the 1920s, the discursive exchange among artists, philosophers, and religious thinkers that initially sought to synthesize worldviews culminated in the pragmatic construction of modernist artificial or "synthetic" wholes. This is a story of the British modernists and a study of their work, and, even at a cursory glance, it raises the following questions: What do Virginia Woolf's notion of character and Walter Pater's curious interest in the *Mona Lisa* share? What does a cadre of renegade priests have in common with the control of language in George Orwell's *Nineteen Eighty-Four*? What sort of thread weaves together Joan of Arc, *The Golden Bough,* and the advent of New Criticism? What link, beyond a mere study of statistics, connects compulsory chapel attendance at Cambridge with Keynesian economic theory? The answer to each of these queries is, in a word, heresy. The claim may seem bold and tenuous at first, but this common denominator underpins a forgotten dimension of the origins of modernism, one deeply entrenched in Victorian blasphemy and the crisis in faith, and one pointing to the censorship of modernist literature and some of the first doctrines of literary criticism.

In April 1933, Hitler promulgated the policies of National Socialism, FDR was in the midst of the first hundred days of the New Deal, and T. S. Eliot traveled to the University of Virginia to deliver a series of lectures denouncing the modernist trend to insert the "diabolical" into literature. Though paltry in comparison to these worldly affairs, Eliot's lectures, which would be published as *After Strange Gods: A Primer of Modern Heresy* (1934), are not as disparate as they may seem. Each platform positioned itself as a corrective to unwanted turns in twentieth-century history. Eliot's self-righteous primer sought to teach readers how to discern whether an author wrote with a "proper" moral sense, and in such matters, he declared that "a spirit of excessive tolerance" was "to be deprecated" (20). April that year indeed was the cruelest month. For Eliot, orthodoxy could and should modernize tradition, which he claimed "implies a unity of religious background" and "makes any large-number of free-thinking Jews undesirable" (20). The next winter fed a little life to tolerance when the U.S. Congress repealed Prohibition, and Judge John Woolsey overturned the censorship, on obscenity charges, of James Joyce's *Ulysses* (1922).

Critics have handily debunked the intolerance, myopia, and anti-Semitism of Eliot's claims, and Eliot himself later disavowed many of the sentiments expressed in *After Strange Gods*. Nevertheless, the question remains: why would a major critic of the time frame modernist literature in terms of heresy? In answer, I find myself in accord with Eliot on three premises: religion is recurrently an important subject; heresy treats it as such; and scholars are responsible for confronting literary engagements with religion. At the same time, criticism handicaps itself if it assumes the rectitude of any orthodoxy and simply dismisses the opposition as wrong, or, as Eliot did, offers a sketchy and polemical moralization. In 1933, though, authoritarian answers won the day, and many modernists found themselves at the pulpit of prophecy, largely because for fifty years heretical discourses had confounded traditional accounts of the world. Part of Eliot's frustration with modernism arises from this and from the fact that he could only define heresy as "wrong" and a characteristic result of "an exceptionally acute perception, or profound insight, of some part of the truth" (26).

For purposes of this study, heresy should be understood, to quote the *OED*, both as "religious opinion or doctrine maintained in opposition . . . to that of any church, creed, or religious system, considered as orthodox," *and* "by extension, opinion or doctrine in philosophy, politics, art, etc., at variance with those generally accepted as authoritative." Since the modernists accentuated the use of religious images, concepts, and festivals in their art, heresy, for them, shuttled with ease between religion and aesthetics. Religion and philosophy, conversely, never can escape the poetics of language. Heresy from 1883 to 1924, therefore, should be understood liberally, in that it was both a common interdisciplinary discursive mode and a rallying cry for the general critique of establishmentarian positions. Etymologically, "heresy" means a "choice one makes" or a "school of thought," and a guiding principle for my investigations is to ask what happens when conflicting value systems or scholarly disciplines are placed in dialogue with each other.

While heresy usually arises over differing interpretations of scripture or doctrine, often the interdicted discourse eventually becomes tolerated or even made orthodox. From 1883 to 1924 (a utilitarian demarcation explained in the introductory chapter), the prominent modernist heresy involved an attempt to syncretize contradictory schools of thought in resolutions which would theoretically dissolve the distinction between orthodoxies and their contestation. Such a paradox saw synthesis itself become almost the *de rigueur* mode of transgression. Theory and criticism evolve through synthesis, and this study hopes to offer its own progressive dialectic of varying "schools of thought." By linking rigorous textual analysis with reception theory and the examination of interwoven cultural discourses, particularly those of the Cambridge Heretics Society, 1909–32, I argue that the literature and culture treated here reveal a modernist sensibility influenced by theological concerns yet committed to the liberation of the body, women's rights, and the concerns of "this world." Such a pluralistic view of the world is antithetical to the intransigence of orthodoxy. From 1883 to 1924, though, heretical discursive modes were still able to underwrite significant religious debates and literary dramatizations of religious questions. The heretical discourses discussed in what follows still teach us about the need and reward for encouraging and defending dissent, tolerance, and diversity.

My narrative of the Cambridge Heretics Society intersects with virtually all strands of modernist thought. Founded by C. K. Ogden at Cambridge University in 1909, the Heretics witnessed, until the Society's dissolution in 1932, an impressive and diverse set of lectures by scores of influential modernists. There are the philosophers, Bertrand Russell, G. E. Moore, James McTaggart, Ludwig Wittgenstein. John Maynard Keynes stood at the forefront of the Economics Section. Bernard Shaw was perhaps the most famous literary figure. Jane Harrison brought cultural anthropology into the fold. But if you were to name any famous modernist figure from W. B. Yeats to

E. M. Forster to F. T. Marinetti to Marie Stopes, it is remarkable how many were members of the Heretics or in dialogue with this group. This fascinating slice in time has been overlooked by criticism this far, and my discourse history of this discussion society draws connections between heresy and these major modernist figures, especially those associated with the Bloomsbury group. In particular, I examine how Lytton Strachey, Clive Bell, and Virginia Woolf used Moore's influential *Principia Ethica* (1903) to steer modernist thinkers toward aesthetics and away from social and political concerns. The history of the Heretics has been an untold story, and recuperating the work of the many famous modernist personalities involved in the group leads to a new genealogy of modernism and its champion, New Criticism. In fact, I. A. Richards and William Empson were Heretics, and this influence can be seen in their early works *Principles of Literary Criticism* (1925) and *Seven Types of Ambiguity* (1930). These were modernist primers of critical heresy, and Eliot had to respond with his treatise.

In illustrating the discursive continuities between 1883 and 1924 through my analysis of heresy, I am positioning *Modernist Heresies* against stratifying and reductive periodization of Victorianism and modernism by tracing the dialectic of heresy and orthodoxy, and the pragmatic shifting of both heterodox and authoritative discourses. From Captain Cuttle's refrain in Dickens' *Dombey and Son* (1848) "overhaul the catechism" (182ff.) to the self-reflexive dictum in Joyce's *Finnegans Wake* (1939) "Renove that bible" (579.10), proto-modernists and modernists made extensive renovations to religious thought without removing tradition. The many cultural and literary instances of heresy and synthesis establish continuities between Victorian blasphemy and modernist obscenity, and I show that the mode of heresy shifts over the course of this time from one of syncretism to one based on discretionary "choices." As Althusser and Jameson suggest, current literary history should strive to produce the "concept" of its object.

While I trace the same historical trajectory of heretical discourses in the two parts of *Modernist Heresies,* Part I focuses on cultural phenomena, and Part II on literary manifestations. The introduction foregrounds the construction and reading of heresy in modernist literature, the "synthetic" approach of the Edwardians, and the modernist development of works of art which were putatively self-contained "wholes." As an illustrative context for this study, a brief examination of the "modernist" crisis in the Catholic Church introduces the debates under consideration here and generates a suggestive set of implications for the literature of the period. The "modernist" clergymen had tried to reconcile Church doctrine with the results of nineteenth-century German higher criticism, the array of historical "Life of Jesus" studies, and evolutionary thought. To date, modernism has been the last heresy condemned by the Vatican, and in 1907 Pope Pius X in fact used a phrase emblematic of the historical context in denouncing modernism as "a synthesis of all heresies."

Part I considers the Cambridge Heretics Society as a cultural phenomenon, and examines the birth of the Heretics, the administrative work of C. K. Ogden, and several addresses given to the Society. Through an examination of the papers of major figures in the Society and of other archival material, I seek to provide a thorough account of the Heretics, and demonstrate that these artists, academics, and philosophers central to defining the intellectual climate of the time found in heresy an intellectual frame for their own activity. According to its regulations, the objective of the Heretics was "to promote discussion on problems of religion, philosophy, and art," and the members rejected "traditional a priori methods of approaching religious questions." As a history of the Heretics Society, my account moves from its humble epistolary inception after what was known as the "Prove All Things" controversy, to Woolf's dismissal of the Edwardians in her address "Mr. Bennett and Mrs. Brown," to Empson's presidency of the Heretics in 1928–29, when he began writing *Seven Types of Ambiguity* with what Christopher Norris describes as a "'heretic' outlook" (*Philosophy* 4). Originating in the Edwardian period, the discussions of the Heretics Society illustrate how the discourse surrounding heresy continued through the 1920s, the time of "High" Modernism in literature.

Beginning Part II, the fourth chapter discusses the historical reception of heresy while considering the debate between Shaw and G. K. Chesterton at the Heretics Society, Shaw's play *Saint Joan* (1924), and the figure of Giordano Bruno. In his play, Shaw draws on his address before the Heretics and recasts heresy as a positive value and claims that religion must eventually respond to an evolving world since he believes "the law of God is a law of change" (38). Shaw sees "the law of change" as underwritten by the gradual reception of heretics and other people he considers forward-minded thinkers and doers. The figure of Joan of Arc presents a unique composite illustrative of historical revaluation, for Joan is successively perceived as a hero, a heretic, and finally a saint. The hegemony of orthodoxy comes to the foreground in my discussion of the processes of canonization, rehabilitation, and accommodation used by the Catholic Church in its treatment of her. Additionally, in this chapter, I discuss Bruno's recuperation from 1883 to 1924 by scholars, writers, and Italian nationalists who saw him as a martyred

prophet of the synthetic agenda; the literary use of his pantheism as a means
to explore paganism; and the aesthetic development of his leading modernist
disciple, James Joyce.

Chapter 5 explores the prevalence of the heresy of syncretism in the
portrayal of paganism in late Victorian and Edwardian literature. As a common ideological structuring element, paganism arises in literature due to the
prominent historical sense cultivated by the modernist clergy, evolutionists,
and cultural anthropologists. The historical study of religion uncovered the
buried pagan past in much of Christianity, and literature by Walter Pater
and Thomas Hardy exploited this connection. Syncretic heresies require
paganism as a supplement and use it as a primary structuring device. As if
not wanting to be left out of the discussion, literary paganism undermines
orthodox interpretations and foregrounds competing visions of the world.
Chapter 6 begins with an examination of the place of religion in the development of English as a discipline. After a discussion of the appropriation of
I. A. Richards' heterodox ideas by New Criticism, I analyze D. H. Lawrence's
use of synthesis, simile, and the sublime to construct a heresy of the doctrine
of transfiguration in *The Rainbow* (1915). The chapter ends with a coda for
this literary history by sketching T. S. Eliot's and E. M. Forster's polarized
play with etymology in *The Waste Land* (1922) and *A Passage to India* (1924).
Linguistic roots become the site at which religious discourses are included or
excluded.

In the Afterword, I return to Ogden, the founder of the Heretics Society,
with a discussion of his development of Basic English, a universal language
he later espoused as a product of "orthology." After analyzing his translation
of an excerpt from *Finnegans Wake* into Basic, I relate Ogden's preoccupation
with eliminating ambiguity in language to its reflection in George Orwell's
Nineteen Eighty-Four (1949). Basic English and Orwell's Newspeak share
many similarities, and I read Orwell's dystopic novel and the "compendium
of all the heresies" within the book as a response to Ogden's orthodox turn
and as a statement on the continued need for heresy. What gradually comes
clear in this literary history is that the displacement of heresy into political
and linguistic realms also reflects the relative decline of heresy as a religious
issue.

Acknowledgments

SECTIONS OF CHAPTER 5 have been previously published in somewhat differ-ent form. "The 'Curious' Pagan Spirit of Pater's *The Renaissance*" appears in *Nineteenth-Century Prose* 31.1 (Spring 2004): 170–90; reprinted by permis-sion of Barry Tharaud, Editor and Publisher. "Hardy's Ur-Priestess and the Phases of a Novel" appears in *Studies in the Novel*, v. 39, no. 2, Summer 2007, copyright © 2007 by the University of North Texas; reprinted by permission of the publisher.

Virginia Woolf's letter of 22 August 1929 to Julian Trevelyan is repro-duced with permission of the Society of Authors as the Literary Representa-tive of the Estate of Virginia Woolf. Extracts from the Chawner papers are made with the permission of the Master and Fellows of Emmanuel College Cambridge. For permission to quote from other material, I thank the Mas-ter and Fellows of Trinity College Cambridge; the Syndics of Cambridge University Library, the Department of Special Collections; Young Library, University of California, Los Angeles; and the William Ready Division of Archives and Research Collections, McMaster University. The archivists at these libraries have been invaluable, and I am very grateful for their gracious assistance. Special thanks are due to Kathleen Garay and Carl Spadoni of McMaster University for their acuity and felicity since my first forays into the archives of the Heretics Society.

I am also in debt to the T. Anne Cleary, Frederick F. Seely, and Seashore Fellowships awarded by the English Department and Graduate College at the University of Iowa, which enabled me to do research at the various archives. This book would never have been written without the encourage-ment and intellectual stimulation of my mentors. Since undergraduate days, John Bishop has been an inspiration in both his teaching and his collegiality.

Adam Parkes has been a vital part of the growth of ideas for this work since its nascent stage. I have drawn much of my approach to literary analysis from Garrett Stewart whose advice and example in the classroom and on the page checked my excesses and steered my thought and my writing to more refined heights. Finally my greatest gratitude goes out to Florence Boos whose encouragement and advice kept me on task and secured my confidence in this project. Her scholarly and political insight has helped me mature as a critic and as a citizen. She read and edited every sentence in this book numerous times with such thorough attention that the book is hers too. The faults are my own.

I have greatly appreciated the support of my colleagues in the English Department at the University of Southern Mississippi. My research assistants, Jeff Pusch and Carrie Harper, were relentless in tracing down leads and verifying sources. I thank my students in courses that have discussed the texts and issues of this work; in particular Jordan Sanderson propelled my thoughts on Vaihinger and Lawrence. Jameela Lares kindly offered her home during my evacuation from Hurricane Katrina, and I was able to proceed with the project nearly uninterrupted. Kimio Steinberg and Rosa Maria Bosinelli also helped put a roof over my head during my fellowships. Certainly many of the historical figures in this book have inspired me with their creativity, courage, and resolve in confronting intransigent thought.

My sister Cara suggested possible images for the cover, and she remains the ideal general reader for whom I write. For their care, humor, and general enrichment over the years, I owe more than can be said here to Steve Schmidt, John Fielding, Erin Charles, Catherine Hollis, Kelli Lackett, Sarah Walz, Andy Tinkham, Gareth Downes, Barbara Gambini, John Pendell, Vickie Larsen, Mark Dowdy, Gustavo Oropeza, Marina Cacioppo, and John McDonald. I would finally like to thank my present editors at The Ohio State University Press, Sandy Crooms and Maggie Diehl, for their detailed attention to my work and for their guidance that saw it through its final stages.

Iowa City–Ravenna–New Orleans

Abbreviations

ARCHIVES

CUL   Department of Manuscripts and University Archives, Cambridge
University Library

ECA   Chawner Papers, Masters Class of Archives, Emmanuel College
Archives, Cambridge University

MCMA   C. K. Ogden Fonds, William Ready Division of Archives and
Research Collections, McMaster University, Hamilton, Ontario

TCL   Julian Trevelyan Papers, Trinity College Library, Cambridge University

UCLA   C. K. Ogden Papers, Department of Special Collections, Young
Research Library, University of California, Los Angeles

WORKS

AS   E. M. Forster. *Arctic Summer and Other Fiction*. Abinger Edition.
Vol. 9. Ed. Elizabeth Heine and Oliver Stallybrass. New York:
Holmes and Meier, 1981.

BR   Bertrand Russell. *The Collected Papers of Bertrand Russell*. 16
vols. to date. Ed. Kenneth Blackwell et al. Boston and London:
Allen and Unwin, 1983–.

CA   P. Sargant Florence. "Cambridge 1909–1919 and Its Aftermath."
C. K. Ogden: A Collective Memoir. Ed. P. Sargant Florence and
J. R. L. Anderson. London: Elek Pemberton, 1977. 13–55.

CF1   Virginia Woolf. "Character in Fiction." *The Essays of Virginia Woolf*, Appendix III. Ed. Andrew McNeillie. London: Hogarth Press, 1988. 502–17.

CF2   Virginia Woolf. "Character in Fiction." *The Essays of Virginia Woolf*. Ed. Andrew McNeillie. London: Hogarth Press, 1988. 420–38.

CH   P. Sargant Florence. "The Cambridge Heretics, 1909–1932." *The Humanist Outlook*. Ed. A. J. Ayer. London: Pemberton, 1968. 224–39.

GB   James Frazer, *The Golden Bough: A Study in Comparative Religion*. 2 vols. London: Macmillan, 1890.

GBA   James Frazer, *The Golden Bough: A Study in Magic and Religion*. Abr. ed. 1922. New York: Macmillan, 1951.

RF   Bernard Shaw. "The Religion of the Future." Cambridge: The Heretics, 1911.

SJ   A. M. Gibbs, ed. *Bernard Shaw*: Man and Superman *and* Saint Joan. London: Macmillan Education Ltd., 1992.

TCA   Don Cupitt. "The Chawner Affair." *Emmanuel College Magazine* 53 (1970–71): 5–11.

TCP   Don Cupitt. "The Chawner Pamphlet." *Emmanuel College Magazine* 54 (1971): 17–30.

WCL   W. C. Lubenow. *The Cambridge Apostles, 1820–1914: Liberalism, Imagination, and Friendship in British Intellectual and Professional Life*. Cambridge: Cambridge University Press, 1998.

Introduction

The Heretical Vintage
of Modernism

IN THOMAS HARDY'S last novel, *Jude the Obscure* (1895), when Jude Fawley
first acknowledges the complete frustration of his desire to matriculate at
university and become an Anglican minister, he recognizes himself to have
been a foolish dreamer, draws comparison to some poetic lines of Heinrich
Heine, and begins to see Christminster in a new light. He acutely feels the literal blindness of his first night there when, impassioned by the fruition of his
long-sought arrival, he caressed the contours of the buildings in the dark, as
if the city were his newfound Jerusalem. However, Jude's gradual disillusionment with his career prospects actually confirms his initial perception of the
university town in which it "seemed impossible that modern thought could
house itself in such decrepit and superseded chambers" (64). With the heavy
touch of Hardy's use of fate and fatalism, Jude also finds his cousin Sue in
Christminster, who consoles him by dismissively noting that the "intellect at
Christminster is new wine in old bottles" (120). As she uses the phrase from
Matthew to admonish academia "to put new wine into fresh skins" (9:17),
Sue at once condemns the university and indirectly reflects Hardy's narrative
desire to synthesize traditional and modern thought, the flesh and the spirit,
form and content.

Jude touched a nerve deeply rooted in the late Victorian consciousness,
and the issues the novel raised challenged orthodoxy on several levels and
elicited a general and vague fear of change. William E. Buckler points out
the influence of Matthew Arnold's thought on the novel, and he suggests that
Sue's biblical allusion recalls Arnold's essay on Heine, which had included the

1

same reference in a description of "the awakening of the modern spirit" and its revolt against archaic dogmas and customs:

> The want of correspondence between the forms of modern Europe and its spirit, between the new wine of the eighteenth and nineteenth centuries, and the old bottles of the eleventh and twelfth centuries, or even of the sixteenth and seventeenth, almost every one now perceives; it is no longer dangerous to affirm that this want of correspondence exists; people are even beginning to be shy of denying it. To remove this want of correspondence is beginning to be the settled endeavour of most persons of good sense (109).[1]

This attempt to harmonize form and content dominated the "modern spirit" from 1883 to 1924 and explicitly challenged orthodox tradition and custom. In a strategy similar to the writing praxis T. S. Eliot commends in "Tradition and the Individual Talent," a new religious discourse often will draw subversively on extant traditions and the resultant heresy will function as old wine in new bottles. Arguing that heresy is a configuration repeated in various fictions of modernism, *Modernist Heresies* illustrates that this interdicted discourse is a critical part of the modernist gestalt, preoccupying its thought and underwriting its forms. Modernism owes much of its legacy to the literary, religious, and academic heretics discussed herein.

Hardy's and Arnold's use of the enological metaphor speaks to the fermentation during these years of a ubiquitous methodological approach used by these self-styled heretics in developing a coherent historical sense of aesthetics and metaphysics. While confronting the developments in natural science, linguistics, and cultural anthropology, artists, clerics, and philosophers sought to advance humanitarian concerns without having to forsake the past. Sniffing to nose out what was age-worthy, the modernists opened everything they could find in the cellar of history. The questioning of the nature of tradition and orthodoxy (what exactly was the old cultural "wine"?) engendered the rise of various heresies as alternative options and led to large-scale repercussions in the modernist reinvention of tradition.

As the biblical passage suggests, the new cannot be funneled wholesale into the old, e.g., the "good news" of New Testament spirituality needed accommodating new ritual forms. Anglicanism perhaps is the grandest example of a religion changing its fundamental tenets while retaining old ritual forms. In the eyes of Roman Catholicism, Anglicanism is therefore a revolutionary heresy. Sue's diagnosis of Christminster reflects this result of the Reformation and parallels Cardinal Newman's implication during the

Oxford Movement that Anglicanism is an untenable form of new wine in old bottles. Amid the "spectres" of the Oxford Movement haunting the university, Sue recoils from the persistent stultifying effects of the Church of England. In making a variant recension of the New Testament, Sue manifests the religious preoccupation of the time by packaging an old spirituality in a new form. As she tells Jude of her "*new* New Testament," she made it "by cutting up all the Epistles and Gospels into separate *brochures*, and re-arranging them in chronological order as written." Sue maintains that "people have no right to falsify the Bible," and that reading her truer new version "afterwards made it twice as interesting as before, and twice as understandable" (121).

Similarly *Jude the Obscure* as a whole achieves a heresy that pushes subsequent literary experiments to attempt further syntheses that avoid both orthodoxy and a nihilistic avant-garde. In the novel, Hardy had discovered that collocating the dual Bildungsromans of Jude and Sue, with their oppositional trajectories, presented a formal suspension of the problem of time by using two mutually obliterating storylines to show how religious values change throughout history. Sue's conversion and Jude's fall emblematize two heretical and historical threads—the rise of Christianity out of pagan antiquity and the advent of modern secularization. The narrative tension between the two is like the "intellect in Christminster," one religious impulse "pushing one way," one "the other; and so they stand stock-still, like two rams butting each other" (120). However, the *ressentiment* fermenting in this "stock-still" narrative creates unstable readerly effects felt in the explosive reaction to the novel. Hardy could hold these inverse storylines in balance as two versions of historical teleology of different but equal merit, interest, and problematic effect; the readers of *Jude* could not abide the heretical implications.

New ways to synthesize oppositional modes of thought abound in literature of this period, but major critical works also employed a similar and more direct method. Balance is the keynote of Nietzsche's *The Birth of Tragedy* (1872) and its English counterpart, Arnold's "Hellenism and Hebraism" (1869). James Frazer's *The Golden Bough* (1890–1915), William James' *The Varieties of Religious Experience* (1902), and Emile Durkheim's *The Elementary Forms of the Religious Life* (1915) all sought to reconcile religious difference with a universalizing theory. T. S. Eliot's essays, "Tradition and the Individual Talent" (1919) and "*Ulysses*, Order and Myth" (1923) advocated a mode of writing that synthesized past and present by affirming tradition. Georg Lukacs' *The Theory of the Novel* (1915–16) points to Dostoevsky's fiction as a resolution of the oppositional and incomplete forms, abstract idealism and the romanticism of disillusionment, which plagued the genre since its progenitor, the epic, no longer corresponded to an integrated civilization. As Michael Levenson states in *A Genealogy of Modernism* (1984), "[o]ne of the most notable features of the period was the continuity between genres and between disciplines, the self-conscious attempt to construct a unified theory of modernity" (viii).

In varying significance, synthesis as an ideal became vital to various influential modernist schools of painting, economics, philosophy, drama, and literary criticism. As a reaction to the pointillism or divisionism of Seurat and his circle, Paul Gauguin, along with Emile Bernard, launched a school of "Synthesism" in art, before moving to Tahiti to paint primitivist themes often with Christian titles. In the preface to the catalog for the famous 1910–11 Post-Impressionist exhibit in London, Desmond MacCarthy explained that the "primitive art" of Cezanne, Gauguin, and Van Gogh seeks a pure self-expression in relating to the subject, one which can be hindered by devotion to representation. Therefore, these "Synthesists," a term which expresses "a quality underlying their diversity," "simplify the drawing and painting" and aim "at *synthesis* in design" (101). MacCarthy argues that this approach means that the artist "is prepared to subordinate consciously his power of representing the parts of his picture as plausibly as possible, to the expressiveness of the whole design" (101).

John Maynard Keynes, MacCarthy's fellow traveler in the Bloomsbury Group, founded his inductive approach to economic theory on synthetic a priori truths, synthetic in that substantive truths attach a predication beyond their simple expression. G. E. Moore's influential study of ideal "goods," *Principia Ethica* (1903), a Bloomsbury bible, championed a synthesis in human relations and the appreciation of art. In 1915, F. T. Marinetti called for a Futurist Synthetic Theater that would "compress into a few minutes, into a few words and gestures, innumerable situations, sensibilities, ideas, sensations, facts, and symbols" (124). As the action unfolds on a fixed and constant stage, a chaotic simultaneity putatively could convey the pulse of "life." During the 1920s, I. A. Richards developed a critical methodology for unpacking analogous complex relations within poetry that creates an "equilibrium of opposed impulses." For Richards, to organize reading literature by "synthesis" and "inclusion" widens the possibilities of experience, and "the experience of great poetry" can beget "moments of completed being." The heterogeneity of a synthetic, inclusive poem exposes "more facets of the mind" and lends itself to "ironic contemplation, "a characteristic of poetry of the "highest order" (*Principles* 249–52). The synthetic, heretical vintage of modernism in the years from 1883–1924 suggests the last gasp of a widespread belief in a unified world.

To speak of heresy in the modern world may initially have the ring of anachronism, conjuring up images of the Inquisition or the auto-da-fé. The decided religious associations of heresy seem to have had their import outmoded by the advance of the scientific method and the exponential growth of academic disciplines. Such intellectual perspectives nevertheless ignore the struggles of those who fought against the oppression of orthodoxy. Moreover, during the key transitional period in Britain from 1883 to 1924, religion still held popular sway in determining the values and customs implicit in social interaction and personal responsibility. The significance and cultural context of religion in the late Victorian and Edwardian periods need to be recognized in order to understand the strategy and philosophy by which heterodox literature challenged orthodoxy while still including religious tradition in its discourses.

As a study of heresy and paganism in Britain during this period, *Modernist Heresies* employs a genealogical mode of discourse analysis to explore the material history of religion and the literary experiments that accompany the changes of modern thought. As such, this work addresses the ideological questions of literary and cultural texts by discussing how people thought of religion and morality in the later part of the nineteenth century and the beginning of the twentieth, and how and why those conceptions have changed. While heresy and heterodox uses of paganism are of central import here, these discourses function not to negate the value of religious experience, but rather to ponder competing visions of the world and social relations. In general adversity to conventional opinion and orthodox doctrine, heresy defines the British cultural climate from 1883–1924 and commonly appears in literature as a discursive trope. In its desire to work within extant systems and blend traditional and modern thought, heresy through its synthesis and syncretism functions as a discourse in the logic of modernism. Two cultural movements reinforce the literary analyses discussed herein: the modernist crisis within the Catholic Church, and the Cambridge Heretics Society (1909–32). Since several highly influential figures of the modernist literati were members of the Heretics or in dialogue with the group, heresy also becomes crucial to an understanding of modernist aesthetics and ethics.

In considering the loaded term "heresy" and the cultural play it enjoyed during this period, it is obviously useful to scan reactions within organized religion itself. The late Victorian and Edwardian attempt at synthesis was also part of the "modernist" movement in the Catholic Church, which Pope Pius X (1835–1914) nonetheless vehemently defined as heretical in 1907. In the "modernist crisis," the Vatican fought its last major battle over heretical doctrine. The attempt to harmonize religious dilemmas and oppositions is certainly not a new one, dating at least from those banned and burnt heretics Pico della Mirandola (1463–94) and Giordano Bruno (1548–1600). However, an examination of the modernist crisis accentuates the central debates under consideration here and generates a suggestive set of implications for the literature of the period.

The modernist clergymen tried to reconcile Church doctrine with the results of nineteenth-century German higher criticism, the array of historical "Life of Jesus" studies, and evolutionary thought. What each of these modes of thought had done was to expose contradictions within scripture, between scripture and tradition, or between Genesis and geology. For example, Ernest Renan's La Vie de Jésus (1863) questions the sanctity of the Gospels by claiming that the life of Jesus was only exemplary in its humanity. In Catholic orthodox eyes, modernism was a heresy since it questioned the biblical canon and the validity of the Gospels as the Word of God. Modernists such as the French cleric Alfred Loisy challenged the historicity of Christ and the immutable nature of the canon, and in Britain, George Tyrrell and Baron Freidrich von Hügel embraced history and appealed to the Catholic Church's amenability to change over time. In 1907, for instance, Tyrrell published his treatise Through Scylla and Charybdis, which sought to steer Christianity between the rock of Catholic tradition and the whirlpool of modern thought by presenting the human mind as a synthetic site capable of paradoxically accommodating these two separate spheres of thought.

With the rise of scientific and historical methods in scholarship, some members of the Church felt that the representation of the life of Christ needed to be reevaluated since the disciples were subject to the same pitfalls as all historians. Moreover, these modernists believed that the Christian faith could be reinvigorated if doctrine was revised to conform to modern scholarship. In effect, the modernists deployed evolutionary theory and the idea of an ever-becoming world for their own pious purposes. The Church could evolve over time too. In response, however, the Vatican authorized an organization of spies, the Sodalitium Pianum, to out "modernists"; eventually excommunicated several of the "modernist" clergymen; and placed their works on the Index of Prohibited Books. During the late Victorian and Edwardian periods in England, an analogous attempt at synthesis preoccupied the work of religious scholars who sincerely engaged Darwinian thought and the developments in biblical hermeneutics. From the controversial bestseller Essays and Criticism (1860) to Edmund Gosse's Father and Son

(1907), liberal Protestantism in England grew to share the same concerns with the progressive Catholic modernists. When the Vatican labeled this thought "heresy" in 1907, the Cambridge Heretics Society quickly assembled a wide variety of avant-garde thinkers who proudly chose the interdiction as a sobriquet.

As a result of the modernist use of "scientific criticism," the clergy had to scramble to counter the perceived threat to the immutability of Christian dogma. Initially, the Vatican's response to these contradictions chiefly came in the form of the declaration of papal infallibility at the Vatican Council in 1870, and in the promotion of a Thomistic scholasticism defined by its opposition to modernist thought. In 1893, Pope Leo XIII moved away from both his encouragement of intellectual pursuits within the Church and his conciliatory measures toward the modernists. He further championed Thomistic scholasticism, and his *Providentissimus Deus* reminded clerics to revere scripture and avoid "the fallacies of science" (Kurtz 43). The modernist clerics continued to pursue their rigorous biblical hermeneutics, albeit more cautiously. Then on December 17, 1903, Pius X initiated what his more liberal predecessor had not been willing to do; he brought to the foreground the heresy of "modernism" within the Church by authorizing a decree of The Holy Office placing five works of Loisy on the Index of Forbidden Books. Appealing to the working class, Pius called for a return to traditions and a reaction against scientific advances. Finally, in the summer of 1907, he issued two encyclicals which sealed the fate of the Catholic modernists. First, in July, the *Lamentabili Sane Exitu* condemned sixty-five modernist propositions which pointed out specific inconsistencies in the Bible and challenged Church authority and infallibility. Many of the propositions reflected the common modernist thread of emphasizing the evolving nature of the Church, humanity, and the canon. Finally, in September, Pius X issued the encyclical, *Pascendi Dominici Gregis,* which condemned "modernism" as a "synthesis of all heresies" (89). The *Pascendi* asserted the Vatican's duty bestowed by Christ onto it through apostolic succession to guard against "enemies," even those "in her very bosom," with "the greatest vigilance the deposit of the faith" (Carlen 89; 71).

In condemning the modernist school of thought as the "synthesis of all heresies," the *Pascendi* built on the associative labeling of the *Lamentabili* and made the modernist school of thought more coherent than it actually was. In this ironic slice of rhetoric, the encyclical used a synthesis of its own to proscribe the synthetic turn of the century climate. In fact, the decree further suggested that modernist doctrines only appeared self-contradictory, "without order and systematic arrangement," when in fact these were the result of a deliberate plan to effect "the mutual separation of science and faith" (Carlen 72; 78). The unilateral homogenization of the work of highly divergent modernist clerics enabled the Church to denounce them all in one bold paraphrastic stroke. As George Orwell illustrates with the "compendium of all the heresies" in *Nineteen Eighty-Four* (15), one effective method used by orthodoxy to contain heresies is to lump them together in one denunciation. Umberto Eco's *The Name of the Rose* (1980) suggests that this has been a long-held stratagem of orthodoxy because "[t]o present to the eyes of the people a single heresy . . . shows the heretic as one jumble of diabolical contradictions which offend common sense" (200). In the *Pascendi,* Rome had misleadingly fashioned modernism into a grand conspiracy that defined Catholic orthodoxy simply by opposition. In particular, Pius X opposed both the modernists' use of reason solely for analyzing natural phenomena, and of their notion of a "*vital immanence,*" which manifests a need for divinity and creates a "special *sentiment*" that possesses "the *reality* of the divine" (Carlen 73). As William James' *The Varieties of Religious Experience* had posited a few years earlier, the modernists emphasized the roles of lived experience and the psyche or conscience in creating and confirming faith.

In addition to an influential dialogue with advances in psychology, what modernism in the Catholic Church and literary modernism shared was the basic philosophical tenet that individuals can judge truth and the good based on their own experiences without deference to custom and orthodoxy. One of the definitive laws of the Heretics Society captures this mindset; members had to "reject traditional a priori methods of approaching religious questions" (see table 1 in chapter 1). Drawing on the Church's recent ostracism of "modernism," James Joyce's broadside, "The Holy Office" (1904), satirized the function of the Vatican institution as the purifying force behind orthodoxy by applying its methods to the Dublin literary scene. Joyce proclaims that he too will perform the "office of Katharsis" (<Gk. *kathairein,* "to purge"). Abhorring superficiality and deception, the poetic voice, rather than "by proxy," directly "[h]azards extremes of heterodoxy" (150–51). As I discuss in subsequent chapters, the Catholic modernist movement also directly influenced the Cambridge Heretics Society, Shaw's *Saint Joan,* and the attempts to recuperate Giordano Bruno.

The same month and year that modernism was declared a "synthesis of all heresies," Edmund Gosse published *Father and Son* (1907), an Erziehungsroman narrating his relationship with his father, Philip Gosse, who had been both a fundamentalist Christian and an eminent zoologist. The figure of Philip Gosse embodies the conflicting issues embedded in the modernist crisis, since he was a fundamentalist who nevertheless thought he could reconcile the implications of geology and zoology with the Bible. More importantly, since the Gosses were of the Plymouth Brethren faith, *Father and Son* underscores the fact that the religious modernists posed questions applicable not only to Catholicism but to many varieties of Christianity. Walter Pater, Jane Harrison, Thomas Hardy, and Bernard Shaw also show how modernist issues could be addressed in a variety of ways by non-Catholics, and similar issues surface in heretical responses to Anglican and dissenting orthodoxies of the period.

Writing at a time when the modernist crisis erupted, Edmund Gosse offers his book as a factual *"document"* that delivers a "diagnosis of a dying Puritanism" (33). *Father and Son* should be read in the light of the modernist crisis not solely because of its shared concerns and proximate date of composition, but because the "Son" delineates in his scrupulously honest and generally self-effacing manner how someone can reject the attempt to synthesize Christianity and science and "let sleeping dogmas lie" (185). He describes his book as a "record of a struggle between two temperaments, two consciences and almost two epochs" (35), by which "two" he means, in part, Father and Son. On another level, "two temperaments" and "two consciences" reflect the conflict between Edmund Gosse's desire for a modernist brand of exactitude and the residue of deference to Victorian propriety. The "two consciences" also inhabit the figure of the Father alone. Indeed, Philip Gosse also lives across "two epochs," for his career as zoologist began in the relative calm and wonder before the monumental publication of *Origin of Species* (1859). In the aftermath, the elder Gosse rejects the theory of natural selection and puts forth his own attempt to synthesize Genesis and geology. His theory, referred to as "Omphalos," posited that, "when the catastrophic act of creation took place, the world presented, instantly, the structural appearance of a planet on which life had long existed" (104). Philip Gosse did not have to face the Holy Office for his exposition, but the cold and mocking reviews served just as well.

As a literary history of the transitional period from 1883 to 1924, *Modernist Heresies* is designed partly to bridge recent studies of the history of interdicted discourses. Joss Marsh's *Word Crimes* (1998), centering on a landmark 1883 trial, analyzes the function of blasphemy in English law and literature during the Victorian period. In what amounts to a bookend to Marsh's work, several studies, including Adam Parkes's *Modernism and the Theater of Censorship* (1996) and Allison Pease's *Modernism, Mass Culture, and the Aesthetics of Obscenity* (2000), examine the obscenity trials from 1915–28. Between these periods highlighted by legal sanctions taken against texts on the grounds of blasphemy and obscenity, heresy was an important concept for both religious and literary writers from 1883–1924. In their varied forms, heretical discourses from literature and culture of the fin-de-siècle and the Edwardian period provide a cognitive map illustrating the continuities between Victorian blasphemy and modernist obscenity. Initially prompted by a general crisis in Victorian faith and the modernist movement in the Catholic Church, a concern with heresy becomes prominent in litera-ture of the period because there were shared concerns among the religious and literary-minded.

Marsh's study uses a detailed history of nineteenth-century blasphemy not only to reread Victorian ideology, but also to understand the continu-ing legacy of interdicted discourses. Drawing on her reconstructed account "from the close of the Napoleonic Wars to the *Freethinker* case and its after-math," Marsh argues that understanding the production and punishment of blasphemy reveals "a unique key to what made Victorian fiction tick" (7–12). In particular, she brilliantly revisits the "celebrated" case of G. W. Foote, the editor of the *Freethinker*. At Foote's 1883 trial, Marsh believes that the fol-lowing "historic ruling" of John Duke, Lord Coleridge, "insured blasphemy's survival into the twentieth century": "I now lay it down as law, that if the decencies of controversy are observed, even the fundamentals of religion may be attacked without a person being guilty of blasphemous libel" (28). Marsh then shows how this emphasis on decency functioned as a class-based interdiction that sought to muffle a plain-spoken working class whose words manifested a perceived absence of decorum and respectability. While the sanctions criminalized vulgarity, they also allowed for intellectual and liter-ary forms of heresy which questioned the principles of religion.

Since heresy is strictly speaking a religious offense, this crucial distinc-tion enables an understanding of why heresy was so prevalent in the period from 1883 to 1924. In contrast to "an awareness of offensiveness," to use Marsh's words, that heightens the crime of blasphemy (277), heresy treats religion more subtly and seriously. Through a dialectic with orthodoxy, the heresies in literature from Hardy to Joyce reflect a newfound stratagem for simultaneously critiquing religious tradition and subverting the censor. Blas-phemy and obscenity were secular offenses punishable in a court of law. Literature, at least in theory, could be heretical with relative impunity. For example, as Marsh well notes, novelists could develop the practice of "insert-ing edgewise . . . their unorthodoxy in what we might call the heretic trope of the Book-within-the-book" (181–88). Unlike blasphemy and obscenity, the fact that the heresies of the time did not have a dramatic day in a late Victorian or modern court also partially accounts for their critical neglect. However, the forms of literature, the cults surrounding historical heretics, and the cultural and religious movements during this period all consistently put orthodoxy on trial with ennobled heretical discourses as their chief witnesses.

While Marsh discusses some contemporary instances of blasphemy and its punishment, her account primarily ends in 1895 with an analysis of how *Jude the Obscure* summarily demonstrates the importance of blasphemy to nineteenth-century literature and culture. *Jude*, then, functions as "proof" that "those restraints on freedom, which a society will always impose upon its 'most influential' medium fell, in Victorian times on the novel" (11–12). In particular, Marsh acutely shows the "direct imbrication" by *Jude*'s "class tragedy of thwarted aspiration" in the 1857 trial of Thomas Pooley, who, in a response similar to Jude's, scrawled blasphemous graffiti on a rector's gate in Cornwall (296). For each case, Marsh explains how institutional forces could not abide the implications of these "crimes" and relegated the poor laborers to further "obscurity." In early 1890, Hardy wrote "Candour in English Fiction" to critique the institutional forces which stifled sincere literary discussion of theology and sexual relations, and claimed that "the position of man and woman in nature, and the position of belief in the minds of man and woman—things which everybody is thinking but nobody is saying—might be taken up and treated frankly" (133). After twenty years of using euphemism in his literary battle with orthodoxy, Hardy decided to be candid. In a sense, for his last novel, Hardy let the refined heresies in such novels as *Tess of the d'Urbervilles* speak with a vulgar and relentless tongue.

In contrast to the explicitness of blasphemy, heresy needs to be detected by close interpretation, as in the case of Mr. Tate, the English master, who finds heresy in the particular word choice of young Stephen Dedalus's essay. Even as late as 1933, T. S. Eliot sought to continue the interpretive practice of heresy hunting. In *After Strange Gods: A Primer of Modern Heresy*, Eliot tried to rescue the reading public from the loss of tradition and orthodoxy. By having these distinct forces cooperate, he believed modern thought and feeling could be reconciled.[2] This teaching text concludes with an appendix comprised of four "modern" passages designed to help students practice recognizing heresy for themselves. In one section, Eliot examines the work of Hardy and D. H. Lawrence to denounce the rise of personality in the novel, a symptom of the fact that morals are no longer associated with tradition and orthodoxy. Eliot finds that both authors insinuate the "diabolic" into literature and illustrate that "modern blasphemy is merely a department of bad form" (55). Modern heresy, however, appears more subversively in the department of content and need not deploy the blatant forms of blasphemy or obscenity to work its effects.

Whatever the degree of change from reticence to candor in Hardy's writings, this shift certainly does not preclude the centrality of heretical discourse to an interpretation of *Jude*. In addition to the instance of Sue reordering the New Testament, Hardy's last novel as a whole reflects one last heretical attempt on his part to synthesize "wine" and "bottles." As Carla Peterson states, "Jude and Sue fail in their quest for intellectual and spiritual complementarity, and their failure marks the complete breakdown of" the belief in the reconciliation of "pagan and Christian cultures" (85). In those twin soulmates, Sue and Jude, who are "just the same" (13) and "such an obscure pair" (243), the novel briefly achieves a synthesis in the unconventional marriage of these misfits. However, these brief unnarrated years, during which they were "almost the two parts of a single whole" (229), cannot be told because their very obscurity enables the happiness of the couple. Their blasphemous past, though, rears up to finish the story. As I show in Chapter 5, Hardy's candid method used at once to avoid and create obscurity in *Jude* only helps to illuminate the heresies in *Tess*.

Where Marsh leaves off in 1895, Adam Parkes begins to trace the origins of the censorship of modernist literature in the trials of Oscar Wilde, which saw his "crime" as intrinsically linked to literary "obscurity." Since the "press accounts sheltered their readers by using references to literary obscenity to censor the unspeakable crimes for which Wilde was convicted," Parkes considers the trials "obscenity trials" which blurred the boundaries between art and life, the appearance of indecency and indecency itself (11). Noting that the origin of the case sprang from the Marquess of Queensberry's postcard to Wilde accusing him of "Posing as a Somdomite [*sic*]," Parkes states: "*Dorian Gray* did not divulge specific acts, but it posed as if it did. Obscurity implied obscenity, a suspicion revived by the appearance in November 1895 of Thomas Hardy's novel *Jude the Obscure,* or 'Jude the Obscene,' as it was called in the *Pall Mall Gazette*" (8–9). Further arguing that literary modernism from 1914–30 needs to be read in the light of a "theater of censorship," Parkes states that, "especially in their responses to contemporary sexual discourse, such novelists as Lawrence, Joyce, and Woolf anticipated and subverted the moral, political, and aesthetic premises on which the culture of censorship was operating" (viii).

In the trials that censored *The Rainbow, Ulysses,* and Radclyffe Hall's *The Well of Loneliness* on grounds of obscenity, the "judges and lawyers often invoked the so-called Hicklin rule, established in Britain in 1868, which defined as obscene works tending 'to deprave and corrupt those whose minds are open to such immoral influences and into whose hands a publication of this sort may fall.'" Finally, in 1928 after the defense for Radclyffe Hall's novel sought to call artists as witnesses to the stand and explain its merits, the judge, Sir Chartres Biron, declared the irrelevance of such testimony since a "book may be a fine piece of literature and yet obscene" (qtd. in Parkes 4). Great literature *could* have sex and sexuality in it, but it would be censored. As Parkes shows, concomitant with the rise of modernism, a new form of "indecency" often played a central role in the literary dramatization of religious controversies. Joyce and Lawrence, in particular, accentuated the dialogic exchange between religious and sexual discourses, and this prevalent development owes much to the return of paganism and the heresy of syncretism in the intellectual desire to synthesize Hellenism and Hebraism.

By indirectly authorizing a reserved debate between paganism and Christianity, blasphemy law had curtailed making the sacred profane on a linguistic level, yet allowed for subject matter that drew on ancient cultures and proclaimed the sexual divine. For example, in his play *Salome* (1891), Wilde positions the audience in Herod's perspective, foregrounding the incestuous desire of the biblical passage, and forces it to reconcile the divine word with the beheading of John the Baptist and Salome's erotic dance of the seven veils. Or, in an example of Marsh's idea of the "heretic trope of the book," there is the influence of the decadent, synthesizing book in Wilde's *The Picture of Dorian Gray* (1891), the book of which one "hardly knew at times whether one was reading the spiritual ecstasies of some mediæval saint or the morbid confessions of a modern sinner" (110). In cases similar to these, Parkes invokes Hans Robert Jauss's point that "a new aesthetic form . . . can have the greatest conceivable impact on a moral question" (Jauss, *Toward* 42). Arguing that Wilde's art "was experimental, yet his innovations were intelligible only in relation to traditional notions of form and style," Parkes then suggests that the critical reception of Wilde often recognized a "calculated deceit" on his part, that through his puns and epigrammatic style he was simultaneously working within and against culture (6; 14; 17). In a parallel argument, Rita Kranidis's *Subversive Discourse* uncovers shared counterhegemonic strategies in feminist novels of the 1890s. In order to escape the censorious effect of authoritative discourses, feminist writers, Kranidis illustrates, developed literary forms that critiqued traditional notions of femininity and patriarchal exclusivity.[3] Other types of experiments with literary forms can also achieve these ends, and heresy exemplifies this ability to work within and against culture, because, in its relation to orthodoxy, heretical thought can often mask itself beneath traditional forms. Between the legal statutes condemning blasphemy and obscenity, heresy took the subtle, subversive road connecting the two. Striking at the very doctrine and ideology of religious institutions, heterodox writers could affect their readers less overtly but more fundamentally.

The prurient subject matter that brought the reactionary censor down on Lawrence, Joyce, and Hall grew out of a liberating heretical approach toward the body, an approach that owes much not only to psychology but to the rediscovery and gradual literary experimentation with paganism. As a common structuring element in British literature from 1883–1924, paganism, a specific heretical discourse of chief interest here, arises from the prominent historical sense cultivated by the modernist clergy, evolutionists, and cultural anthropologists. The analysis of the synthetic philosophies during this time helps to reveal the methods by which literary writers collocated paganism and Christianity. For purposes here "paganism" refers to religions appearing prior to the advent of Christianity such as those of the Celtic, Roman, Greek, and Egyptian peoples. The high time for this aesthetic experimentation was 1890–1914, but the modernist elision of their antecedents has helped to occult the pervasive influence of the Edwardian heretic position. By neglecting or distancing themselves from their predecessors, leading modernist critics defined a lasting vision of a self-contained art or claimed a radical newness in the spirit of the times. To counter this disservice to an understanding of the fluid processes of history, we can now perceive heresy as a discourse that allows us to theorize and historicize the literature and culture across this transitional moment in history.

In particular, the cultural contexts of the Cambridge Heretics Society and the Catholic modernist movement provide transhistorical links between the ideology of such texts as Hardy's *Tess of the d'Urbervilles* (1891) and Shaw's *Saint Joan* (1924). A movement branded heretical in 1907 and a society defiantly donning the brand, these two slices of history let us reconceive the literary period under question. By placing this historical 1907 moment in dialogue with the founding of the Heretics Society in 1909, we can begin to see how modern religious, literary, and philosophical thinkers clustered around the discursive function and positioning of heterodoxy.

Heresy held such sway in the 1890s that, in the year before *Jude* appeared, a ninety-year-old William Gladstone returned to his study and sought to remedy one last theological difficulty. In his contribution to *Nineteenth Century*, "The Place of Heresy and Schism in the Modern Christian Church" (1894), the former Liberal prime minister applied to these divisions within Christianity the notion that historical change enables one to disregard certain "laws of religion," such as the proscription of idolatry and usury, that "have been modified by circumstance" (158–59). Gladstone, the writer of such previous works as *The Impregnable Rock of Holy Scripture* (1891) and *Homeric Synchronism* (1876), an attempt to harmonize Homer with the Gospels, subsequently felt that all the modern heresies, the "Babel of claimants for the honour of orthodoxy and catholicity" (172), should unite in defense of Christian belief. Therefore, he recommends a "readjustment of ideas, and not a surrender . . . of *established* laws and practices" (173, emphasis mine). For Gladstone, a united Christian apologetics is imperative because of the "signs of the times" which tell "the champions of religion" that "their duty [is] to equip themselves with knowledge, and use it as an effective weapon in regard to the ancient history of our planet and of man" (174). Evolution and the "historical method" were in the air, and he agrees with the Catholic "modernists" that scripture can defend Genesis from geology by synthesizing knowledges.

In effect, Gladstone acknowledges that the history of Christianity is a history of sectarianism, and he calls for an ecumenical tolerance between "orthodoxy" and all the sundry heresies that have endured. Not only does the Grand Old Man note that the "evidence which condemns heresy and schism has been . . . greatly weakened" (159), but he also extols the virtues of nonconformity in perpetuating faith while also advancing humanitarian causes. In Gladstone's high Anglican mind, the place of heresy in the modern world is a secure and salutary one. However, in affirming this view, he redefined "heresy" as a "changeable and short-lived" phenomenon divested of doctrinal controversies (172). Gladstone states: "If and so far as the heresy involves in itself perversion of the Christian dogma, they are the sufferers. But here we are dealing with error, not heresy" (164). In such a context, heresy is no longer possible. By eliminating the "unorthodox meanings" from "heresy," Gladstone's insertion into the religious debates functions like a principle of Orwell's Newspeak, in which changing the meanings of words can make "a heretical thought . . . literally unthinkable" (*Nineteen Eighty-Four* 246). Of course, Gladstone would have recoiled from such totalitarianism, and in fact did not want the state to control religion, but the effect of his argument is nevertheless an attempt to subsume and antiquate heresy. His essay, however, testifies to the currency of a heretical spirit in the late Victorian period.

In defining "heresy," the esteemed Eleventh Edition of the *Encyclopedia Britannica* (1910) offers a representative survey of what an Edwardian expert in the field considered important about the subject. In his discussion of the modern use of the term "heresy," Reverend Alfred Ernest Garvie notes that churches are "less anxious about the danger" of heterodox thought because "to-day a spirit of diffidence in regard to one's own beliefs, and of tolerance towards the beliefs of others, is abroad" (360b). However, Garvie neglects mentioning the recent condemnation of "modernism" as a heresy (1907) or the advent of the Heretics Society (1909), and therefore the persistent import of the term is missing from the entry. While these historical events were probably too recent for an encyclopedic perspective, the entry's classification of the three types of heresy in the history of Christianity still delivers a parallel analysis of the forms of heretical thought that appear in British literature and culture from 1883 to 1924. There are "syncretic," "evolutionary," and "revolutionary" heresies. In "syncretic" heresies, such as Gnosticism or Manichaeism, the heterodoxy tries to create "a fusion of Jewish or pagan with Christian elements" (359b). If a doctrine is in the process of formation, "undue emphasis may be put on one aspect, and thus so partial a statement of truth may result in error" (359b). The contested history of beliefs about the nature of the Trinity exemplifies this type of "evolutionary" heresy. In cases such as the Reformation itself, a "revolutionary" heresy opposes "the church, its theory and its practice" (360a).

From 1883 to 1924, all three forms of heresy appear in Britain. The British Catholic "modernists," George Tyrrell and Baron von Hügel, were central parts of the clerical movement which tried to revolutionize Catholicism. Several writers led by Shaw proposed the idea that heresy itself reflects the fact that religion is always an evolving process. Through its extremely diverse set of debates and addresses, the Heretics Society witnessed all three forms of heresy in various manifestations. By far though, the most prevalent form of heresy during the Edwardian period was the syncretic, the attempt to find a new way to put a blend of wines in bottles. The following chapters discuss this concept extensively, but a few examples here illustrate the modernist preoccupation with syncretism. The narrative of Walter Pater's *Marius the Epicurean* (1885) develops a dialectic of ethics and aesthetics that culminates in a synthesis of Christian and pagan values. In W. H. Hudson's *Green Mansions* (1904), the natives of Guyana set fire to the tree in which they had trapped Rima the Bird Girl. She suffers this emblematic burning at the stake because the natives cannot abide her syncretic spirituality. James Joyce's "The Dead" (1914) invokes the shared Dionysian and Christian elements in the history of Epiphany in its search for a grander inclusivity than orthodoxy offers.

In one of the fullest treatments of the Edwardian period, *The Edwardian Temperament* (1986), Jonathan Rose compiles extensive evidential cases of the period's predominant synthesizing or unifying mode of thought. Amid the wealth of his material, Rose declares that the "period produced a remarkable crop of omnibus philosophies harmonizing different points of view" and specifically "responded to the decline of religion by reconciling faith and reason, merging the two in a higher and broader synthesis" (2–3). While this last particular exercise was the basis of the Catholic modernist movement, Rose overlooks the Cambridge Heretics and the fact that heresy is the definitive discourse of this type of synthesis (synthesis <Gk. *suntithenai,* "to put together"). Rose presents an array of fascinating, recondite material, including a brief account of the formation of the Synthetic Society which "undertook the 'construction' of a new foundation for religious faith" (6), and of the origin of the Fabian Society in the Fellowship of the New Life, whose mentor, Thomas Davidson, in 1883 "preached a pantheistic monism postulating a single immanent deity uniting the entire material universe" (22). Among his more canonical examples, Rose foregrounds the appearance of the *Hibbert Journal,* a theological quarterly launched by its editor in 1902 with the claim that "The Goal of thought is one" (9), the scientific advances that suggested universal coherence through electromagnetism, radio waves, and the special theory of relativity (6–8), and the influence of Madame Blavatsky's Theosophy, "a new cult that promised to effect a 'synthesis of science, religion, and philosophy'" (11).

Noting similar historical developments in "The Two Faces of Edward" (1959), Richard Ellmann had already adduced the results of Rose's survey in stating that the "amount of unity which the Edwardians instilled in their work is one of their extraordinary accomplishments" (205). To perpetuate a phrase, Rose suggests that Forster's epigraph to *Howards End* (1910), "Only connect . . ." captures a large part of this synthesizing temperament. By dismissing the Edwardians, though, as merely gathering convergent ideas and "conceiving all things as one" (3), Rose reaffirms the modernist dismissal of their predecessors. However, the various techniques and philosophies surrounding the notion of "synthesis" from 1883 to 1924 are much more profound, diverse, and lasting than Rose allows them to be.

Let us take, for example, the most famous claim for the revolutionary newness of modernism in Virginia Woolf's "Mr. Bennett and Mrs. Brown" (1924). Woolf's words, "On or about December 1910 human character changed," now appear in nearly every critical commentary on the Edwardian and modernist periods as evidence of how the modernists saw themselves as breaking from their ancestors. What is neglected in criticism is the fact that she delivered a substantive version of this essay, "Character in Fiction," before the Heretics Society in 1924. In Chapter 3, I analyze the manuscript changes in this famous modernist manifesto in order to show how the audience of Heretics informed her discussion of periodization, obscenity, and character. In ranging the "Edwardians and the Georgians [modernists] into two camps," Woolf inserted "December 1910" as her chosen date of rupture after addressing the Heretics (CF2 421). Many studies perpetuate this false presumption of a radical epistemic break by ascribing it to a number of historical events: the death of a king, the outbreak of sundry manifestoes on the "isms," the exhibition of one of those in London in 1910, and the shock of the declaration of war.[4] Recent criticism has begun to argue against Woolf's claim, and heretical discourses provide a new historical perspective for understanding the particular continuities and discontinuities of late Victorian and modernist literature and culture.

In their 1996 revisionist history of the relations between the Edwardians and the modernists, *Seeing Double*, Carola Kaplan and Anne Simpson militate against the modernists' influential and homogenizing assessment of their predecessors as "socially conscious" but "simple-minded" "hacks" (viii). Through the lens of reception theory, Kaplan and Simpson illustrate how the Edwardian period typifies the shifting of critical interpretations, and in particular they oppose Rose's study whose poststructuralist influences lead to a denigration of the synthetic character of Edwardian thought. In contrast to the "intellectual honesty" and "healthy development" of the fragmented modern self, Rose finds that the Edwardians did not face "up to hard philosophical choices" and only "achieved an inner wholeness by affirming unity everywhere" (210–12). Since the Edwardians, in Rose's mind, "presumed the reconcilability of everyone and everything" (72), this "synthesizing impulse, carried to its final conclusion, would dissolve all intellectual distinctions into metaphysical slush" (210). However, the Edwardian impulse was just that, a search and a desire, not an a priori assumption.

In fact, the Edwardians discovered validity in the idea of an organic society, and this philosophical approach prompted some advances in the welfare state based on the "synthetic" belief that people exist in their relationship to others. Rose, though, will not credit Hardy's observation that the ethical implication of the origin of species calls for the Golden Rule to all (64), or the general idea that "people shared a common 'social citizenship' and were therefore entitled to common social services" (58). Noting that the First World War reversed these reconciling trends and that a new divisiveness appeared in postwar aesthetic forms, Rose even claims that the Edwardian "tragic flaw" consisted of not anticipating "the holocaust that would explode their cherished ideal" (72). Yet surely the Edwardians cannot be blamed for not foreseeing the future, and the shock, horror, and repercussions of war do not retroactively discount an entire preceding body of intellectual thought.

Recognizing the deleterious effects of some of the choices made by the modernists, this work builds on Kaplan and Simpson's admiration for the social advances and synthetic character of the Edwardians, a character which owes much to contemporary developments in physical science, linguistics, comparative mythology, and cultural anthropology. As they state, the "ability to hold in tension competing philosophical positions on contemporary culture" is "one of the most fascinating aspects of Edwardian literature, and one of its most pressing aesthetic claims" (x). A literary instance of this desire occurs during the debate over Shakespeare's life and work in *Ulysses* (1922), set in 1904, in which Thomas Lyster, the Quaker librarian, tolerantly observes, "All sides of life should be represented." However, the modernist tenor of Joyce's novel does not refrain from poking at this inclusive diversity, and the next line mocks Lyster's appeal: "He smiled on all sides equally" (162–63). The Edwardian syncretists brought issues into play with each other that the modernists tended to sort out in their aesthetic "choices" (heresy <Gk. *hairesis,* "choice"). Each type of response is a form of heresy, one unitarian, the other sectarian.

Kaplan and Simpson point out that, whereas the Edwardians engaged history and attempted to come to terms thematically with the perception of change and instability in the world, the modernists deified art, claiming that it must be more discrete and assume precedence over politics or philosophy. They undercut this modernist dismissal of the Edwardians by arguing that the chief difference between these groups consists not in artistic quality but in their views of history. The prominent current critique of modernist ideology, as Marjorie Perloff illustrates, uncovers fascist tendencies in its aesthetic sensibility, which construct a totality out of spatial metaphors or the idea of tradition. In retrospect, we can better see the myopia of the constructed totalities. Perloff further reminds us that the emphasis on form central to ahistorical views of literature is born out of a "self-destroying" view of modernity, to quote Paul de Man, that "exists in the form of a desire to wipe out whatever came earlier in the hope of reaching at last a point that could be called a true present, a point of origin that marks a new departure" (162).

In D. H. Lawrence's essay "Surgery for the Novel—or a Bomb" (1923), he declares that the modern novel should lay waste present modes of thought by finding "a new impulse for new things in mankind" and by presenting "us with new, really new feelings, a whole line of new emotion, which will get us out of the emotional rut" (520). Chiefly, he attributes the "senile-precocious," "sloppy" style and "self-consciousness" of modern novels to the "split" of "philosophy and fiction" which "used to be one, right from the days of myth" (518–20). By synthesizing the two, having them "come together again," Lawrence believes that readers will be estranged, but "a new world outside" will open to them (520). In different strains of this attempt to make things "new," Pound's Vorticism, Eliot's Individual Talent, Lewis' bold straight line, and fascism's national borders all professed themselves to be corrective measures to the fragmented modern world.[5] Michael Levenson sums ups "the English modernists" as "inclined to definitive opinions expressed in vehement tones" (viii). A common method used to promote the modernist manifestoes involved isolating themselves from competing systems of thought and idealizing a remote past—or blasting the past away. As a result of this self-righteous violence done to the continuities of history, an orthodox backlash based on a "right-mindedness" pervaded the period.

The Cambridge Heretics Society was not immune from such a critique. After his address before the group in 1911, G. K. Chesterton, the conservative watchdog of heresy in such books as *Heretics* (1905) and *Orthodoxy* (1908), wrote a letter to the president of the Society explaining his antagonistic interest in the group: "[F]irst and last, I should like to ask them why they are so weak-minded (if you will forgive the phrase) as to admit that they *are* Heretics. You never really think your own opinion right until you can call it Orthodox" (MCMA 113.36). What Chesterton failed to realize was that in the Edwardian age heresy foremost implied synthesis, and the desire not so much to remain *opposed* to orthodoxy but to *subsume* it. Reconciliation and synthesis were the predominant modes of transgression of the age. Nevertheless, Chesterton's rhetorical point prophetically anticipated the modernist turn in which heresy slowly declined as an important philosophical position, and the didactic modernist manifestoes abound with self-satisfaction and decree. In many respects, the dialectic of heresy and orthodoxy is akin to Jameson's conception of the dialectic of utopia and ideology. As in the utopian impulse, syncretic heresy in our transitional period of concern strives for a larger unity of collectivity than orthodoxy allows, while the latter develops strategies to appropriate the appeals toward synthesis and inclusivity.

One of the difficulties in discussing periodization, even negatively, is

that there is still an initial need to create order through arbitrary but functional dates. Criticism has delimited the Edwardian period, in particular, in
a highly fluctuating manner. Kaplan and Simpson consider the years 1895–
1920 for their study; Rose's *The Edwardian Temperament* uncovers material from 1895–1919; Ellmann's essay and Samuel Hynes' numerous studies
each employ the parameters of Edward VII's reign (1901–10); and Harold
Bloom offers the most inclusive span in his critical collection *Edwardian
and Georgian Fiction, 1880–1914.* In choosing the years 1883 and 1924 as
bookends to this literary history, *Modernist Heresies* incorporates the traditional *anni mirabili* of the decadent Nineties (1891) and of High Modernism
(1922), but the most important aspect of the selections derives from their
temporal demarcations well into the Victorian and modernist periods. Like
Wittgenstein's ladder, the dates are to be discarded after achieving a new
knowledge of the origins of literary modernism. Heresy certainly exists both
before and after these dates of Kafka's birth and death, but during these forty
years the intellectual climate and the discursive control which first put Foote
behind bars and then banned *Ulysses* foregrounded heresy as an appealing
and viable alternative discourse.

Foote's blasphemy trial initiates the context of my study, and several
changes took place in 1924 which suggest a turning away from heresy. First
and foremost, C. K. Ogden, the force behind the Heretics Society, resigned
his thirteen-year presidency of the group in order to devote himself to his
ideas of language reform. Two texts that I discuss later, Shaw's *Saint Joan*
and Forster's *A Passage to India,* first appeared in England in 1924 and presented solutions to heretical problems. In that same year, Woolf delivered her
address to the Heretics, which attempted to steer modernist art away from
Edwardian synthetic heresies and toward stricter aesthetic "choices." In the
first "Manifesto of Surrealism" (1924), André Breton declared his belief in
the "future resolution" of "dream and reality" into "a *surreality*" (14), which
by his definition of the movement, would be "exempt from any aesthetic or
moral concern" (26). Courting the desire for this synthesis, surrealism however would distance itself from heresy, which was vulnerable to orthodox
appropriation, by asserting its "complete *nonconformism* clearly enough so
that there can be no question of translating it, at the trial of the real world, as
evidence for the defense" (47).

On this note, Richard Ellmann offers a final, crucial insight needed for
any critical reassessment of the Edwardian period. As Breton had warned,
Ellmann notes the examples of Yeats and Joyce who "are sometimes suspected
nowadays of having been reverted Christians or at least demi-Christians."

He states that this fallacious critical turn happens because Edwardian writers who had actually "rejected Christianity" "no longer made a fuss about being infidels" and "felt free to *use* it [religion], for while they did not need religion they did need religious metaphors." By using the lexicon they knew best, Edwardian writers often fashioned a climax out of a secular miracle or created unifying centers out of a "religious" event or symbol. As Hardy's enological figuration indicates, the prevalence of religious metaphors during this time also informs, in Ellmann's words, "the Catholic modernists, with their emphasis upon the metaphorical rather than the literal truth of Catholic doctrines." While Ellmann's reminders certainly do not hold for all writers during this period, they serve to highlight the difficulties of interpreting synthetic literature and the importance of reception in determining its orthodox or heretical valence. Nevertheless, when a writer such as Forster "is not for Christ or Pan, but with profoundly Edwardian zeal, for the deities reconciled" (Ellmann, "Edward" 192; 195), on paper at least this is strictly a syncretic heresy, and the writer's particular religious inclination is of less importance than the textually manifest influence of the cultural context. The desire for synthesis flavors British literature from 1883 to 1924 with heretical and religious metaphors bottled as a new vintage blend.

PART I

The Academy of Modern Heretics

Chapter 1

A Society of Heretics

ON DECEMBER 8, 1909, during her lecture inaugurating the Cambridge Heretics Society, Jane Harrison (1850–1928), the classical scholar and anthropologist, rejoiced that the "word 'heretic' has still about it an emotional thrill" and that "[t]o be a heretic to-day is almost a human obligation" ("Heresy" 27–28). Historical progress, in Harrison's mind, had made the Edwardian period conducive to a relentless dialectic between maverick heretics and the orthodox herd. Fresh in her mind was the condemnation of modernist religious thought as a "synthesis of all heresies." For Harrison, the dialectical relationship between heresy and orthodoxy would subsume orthodoxy in a broader synthesis and propel human intellectual endeavor. The dialectic would produce new syntheses from which society could choose a more enlightened course for subsequent thought and action. Harrison found that the inauguration of the Heretics Society was a welcome first step on this path. The previous critical neglect in acknowledging the vital and formative influence the Heretics had on modernist thought may be one of the more glaring omissions in our understanding of twentieth-century intellectual history, for the Heretics effectively dominated the intellectual climate in Britain from the end of the Edwardian period through the height of the modernist era.

The critical oversight is all the more surprising when one considers the impressive and diverse lists of people who were either members of the Heretics or addressed the conversation society under the rubric of heresy. The active and wide-ranging Honorary Members included Harrison, the dramatist Bernard Shaw, the historian G. M. Trevelyan, the economist J. M. Keynes, the mathematician G. H. Hardy, the political scientist G. L. Dickinson, the literary critic I. A. Richards, the classicists F. M. Cornford and

Arthur Verrall, and the philosophers G. E. Moore, John McTaggart, Bertrand Russell, and George Santayana. While most of these persons had established themselves as reputable national figures by the 1909 inception of the Heretics, several, including Keynes, Trevelyan, and Richards, rose to intellectual prominence while participating in the Society until its dismantling in 1932. Two Cambridge undergraduates, C(harles) K(ay) Ogden (1889–1957) and William Empson (1906–84), would begin their long and opposing studies of language while serving as presidents of the Heretics. Even more command-ing a claim for the centrality of the Heretics during this time perhaps is the composite of artists and intellectuals outside academia who, while not all becoming Heretics, came to Cambridge to address the group. Most of the pre-eminent figures of the Bloomsbury Group exchanged ideas with the Heretics; Roger Fry, Clive Bell, Lytton Strachey, Edith Sitwell, Leonard and Virginia Woolf all sojourned by the Cam to dab a little in heresy. Even E. M. Forster, as I illustrate in chapter 2, engaged the Heretics in his novel, *Arctic Summer,* which he abandoned unfinished at the outbreak of the First World War. Other noteworthy guest speakers included Rupert Brooke, Vernon Lee, Rebecca West, Walter de la Mare, F. T. Marinetti, Bonamy Dobree, Marie Stopes, Wyndham Lewis, Arthur Machen, and Ludwig Wittgenstein. (See the Appendix for a list of the meetings and addresses of the Heretics Society.)

This impressive roster not only establishes the fact that a proper his-tory of the Heretics has long been warranted, but it also indirectly suggests that the particular subjects of heresy and religion have been received with a peculiar form of silence by academia.[1] Until recently, religious heterodoxy has been virtually a taboo subject in criticism, particularly in discussions of the modernist period. Our immediate intellectual precursors often openly defended or denounced religion until people of varying pious and secu-lar inclinations no longer wanted to offend each other's sensibilities. As a result, in the postmodern age, religious issues have been muted because they are still controversial topics. However, several recent studies have begun to illustrate that the subject is indeed important, even if not to hold religious debates once again, then to understand our intellectual history.[2]

In the previous cursory accounts of the Heretics, a memoirist or historian briefly mentions the existence of the Heretics and possibly records an anec-dote about their meetings. Sometimes the reports make erroneous claims, such as naming Cornford the founder or calling the group the "Heretics Club." The most significant yet innocent negligence lies in not identifying the Heretics at all. Over the course of the Society's twenty-three years, sev-eral landmark essays and nearly every tangent of modernist thought were initially promulgated in this freethinking atmosphere. The Heretics Society brought forth such a diverse and expanding set of topics and allowed for such a variety of perspectives that a complete account of the Heretics is impractical for purposes here. However, the following discourse history highlights the origins and first five years of the Heretics before the First World War in order to demonstrate that heresy was not only fundamental to Edwardian Britain, but that the Heretics themselves embodied and enacted the ability and desire to coordinate conflicting schools of thought. In the historical moment from 1909–14, the umbrella platform of the Heretics Society was able to balance competing tensions and oppositional views. Isolating this coalition of heresy in the "Georgian" period enables us to draw historical continuities from the Edwardian to the modernist periods. In contrast, an account of another five-year period, 1919–24, illustrates the prevalent shift at the Heretics from a desire for synthesis to a more divisive form of heresy in which modernists defended the "correctness" of their positions.

When previous general histories, memoirs, or literary studies do mention the Heretics Society, they tend to deflect the impetus for the radical group onto C. K. Ogden. Those who remember him fondly for his administration of the Heretics, his editorships of *The Cambridge Magazine* and *Psyche,* or his invention of Basic English often use the word "polymath" to describe him. Those inclined to dismiss the Heretics invariably label him "eccentric." For instance, in his multi-volume *A History of the University of Cambridge,* Christopher Brooke mentions, only once, "the formation of the society of Heretics," and attributes this achievement to the "plotting" of "that celebrated eccentric C. K. Ogden" (126). On the other hand, in the one substantive account of the Heretics, a memoir essay, P. Sargant Florence, Ogden's right-hand man at the Heretics from 1909–24, attacks the "superficial tag" placed on Ogden that he was "a mere eccentric who happened to have tossed off the *The Meaning of Meaning* and Basic English." Instead, Florence chooses to underscore additionally his "importance as a heretic and a creator of heretics, among at least six generations of Cambridge men and women" (CH 227). Similarly, in the most thorough account of Ogden's work, W. Terrence Gordon also seeks to recoup Ogden's heretical influence on modern thought, stating that by 1932 "an incalculable effect of intellectual ferment had been exerted on a whole generation of future writers and thinkers, many of whom would transform heretical views into received wisdom" (7–8).

During his second year at Magdalene College, Ogden and several other Cambridge undergraduates formed the Heretics in the Michaelmas term of 1909. Though he was a keen recruiter of heretics and the paragon of a marketing publicist, Ogden could not have helped solidify the birth of the Heretics without the widespread encouragement of the faculty. Considering the difficulties that an undergraduate-based organization faces in recuperating lost membership each year, the Society would not have maintained itself for twenty-three years without having touched a nerve in the culture of the times. To attribute the Heretics solely to Ogden credits his influence, but also does a disservice to the cultural contexts of the Edwardian and modernist periods.

Ascribing the creation of the Heretics to a single person is a facile explanation for a much more complex and widespread phenomenon. Edwardian Cambridge in 1909 already teemed with heterodox ideas and affiliations influencing college life. Perhaps most flamboyantly, Rupert Brooke and his circle of Neo-pagans romanticized love, nature, drama, and the possibilities for social transformation. For several years on campus, a group of academics known as the Cambridge Ritualists had been cultivating a new approach to the study of classical pagan literature and culture. These "Ritualists," Jane Harrison, Francis Cornford, Gilbert Murray, and Arthur Cook, all were developing methodologies for confirming the primacy of ritual over myth in ancient cultures. Harrison and Cornford would become Heretics; Murray and Brooke each would later deliver a paper before the Society. In this context, it is no wonder that Jacob Flanders in Woolf's *Jacob's Room* goes up to Cambridge in 1906 and finds the study of Greek, science, and philosophy to be the "light" that "burns above Cambridge" (39). However, the narrative voice soon adds the clarification: "if you talk of a light, of Cambridge burning, it's not languages only. It's Julian the Apostate" (49).

The list of Heretics and their associates also illustrates that these same people were often also members of the more widely received Cambridge Apostles and travelers in the famed Bloomsbury Group. Underscoring the fundamental connections between the latter two groups, Quentin Bell claims that Bloomsbury was born at Cambridge in the autumn of 1899 when Leonard Woolf, Lytton Strachey, and Clive Bell first became friends sympathetic to each other's intellect, and he adds that of these "young men who formed the nucleus of Bloomsbury, all save Clive Bell and Thoby Stephen were members of that semi-secret Cambridge society The Apostles" (*Bloomsbury* 23; 37). In her exemplary study of the epistemological discursive exchange between Russell, Fry, and Virginia Woolf, Ann Banfield intricately elucidates the "Cambridge Apostolic" influence on the "Bloomsbury family tree," which has "yet to be explored in all its ramifications" (x). One of these ramifications, still neglected, is the role of the Heretics in facilitating this dialogue and widening the sphere of mutual influence between the Apostles and Bloomsbury.

The historical reception of the figures in question highlights these more acceptable groups and effectively distances them from their engagement with heresy. Often in their own memoirs, the former Heretics are complicit in this elision by muting their past associations with the Society. While the agnostic or atheistic Apostles never refrained from admitting their religious doubts, in Bloomsbury the discursive agenda was already replete with their topical concerns—literature, economics, painting, publishing. In their relationship with the Heretics, the Bloomsbury Group would bring these issues to the foreground and concede explicit religious questions to the other Heretics. Nevertheless, this shared dialogue illustrates that Bloomsbury found heresy an important issue and the Heretics a crucial audience. Through a tolerance implicit in the acceptance of heresy, Bell, Strachey, Virginia Woolf, and others could steer the direction of British intellectualism through the avenue of heresy.

Intellectual histories and period studies of modernist literature have accounted well enough for the roles of the Cambridge Apostles and the Bloomsbury Group in directing aesthetic and philosophic thought in Britain during the first few decades of the twentieth century. As Richard Deacon stresses in his history of the Apostles, "the influence of its members has been considerable on both sides of the Atlantic Ocean and in all spheres of life from administration to the arts, from philosophy to politics, from science to medicine" (vii). With its inception in 1820 as the Cambridge Conversazione Society, the Apostles began refining its exclusive membership for prominent roles in British society. Tennyson would commemorate his experience at the Apostles with an apotheosized Arthur Hallam in section 87 of *In Memoriam* (1850). It is particularly fascinating to look at the impressive list of the fifty or so members chosen between Dickinson and Fry in the 1880s and Brooke and Wittgenstein in the early 1900s and wonder at the selection processes at work in so accurately discerning the potential of its members. Nearly half of the fifty Apostles chosen in those thirty years became major figures in the intellectual climate of England. Among those, Dickinson, Hardy, Keynes, McTaggart, Moore, and Russell were also eager Heretics. Through others such as Forster, Fry, Strachey, and Leonard Woolf, who addressed or responded to the Heretics, the Apostles helped to cultivate a triangular and often overlapping dialogue between themselves, the Heretics, and Bloomsbury. The eclectic nature of these various affiliations made possible a dialogue at once heteroglot, negotiable, and identity-based. Similar to the effect of the wide-ranging topics and perspectives of the Heretics, the Bloomsbury Group, as S. P. Rosenbaum believes, "displays a unique complex resemblance that cannot be reduced to a platform or creed" (*Group* ii).

In his study of the Apostles, W. C. Lubenow also finds that the secret society, while "caught up in a struggle for wholeness" that could relate the self and the world, was, however, eclectic and professed "no single ideology." The Apostles brought together members from diverse religious backgrounds, yet Lubenow hazards one conclusion unifying their intellectual endeavors—that "from beginning to end [the Apostles] were bound together in a common sceptical tradition which enabled them to both engage in self-definition and forge a sense of duty" (WCL 411). In seeing their history as "inseparable from the history of religion in the time between Waterloo and the Great War," Lubenow argues that they contributed "to reform when they were of the church and [remained] sympathetic to religious impulses when they were not" (WCL 407). Throughout the late nineteenth century, the Apostles aggressively pursued abolishing religious tests at university and several other significant agnostic and secularizing causes. By 1902, Lytton Strachey reports that they "discussed whether it should crusade against Christianity," and he was among the majority who "seemed to think [they] should" (WCL 400). Lubenow ends his study of this "crucible of heterodoxy," as he calls the Apostles, at the time of the advent of the Heretics when, in a sense, the Apostles' "crusade" became manifest (WCL 400). Lubenow's account loses some of its acuity in erroneously asserting that Moore, Hardy, and Russell "went missing from Ogden's scrutiny" and did not join the Heretics (WCL 405). Knowing them as such, the legacy of the Apostles' skepticism becomes even more clearly bequeathed to the Heretics.

In his biography of Dickinson, Forster remembers the nature of the Apostles' meetings: "The characteristics of such societies vary but little. The members are drawn from the older undergraduates and the younger dons, they meet of an evening in one another's rooms, a paper is read, . . . and finally the reader responds to his critics" (34–35). While the Heretics did share similar practices with this other discussion society, Forster is trying to play down the cache of secrecy surrounding the exclusive Apostles. Therein lies a key difference between the Heretics and the more star-chamberesque atmosphere at the Apostles and Bloomsbury. The discursive exchange amongst (and shared "membership" in) this triumvirate of conversation societies mandates a recognition that the Heretics not only held equivalent import and sway, but did so in a more open, egalitarian, and diffuse fashion. To speak of the Apostles and Bloomsbury is to speak of an elitism characterized by secrecy on one hand and highbrow culture on the other, but the Heretics, while still functioning as a member-based society, often opened their meetings to the public, and published addresses as examples of heretical thought. In a sense, the Heretics provided a forum for making public whatever ideas individuals from the other groups had worked out behind closed doors.

By most accounts, the most exciting and influential school of thought that blossomed at turn-of-the-century Cambridge was the ethics of the Apostle and eventual Heretic, G. E. Moore. For instance, in his account of Bloomsbury, Quentin Bell states, in an echo of Woolf's famous declaration, that by 1900 there was a need "for a new honesty and a new charity in personal relations," and the Group found in Moore's philosophy a liberating approach to life (28–37). Bell believes Bloomsbury was born with Moore's ethos. In his landmark *Principia Ethica* (1903), a thirty-year-old Moore pursued the meaning of "goodness," finding it inevitably indefinable, yet he was still able to outline contemplative states of mind reflective of and conducive to "goodness." Though intrinsic "goodness" cannot be defined without reference to a posited natural or transcendental property, Moore argues that some fundamental principles of ethics, various *goods,* are self-evident and can be illuminated by the conceptualization of "organic unities." These "organic unities" or "wholes" may have intrinsic value, but in Moore's words, "*such a whole bears no regular proportion to the sum of the values of its parts*" (27). Therefore, in this form of holism, reducing a "whole" to its component parts does not lead to a definition of the "good." Only through an analysis of the general and immediate causal relations within a "whole" do "goodness" and "right action" become verifiable. In this vein, *Principia Ethica* further exemplifies the prevalence of synthetic agendas during the Edwardian period.

On the other hand, Moore also laid the seeds of the various modernisms, essentially founded on the belief in the "rightness" of their methodologies, when he affirmed the argument that one could "*declare*" a proposition "untrue, because its untruth is evident" to him or her. While intuition does not validate the "rightness" of an ethical choice, Moore believes, as in the case of denying that pleasure is the only good, that his intuitive supposition, if persuasive enough, "justifies us in *holding* that we are so" (144–45). By bearing in mind how actions will affect the organic whole, that is, whether they will generally make the world a better place, Moore believes that his disciples will be able to determine an immediate course of action. He emphasizes that the "idea of abstract 'rightness'" constitutes "conscience," and a "'conscientious' man [is] one who, when he deliberates, always has this idea in his mind, and does not act until he believes that his action is right" (178–79). Above all, a "common sense" should be used in making the decisions. Moore's own careful deliberations culminated in the famous last chapter in which he defines "The Ideal" in terms of qualities attainable in "this world." In the legendary platitude, Moore declares that the most decidedly "valuable things, which we know or can imagine, are certain states of consciousness, which may be roughly described as the pleasures of human intercourse and the enjoyment of beautiful objects." These "highly complex *organic unities*" link the object of enjoyment with a perceived consciousness of the object, and this appreciation brings together spiritual and material goods and makes them more valuable than the sum of their parts (188–89).

No doubt this conception of human ideals is what led to the dramatic influence of *Principia Ethica*. Keynes claimed that the influence was "the beginning of a renaissance, the opening of a new heaven on a new earth," and he added that the "New Testament is a handbook for politicians compared with the unworldliness of Moore's chapter on 'The Ideal'" (10: 435; 444).[3] Another fellow Apostle, Strachey wrote a "confession of faith" to Moore, and in reference to *Principia Ethica* he exclaimed to Leonard Woolf, "glory alleluiah!" (qtd. in Levy 235; 239). Moore's book elicited these enthusiastic responses laden with religiosity because it not only offered a new ideal of "this world," but he also explicitly questioned the legitimacy of God and heaven. For instance, Moore states: "though God may be admitted to be a more perfect object than any actual human being, the love of God may yet be inferior to human love, *if* God does not exist" (200). As Nietzsche had done twenty years earlier, Moore presented a revolutionary revaluation of traditional morality and wisdom. However, the degree to which Cambridge and Bloomsbury put Moore's theories into practice became a pointed source of debate in the memoirs of figures such as Keynes, Russell, and Leonard Woolf.

In "My Early Beliefs," Keynes reports that the effect of *Principia Ethica* on Moore's coterie of friends "dominated, and perhaps still dominate everything else." On the other hand, he also claimed that they ignored the chapter on ethical conduct and only "accepted Moore's religion" (10: 435–36). Similarly, in his autobiography, Russell states that "those who considered themselves his disciples ignored [the idea of organic unities] and degraded his ethics into advocacy of a stuffy girls'-school sentimentalizing" (71). Leonard Woolf disagrees wholeheartedly and finds Keynes' memoir a "distorted picture of Moore's beliefs." Instead, Woolf argues that in fact when he, Keynes, Strachey, and others became Moore's followers in 1903 they used *Principia Ethica* as a practical guide to ethical conduct, one that used "the more divine voice of common-sense" (161–62). R. B. Braithwaite offers the peaceful solution that

Keynes found Moore's treatise on ethical conduct old hat compared to the exhilaration produced by the new ideal (244). To further clarify this little rift, David Holdcroft presents a diplomatic perspective: "if the *Principia* and its author was not *the* major influence on Bloomsbury, it was undoubtedly *a* major influence" (133).

Although Bloomsbury had Moore's sanctification of the "enjoyment of beautiful objects," he refrained from the "task" of "Aesthetics" and thereby enabled the Group to determine what constitutes the beautiful. Though he admitted that a false evaluation could lead to "an error of taste," he also believed that a proper analysis of art could "satisfy" the observer that his or her taste was "correct" (192–95). He suggested that others could sufficiently avoid the arbitrariness of taste by using a "consensus of opinion" in their value judgments (200). Instead of the analysis of beauty, Moore later concerned himself with refining and elucidating his ethical system, and from 1914–25, he used the meetings of the Heretics as his forum. His addresses to the Society included discussions of "Intrinsic Value" in January 1916 and "A Defence of Common Sense" in January 1925. During the same time period, Bloomsbury gradually congealed and also began using the Heretics Society as a forum to advocate their tastes. Clive Bell in particular deployed Moore's philosophy in his mandarin aesthetic judgments. In Moore's words, the Group came to believe their "judgment" was "right," and this discursive development, as shown later, directly leads to the decline of the centrality of heresy and the Heretics Society.[4]

While Bloomsbury and the Apostles may have begun practicing a secular religion during the Edwardian period, traditional faith and the vision of university life as a place of religion persisted with an equal vigor at Cambridge. Despite confronting an increasingly secular society and the gradual acceptance of evolutionary thought, orthodoxy had held its own during the late Victorian age, especially at universities. Calling the phenomenon of religion at Oxford and Cambridge in the last half of the nineteenth century "one of the deepest paradoxes" (105), Brooke notes how the centrality of religion at university actually strengthened in the face of legislation that facilitated a secular education. After 1856, no pledge of adherence to the thirty-nine articles or other declaration of faith was mandatory for a degree, except in divinity. For the next fifteen years, membership in the governing body of dons, the Senate, entailed affiliation with the Church of England, but the 1871 Religious Test Acts abolished even this holdover requirement. The Second Reform Bill had enabled Gladstone to acknowledge the growth of nonconformists and push this further emancipation through Parliament.

Nevertheless, as Brooke states, "many vestiges of sectarian privilege still clung to the colleges and chapels and divinity professors" (102). Cambridge was founded as a religious institution, and in 1877 the university commissioner reaffirmed in statute that the colleges were intended to be in part a place of worship and theology. The Theological Tripos had appeared in 1874 in the wake of the abolition of the tests, and the educational system was now in place to spawn several key theological studies over the course of the rest of the century.[5] Additionally, fellows and patrons sought to continue the legacy and import of religion at university by investing in the building and restoration of college chapels. In the last half of the nineteenth century, St. John's and Queens' saw new chapels adorn their campuses. King's College Chapel continued, as it still does, to tower majestically over the town.

Filling the pews was not a difficult task on paper since the most salient religious component of university life came in the form of mandatory chapel attendance.[6] Peter Cunich finds that "[r]eligious orthodoxy remained a central feature of the university, with compulsory chapel as its symbol" (204). The dons saw themselves as functioning *in loco parentis,* and they felt that only good could come of forced attendance at services where the gospel might be heard by students disillusioned with punting and pub life. The number of compulsory services attended per week varied by college, but until the time of the Heretics resident undergraduates across the university were officially required to attend several per week and two on Sundays. Enforcing the obligatory attendance was a different matter. The agnostic dons were disinclined to do so, especially if they were skipping out on services themselves. Already in 1838, some Trinity men had formed The Society for the Prevention of Cruelty to Undergraduates, which circulated the attendance records of the master and fellows in response to The Society for the Propagation of Christianity among the dons. At King's since the 1870s, the young men could "sign a book rather than attend" (Brooke 112–15). When the undergraduates did attend, their "rowdy behaviour" and "giggling" undermined the desired instillment of discipline (Brooke 116; Cunich 226). By the end of the century, the administration realized that the problems associated with compulsory chapel required that the system be overhauled, but no adequate forms of maintaining chapel attendance could be seen.

Then in the early 1900s, Francis Cornford, a future Heretic, published a critique, *Compulsory Chapel* (1904), and a classic satire of university life, *Microcosmographia Academica* (1908). In the latter scathing little treatise that promotes itself as a guide for the young academic politician, Cornford attacks the do-nothing bureaucratic policies of the administration that prevent thought and just action. Only "when the Church is in danger" will it act, and that is only to impose "some rules" (9–10). Compulsory chapel repeatedly bears the brunt of Cornford's satire in the following passage exemplifying the handbook's style: "They [young academics] must never be troubled with having to think whether this or that ought to be done or not; it should be settled by rules. The most valuable rules are those which ordain attendance at lectures and at religious worship. If these were not enforced, young men would begin too early to take learning and religion seriously; and that is well known to be bad form. Plainly, the more rules you can invent, the less need there will be to waste time over fruitless puzzling about right and wrong" (10). In exposing the cult of stupidity and the mindlessness of rules that can repress thought, Cornford still reveals his own concern for religious questions.

The next year his colleague William Chawner brought a more staid earnestness to the issue of compulsory chapel, and his address, "Prove All Things," would lead directly to the birth of the Heretics. Compulsory chapel failed to survive the First World War in any college except Magdalene. By 1924, the "ordinary congregation" had "of late years sadly diminished" (Green 338). Though Ogden's college, ironically enough, was the last holdout, the advent and rapidly growing influence of the Heretics suggests the possibility that their presence nailed the coffin on the statute. With heresy becoming more and more intellectually legitimate, the dons could no longer justify enforcing the rule by penalty.[7] In 1921 the rule was changed, even at Magdalene, so as not to require a certain number of attendances or impose sanctions, and instead it simply read: "attendance at College Chapel is expected of all undergraduates" (Cunich 236).[8] In 1909, though, the climate at Cambridge was decidedly less tolerant.

THE "PROVE ALL THINGS" CONTROVERSY

Toward the end of Ogden's first year at Cambridge, William Chawner (1848–1911), Master at Emmanuel, publicly expressed his lingering private doubts about Christianity, and his disavowal of orthodoxy initiated a scandal known as the "Prove All Things" controversy, or alternatively, the "Chawner Affair." More interested in teaching than scholarship, Chawner in nearly forty years had only published a letter on university examinations in Greek since his prize-winning dissertation of 1872, *The Influence of Christianity upon the Legislation of Constantine the Great.* During his time at Cambridge from

1867–1911, Chawner had helped turn Emmanuel into a teaching college, and the general esteem in which he was held eventually led to his appointment as Master in 1895. Behind his face of authority, though, the master had been trying for some years to justify institutional Christian orthodoxy, and at length he concluded that it could not be maintained. At the inaugural lecture of the Emmanuel College Religious Discussion Society, Chawner shared his loss of faith.

On this May evening of 1909, Chawner's argument for the need to "Prove All Things" advocated the transgression of orthodoxy in the pursuit of the "truth" about the origins and destiny of humanity. Chawner felt promise in the return of a scholarly voice to religious debates, and his emphasis on the alienation of intellectuals from orthodoxy suggests that he held "approximately a Unitarian position" (TCA 7). Privately publishing the pamphlet in the same month, Chawner disseminated copies to all who asked. As the newly appointed dean, Charles Raven (1885–1964) remembers arriving at Emmanuel in January of 1910 amid this controversy and being asked to remedy a situation that "came as a thunderbolt among the faithful" (173). A bastion of orthodoxy, Emmanuel had been built on the former site of a Dominican monastery. Its founder, Sir Walter Mildmay, had tried to continue the spirit of the mendicant order by establishing a college in 1584 that would manifest Puritan leanings while remaining deferential to the crown. In 1909 Emmanuel still had close ties with Anglican and evangelical parsonages, and many ordinands were affiliated with the college. The master had originally pleased them sufficiently enough to gain his position. However, the orthodox administration could not have realized that Chawner was of that rare breed that grows radical with age. Raven likens him to "a man who had caught late in life the scepticism that infects most of us at eighteen; and like measles at his age it was a bad attack" (173). The shock of having such an overt heretic among the faculty grew worse once the Cambridge administration witnessed the widespread support Chawner received.

In the opening remarks of his lecture, Chawner tries to evoke a questioning mood by quoting passages from Proverbs, Thucydides, Wordsworth, and Arnold, which refer to the uncertainty of human existence. Immediately, Chawner acknowledges that he does not accept the received authority of the "precise and definite answer" Christianity offers to such questions (3). A single, fixed conception of Creation and Providence is intolerable to Chawner in a pluralistic world. Noting the presence of many world religions and even the divisive sects within Christianity, Chawner declares: "for beings finite and relative, as we are, there is no absolute truth, no ultimate body of doctrine, no rounded logical complete system, that can be comprehended in thought or set forth in words" (4). Such dismissal of logocentrism was not by any means original in 1909; the striking newness was hearing such words from the master of a college in a public forum.

Amid the relativism of belief, Chawner finds no surprise that in a post-Darwinian world there has been a "growing indifference and hostility shown towards Christianity by men of culture and learning and intelligence." Chawner's use of specific gender here seems intentional, for in his view Protestant "churches are half empty and the congregations consist of women only" (5). He further observes an indifference to Christianity in Germany, hostility in France, and a combination of the two in England. Chawner then turns his eyes on Cambridge itself, where he diagnoses a general decline in the value that the student body places upon worship and Holy Orders. An experiment in voluntary chapel attendance tried during the previous "Long Vacation" had failed miserably, leaving the chapel virtually vacant. The clerical profession attracts few, Chawner claims, not because the monetary reward for taking orders had decreased over the previous decades, but because there is "no message to deliver." Among "first class men," Chawner observes a more conspicuous lack of desire for what "ought to be the most coveted of offices" (8). In his mind, the relative ease of winning promotions and honors in the holy profession means nothing to those ambitious for intellectual stimulation. In describing the university climate at the inception of the Heretics Society, P. Sargant Florence reminds his readers: "It must be realised that in 1909 *Jude the Obscure* conditions still prevailed. A child of relatively poor parents, however clever, was virtually debarred from Oxford or Cambridge by reason of poverty" (CA 14). As Sue states in that novel, poor students who have a great "passion for learning" like Jude "were elbowed off the pavement by the millionaires' sons" (120). While economic factors might still have prevented Jude from matriculation, Chawner's paper suggests that, were he able to attend college, the poor naive boy's clerical aspirations soon would have been redirected. In 1909 Cambridge, Chawner, or maybe Ogden, would have been Jude's Sue.

While the students have turned away from Christianity, Chawner finds that the faculty respond to the crisis in faith by maintaining a placid veneer that keeps up appearances. Chawner wants to expose what he calls "a conspiracy of silence" (10), a phrase he might have borrowed from an indictment by Cambridge's own Samuel Butler in *The Way of All Flesh* (1903). After Ernest Pontifex's loss of belief, Overton critiques the self-righteous and prosperous "teachers of truth" who benefit through "a conspiracy of silence" about religious questions (299). In Chawner's Cambridge some of the professors, fellows, and lecturers are "in open opposition" to Christianity, but the general attitude remains one of "benevolent neutrality." Others accept the practical ethics taught by Christ while quietly rejecting the dogmatic underpinnings. The Master of Emmanuel wants a forum "to represent the other side" of the arguments students hear in chapel from its "official defenders." In the public schools, Chawner senses a similar control of religious questions "by artificial means" (9–10). Clerical influence still determines educational policy, and orthodox headmasters rule their intellectual superiors. For Chawner, reason and the intellectual life could not be reconciled with orthodoxy.

At this point in his paper, Chawner clarifies his thesis:

> If you have followed the thread of my argument, you will have seen that my purpose has been to show, that in the three leading nations of Western Europe there is something like a general revolt among men of intelligence against old fashioned orthodoxy, that there is a feeling of unrest and uncertainty in the religious world, that these symptoms have shown themselves as conspicuously here as elsewhere, and that there is urgent need of such a society as you are founding to-day. (10)

Faced with this cultural context, the pedant in the master wants his student audience above all to attempt to cultivate a coherent view of the world, the hallmark of Edwardian thought. For the "men" who are "the salt of the earth" historically have provided life to Christianity through the desire "to coordinate and harmonise" beliefs (11). To achieve such a synthesis of thought, a religious discussion society should use reason as its chief tool and, to validate and refine the reasoning, debate. For a proper debate, Chawner offers some structural and methodological advice for approaching the explosive subject of religion. There should be no delicacies of discussion though. The discussion society should employ "impartial criticism" and "frankness," "secure representatives of every variety of opinion," and "invite distinguished persons from outside to read papers" (11). Almost to the word, the Heretics Society adopted his advice and incorporated its details into its laws and organization. The Heretics would also denounce the orthodox mode of a priori reasoning that ignores the contradictions embedded in doctrine and tradition. Protesting against this method of "the Church," Chawner mandates an acknowledgment of evolutionary thought and comparative anthropology. His vision of the history of religion suggests that heterodox positions serve as refining agents in the development of civilization.

The orthodox voices should still be heard, however, and Chawner notes additionally that agnostics and atheists need not make an open disavowal of faith in order to avoid discomfort for friends or family. Amid all the various philosophical or religious positions, Chawner still affirms the persistence of the "moral sense," and he concluded his speech advocating doing "good" out of "sympathy" for others. By the "moral sense," he meant "the sense of duty, conscience, the categorical imperative whose right to command we admit even when we refuse our obedience" (15–16).

As would be expected, the orthodox contingent at Cambridge moved quickly to respond. Ostracizing reviews immediately appeared in both Christian and lay newspapers and journals.[9] Chawner, though, was more interested in the responses he might have elicited in those outside of the mainstream. On May 15, Chawner sent a copy of "Prove All Things" upon request to the repository at the University Library. He included a handwritten note on the first page welcoming a heated exchange with the Christian establishment: "I have great pleasure in enclosing a copy of my pamphlet. I did not send it to you for the same reason that I did not send it to some of my most intimate friends—for fear of hurting their susceptibilities. I hope that my unorthodox views will not give offence. I am told that I have already been denounced in one College chapel. This pleases me" (CUL cam.c.909.7).

Over the course of the ensuing five months, Chawner received scores of requests for a copy of the pamphlet. In addition to neutral correspondence or acknowledgments of receipt, some seventy letters survive expressing either commendation or disapprobation of his paper, or in some cases, approval of his motives but condemnation of his tactics. The letters came from such a wide variety of people and signaled such a strangely mixed audience that Chawner decided to publish all of them anonymously as a supplement to his pamphlet. Only three people denied permission to print their letters.[10] In November the Cambridge University Press printed thirty-seven letters in the order Chawner received them, with a prefatory note dated October 15. In this, he regrets that he must publish the letters anonymously, especially because twenty-three letters are from professors, fellows, and others at Cambridge "whose position would give weight to their opinion" (2). Some of these are from women teachers at Girton and Newnham. A separate section includes thirteen letters from nonresidents of Cambridge selected for diversity of perspective, which variously report the thoughts of a surgeon, a barrister, a scientist, several headmasters, and both Anglican and nonconformist clergymen. A letter added to the residents' section we know now to be signed collectively by, among others, C. K. Ogden and C(yril) M(oses)

Picciotto, the two key founders of the Heretics Society.

Nearly all of the letters express their interest in the subject matter and thank him for having sent a copy of the pamphlet so readily. The fact that many have read borrowed copies testifies to the interest in the rumor mill and uproar surrounding the Chawner Affair. Some want the further dissemination of "Prove All Things" to more remote communities and wish that Chawner would make more copies available for purchase. Indeed, the first letter writer questions Chawner's gender-specific appeal and suggests that women too should be equally confronted with "the truth" (4). The predominant tenor of the correspondence as a whole supports Chawner, appreciates his frankness and sincere tone, and particularly admires the courage of someone in such an influential and scrutinized position who is willing to proclaim such views.

A few letter writers predictably feared for the souls of young impressionable minds. One member of Cambridge suggests that, if there is "no standard of orthodoxy," the best undergraduate minds would not receive the stimulation of a consistent discussion, and the remainder would not be able to make sense of "fragments of disconnected philosophies." People would end up adopting the "*dogma* that there is no answer" (8). Aside from the intellectual arrogance of this perspective, the writer reveals a prevalent belief that heresy inevitably leads to the loss of faith. Several letters wonder what new morality could arise if the old creed is lost. One correspondent feels that a new, humanist ethical code is not enough and still wants a metaphysical unity for humanity, even if it is an "abstract God." One self-proclaimed independent thinker still doubts "whether it is wise to offer this meat to babes," and another worries about "what happens to a youngster when he goes out into the world with his religious principles gone" (19–21). Certainly, forecasts about the future of tradition and the effects of open debate both are dubious at best, and literature of this period decidedly illustrates that the etiology of changing values is moot. (Does the questioning young scholar fall into the abyss with Kurtz? Does he grow full of melancholy or troubled by the "ache of modernism" like Stephen Dedalus or Angel Clare? Or does one discover a way to cultivate a "moral sense" akin to that of Dorothea Brooke, Lord Jim, or the Schlegel sisters?) Several of the letters acknowledge doubt and the implications of modernist thought, yet some writers remain content in their faith. One cleric appreciates being kept abreast of the currents in lay interests, and another remains orthodox despite "many disquieting thoughts" (22). The pious need not defend what they believe since, for example, faith may be "of the nature of a conflict—not of a conflict with truth but with obstacles to truth which for a time appear to be true" (16). One of the faculty correspondents echoes this sentiment in believing Christianity to be "a progressive revelation," so it can only benefit from "the fullest possible discussion" (5).

Above all, the most striking condemnation concerns Chawner's position as master. The writer who denied Chawner's perception of the prevalence of agnosticism also thinks "Prove All Things" is "a distinct abuse" of Chawner's "position" and states that he has "no moral right to upset a boy's religious beliefs unless [he has] a higher religion to offer" (21). Responding to a suggestion in this letter, Ogden later joked with Chawner: "I hope the idea of leaving youngsters till they are 35 will not make much headway" (ECA 2.3.6). The credibility of the writer is further tempered by his conviction that drunken debauchery has grown in Germany ever since the people "abandoned their religion" (21). The responsibilities of masterdom remain in debate today. In his account of the Chawner affair, Brooke can admire the "basic purpose—to foster candour and openness in religious discussion," but he questions the wisdom of condemning compulsory chapel and of distributing "pamphlets attacking the orthodox from the master's lodge" (124).

While Chawner reports that his motive in publishing the letters was to offer the interested readers of "Prove All Things" more information on the state of religion, publishing the correspondence suggested to the administration that the furor might not die down and that the master's lodge now housed a loose cannon. During the Heretics' formative academic year of 1909–10, the Chawner crisis brewed at Emma. Two factors, though, checked any further plans for reform Chawner might have had in mind, his ill health and the stealing of his thunder by the Heretics.

One of the letters in the residents' section is a brief statement of interest and deference signed by twelve undergraduates from across the university on May 23, 1909. Of the new disciples of "Chawner's heresy," five were from Trinity, three from Sidney, two from Magdalene, and one each from Queens' and Caius (see figure 1). This intercollegiate student group wrote to Chawner: "We have been much interested in your pamphlet 'Prove All Things,' and should be glad to know if copies may be anywhere obtained: we feel sure that many undergraduates would be glad if it were made accessible" (ECA 2.3.6). Like the Apostles nearly a century earlier, these twelve young men had just sown the seeds of an intellectual society that would participate in determining from a privileged position the British stance on philosophical, religious, and aesthetic questions. The society would not be secret in nature, though, and the discussion forum would be open. These new "apostles" were so sure of the sentiment of the student body that at least four of them, including

Figure 1. The founders of the Cambridge Heretics Society, 1909–10. C. K. Ogden is seated second from the right. (*Source:* C. K. Ogden fonds, McMaster University Library, MCMA 114.28)

Picciotto and Ogden, used the summer to plan the birth of their prospective "Heretics Society." In the fall, Ogden began a fascinating correspondence with Chawner, soliciting his advice on how to canvass sympathetic members of the faculty and convince them to join the Heretics.

The Cambridge Heretics Society

In his account of the beginnings of the Heretics, Sargant Florence remembers that in the Michaelmas term of 1909, as a freshman, he went to "a mysterious gathering over the Pepysian Library at Magdalene . . . intent on forming a constitution and finding a name for a society to oppose compulsory college chapel and to discuss religion freely" (CA 13). Though Ogden had attended Rossall prep school in Fleetwood, Lancashire, Picciotto was from St. Paul's in London, and Florence labels the rest of the attendees of the meeting "Paulines" as well. He also describes Ogden as the "moving spirit" of the meeting in steering its course of action (CA 3; 13). The meeting profoundly influenced Florence, who immediately would become central to the workings of the Heretics and continue so for fifteen years.

At the same time that Chawner was preparing the supplemental letters for publication, Ogden and Picciotto had already discussed their plans with him and begun fishing for potential Heretics. By the time the collected letters appeared, the Heretics had already met several times, formed a constitution, and swayed several professors to join their cause. In the months from October to December of 1909, Ogden and Chawner conducted a remarkable correspondence. Ogden's alternately sophomoric and sophisticated voice in the letters illustrates the mixed exhilaration and frustration involved in starting a movement or organizing a society. He writes to Chawner as a son to father, seeking advice, courting approval. In an October 6 letter, Ogden told Chawner that the Heretics had already attracted such Honorary Members as Harrison and John McTaggart (1866–1925), two scholars who in December would deliver the pair of inaugural lectures of the Heretics Society. Ogden lists the honorary members after parenthetically stating "besides yourself." On November 1, Ogden again writes: "It was unanimously decided that the Master of Emmanuel be elected an Honorary Member" (ECA 2.3.7). Such tactical presumption did work, for "The Master of Emmanuel" soon headed the list of honorary members. Ogden was refining the memorable solicitation and marketing skills that would define and mobilize the rest of his career. Florence notes: "Somehow or other he seemed to find the right approach to the dons we enlisted, as well as to the distinguished speakers we secured" (CA 15). Despite Ogden's artful diplomacy, becoming a Heretic at this point could not have been a wise choice for Chawner, who was already caught in the imbroglio of his own design. He was also already sick, for in the same letter Ogden expressed hope for Chawner's recovery from an unstated "illness" (ECA 2.3.7). Chawner's condition would not abate until at least mid-December.

By the beginning of the Michaelmas term, the Heretics had elected Picciotto as acting chairman and Ogden as secretary, and on October 3 they met to discuss Monsignor Moyes' lecture on "How do we know there is a God?" (ECA 2.3.7). In coordination with this clerical perspective on the subject, the Heretics raised issues from a lecture McTaggart gave on "Agnosticism." Ogden's October 6 letter also described the careful yet singularly self-directed deliberations surrounding the rules for the Society. Despite their deference to faculty opinion, these undergraduates were also self-possessed and assured of their own position. The defiance of their terse manifesto is striking. Perhaps the boldest, and very modernist, assertion required of members initially confronted some dissent, i.e., the proposed rule that members "reject traditional a priori methods of approaching religious questions." Ogden told Chawner that while "to most people this is plain enough, and denotes what we require in an inoffensive manner, philosophers demur." Here Ogden means McTaggart. Though he was readily willing to become a member, McTaggart "objected that he spent 'most of his life approaching religious matters' thus" (ECA 2.3.7). He would suggest an alternative, and on November 15 Ogden sent Chawner the revised set of rules (see table 1).

The new version of laws included McTaggart's amendment to Law 4 regarding types of membership, which Ogden found "quite unobjectionable, neither too vague nor too definite" (ECA 2.3.6). McTaggart's added clause opened up another dimension to the Heretics, Associate status, which would enable the manifold increase in the number of Heretics. Though people may not be "entirely free to be Members," those "in sympathy" could join the Society as Associates. The emphasis on the word "free" may also suggest that the Associate status was, in part, designed to allow for the membership of those simultaneously affiliated with the Free Thought Association, another Cambridge discussion group of which the Heretics' officers disapproved.

At first, Ogden and the others sought to exclude unilaterally all members of this rival group of freethinkers. Without acknowledging the contradiction in philosophical tolerance, Ogden informed Chawner that he regretted this only because the Master of Emmanuel had recommended a member of the F.T.A., one Mr. Lavington.[11] While the Heretics wanted him to join, they would not withdraw their demands for exclusivity, in part because they wanted to distance themselves remotely from Aleister Crowley. Ogden explained to Chawner that when the Heretics "set out we were to endeavor as far as possible to contradict the impression produced by Mr. Crowley's introduction to Cambridge at an early stage of that Society's existence" (ECA 2.3.7). Crowley had become acquainted with the occult while an undergraduate at Cambridge during the "magic revival" of the 1890s, and by 1909, he had established his own society, the Silver Star, and published semi-pornographic manuals for traineeship in magic. If the Free Thought Association could produce "The Beast," as Crowley was known, then the Heretics wanted no dialogue with such a tainted conversation society.

In December, however, the Heretics had reached an agreement with the F.T.A. The Heretics saw promising changes on the latter's executive committee, and Ogden explained to Chawner that the group had expressed the desire "both officially and otherwise to be no more than their name would properly

Table 1. The Laws of the Cambridge Heretics Society, October 1909

I.
OF THE NATURE OF THE SOCIETY.

1. That the name of the Society be "The Heretics."
2. That the object of the Society be to promote discussion on problems of religion, philosophy, and art.

II.
OF MEMBERSHIP AND ASSOCIATION.

3. That the Society consist of Members, Associates, and Honorary Members, who shall be elected by the members.
4. That the Members consist of those who reject traditional a priori methods of approaching religious questions; that Associates consist of those who, while in sympathy with the general principle of open discussion, are not entirely free to be Members.
5. That Members and Associates be elected from members of the University of Cambridge below the degree of M.A. and from students of Newnham and Girton Colleges; that Honorary Members be elected from those not eligible for Membership or Association, owing either to their being above the degree of B.A. or to their not being Members of the University.

III.
OF SUBSCRIPTION.

6. That Members pay 2s. 6d., Associates 1s. 6d. subscription per term.

IV.
OF OFFICERS.

7. That a Chairman, a Treasurer, and a Secretary, be elected at the end of each Term, and that these Officers form a Committee which shall decide all arrangements for meetings.

V.
OF MEETINGS.

8. That meetings be held not less than four times a Term, at any place deemed suitable; and that at all meetings Members, Associates, and Honorary Members may introduce visitors.
9. That if any Member challenge the ruling of the Chairman he may appeal to the members present, a majority of whom shall decide the point.

VI.
OF PRIVATE BUSINESS

10. That all matters of private business be in the hands of Members only.
11. That any change in the laws may only be effected by the vote of two-thirds of all Members of the Society.
12. That any Law, except Law 11, may be suspended for any meeting by a majority of members present at any meeting.

Source: MCMA 114.1

imply." Hence, while full members of the Heretics "remain distinct" and have "sole authority," members of the F.T.A. could participate through Associate status. Ogden added that the Heretics' election of Francis Cornford, who was affiliated with the F.T.A., to Honorary Membership "formed a natural link in the conclusion of this friendly agreement." More importantly, the Heretics wanted to create a united front of freethinking, since "it is undesirable that the outside world should rejoice at any misunderstanding between us" (ECA 2.3.7). Through this process of appropriation, the Heretics began to form an umbrella coalition of dissent and heterodoxy at Cambridge. The alliance would become insignificant as the Heretics grew and came to overshadow the other dissenters. The F.T.A. would lose some of the spotlight as Ogden's managerial skills quickly drew such figures as Shaw, Chesterton, and Russell to the Heretics. Additionally, after several joint meetings between the Heretics and the Emmanuel College Religious Discussion Society, the latter became supernumerary and faded away.

During its formative stage, the Heretics also struggled over some logistical and functional aspects of the laws. When its numbers were so small that the location of the meeting did not matter, the Heretics held their informal meetings in a member's rooms or a pub or coffee shop. Mostly the meetings were held in Ogden's rooms, which at first were in the attic over the Pepysian Library at Magdalene. Since these rooms could only host thirty people, the Heretics initially thought of limiting undergraduate membership to fifteen. Later when Ogden moved in the fall of 1911 to an office over MacFisheries in Petty Cury, the meetings went with him, a fortunate change which precluded the necessity of limiting membership. The flat above this fish business on Trumpington Street, what everyone knew as "Top Hole," would also be Ogden's headquarters for the *Cambridge Magazine*. G. F. Fox of Newnham playfully remembers the effect that the proximity of the fish house had on her: "For long after, the smell of fish recalled the Heretics" (88). In her memoir, Dora Russell recalls that for the meetings "one waded or sat on" Ogden's filing system, which consisted of "a great many books which lay in piles" next to "piles and piles of papers and letters" (43). The Heretics might have been mistaken for sardines in these moments. Every Sunday night amid this atmosphere a member or guest would present a paper on any aspect of religion, art, or philosophy, and then open up the floor to discussion. These lively informal meetings were the forum for introducing visitors for potential membership, since the four or five plenary addresses held each term in lecture halls were not conducive to rapport-building conversation.

The laws of the Heretics Society were slightly modified over its lifespan.

Figure 2. Triptych program of the Cambridge Heretics Society, Michaelmas term 1911. (*Source:* C. K. Ogden fonds, McMaster University Library, MCMA 114.7)

One change allowed nonmembers to hold the Chair at the plenary meetings, and in 1921 an Economic Section of the Heretics was inaugurated. By November of 1909, though, the laws were finalized enough to let the young radicals turn to soliciting further Honorary Members. The faculty then knew exactly what commitment they were making. The Apostles G. M. Trevelyan, Lowes Dickinson, and G. H. Hardy were among the first of their star recruits, while J. M. Keynes replied to Ogden by the 15th that he "would rather not be" an Honorary Member (ECA 2.3.6). Within three weeks Keynes had inexplicably changed his mind, and he was on Ogden's list of fifteen Honorary Members presented at the inaugural lectures of December 8 (ECA 2.3.7) (see figure 2). When the Heretics first issued their green-printed triptych schedule of meetings in the Lent term of 1910, Keynes name is on the right leaf listed among the nineteen original Honorary Members.[12] In early December, these nearly outnumbered the twenty-three undergraduate Heretics. The appetite for heresy was stronger initially amongst the older generation at Cambridge. They had been craving it longer. However, so that their number "may not appear out of proportion," the Heretics decided to limit the Honorary Members to twenty until there were at least fifty regular members and associates. McTaggart's and Harrison's inaugural lectures doubled their size as hoped, and Ogden shared with Chawner his optimism for the growth of the Society since they were "only just beginning to be heard of" (ECA 2.3.7).

The Associate status also enabled the women of Girton to attend meetings, since the College administration forbade them to join the Heretics outright (Fox 88). Chaperon rules also curtailed attendance until Ogden found a way to circumvent the tradition. Dora Black of Girton, who later gave a joint presentation before the Heretics with her future husband, Bertrand Russell, delighted in the glee of escaping holy retreats or College chapel on Sundays with an "exeat permit" she would use to attend Heretics' meetings. The administration could only frown. Black would "bicycle off there . . . with a most agreeable feeling of defiance and liberation" (42). She noted how Ogden would "bolster the self-confidence of the more obscure," and felt that she was "one of those who would not have put pen to paper but for his encouragement" (MCMA 65). She would later be secretary of the Heretics in 1918–19. Looking back and wondering "how women ever managed to free themselves from their corsets . . . and the iron straitjacket imposed on them by religion, morality and social sanctions," Russell, née Black, ascribes part of their success to the Heretics' protest "against authority." She highlights the particular role of the Heretics after stating: "I believe that the metaphysical discussions that went on in Cambridge from 1900 onwards had very great political and social repercussions, not the least of these the emancipation of women" (*Tamarisk* 41–42). P. Sargant Florence reports that Alix, his sister who later translated Freud's papers with her husband, James Strachey, told him that she found meetings of the Heretics "one of the few occasions of real University coeducation" (CA 17). The philosophical ideas heard therein and "the knowledge that heresy is contagious" were the chief weapons in Dora Russell's vision of the war against authority (*Tamarisk* 43).

As a result of Jane Harrison's presence on the faculty, a presence Virginia Woolf calls "formidable yet humble" (*Room* 18), Newnham women could join from the outset. Chaperons were also required there, though. As G. F. Fox of Newnham remembers, the protective elderly mandated that the nubile women be "shepherded by a don" to "such a dangerous debating society" (88). Undergraduate women of both Girton and Newnham held committee posts and contributed important papers at the informal meetings.[13] From inception, the Heretics had sought to include women's voices in the religious debates, as one of Chawner's correspondents had suggested, and by 1911, the Heretics changed the laws in order to ensure representation on the executive committee of at least one student from Girton or Newnham. For the 1919–20 academic year, three of the seven committee members were women, including the secretary, a prestigious post.

When Florence's aunt, Ethel Sargant, "took charge" as an Honorary Fellow at Girton, the college had their counterpart to Harrison, and Girton women could then attend the Heretics unrestricted. The hundredth meeting of the Society took place on January 28, 1913, at Sargant's house, the Old Rectory at Girton. This meeting was actually a dinner party celebrating the occasion with a six-course meal flamboyantly punctuated by arched tongue and fillets of sole à la Cardinal (MCMA 114.5).

The Inaugural Lectures

Despite the maturity of Ogden's correspondence with Chawner, the neophyte heretic still displayed brief moments of tentativeness and insecurity. A few members of the Heretics had expressed reservations about the notorious name by which people would know them. However, when the Heretics Society went public in the lecture rooms of Trinity College on the night of Wednesday, December 8, the members had resolved their nominal qualms. Moreover, Jane Harrison, in her usual stately ebullience, gave the Heretics cause for pride in their choice of name when she "characterised this as 'most inspiring.'" Harrison and McTaggart also eliminated any residual fears the Heretics might have had about their acceptance when "in spite of pressing engagements [they] very kindly promised speeches for about 20 minutes each" (ECA 2.3.7). Then, in their opening remarks, Harrison suggested that the Heretics embodied the spirit of the times, and that at present humans were morally obliged to become heretics, and McTaggart dared his audience to pursue to the furthest extent the implications that "truth" might have on religious questions. Together the inaugural speeches illustrated the two chief strains of thought that would characterize the Heretics before the war. McTaggart brought to metaphysical and ethical questions a rational utilitarianism, infused with notions of love and happiness. In her address, "Heresy and Humanity," Harrison checked any rigidity in McTaggart's colder calculations by claiming that heresy, as "the child of Science," can lead to a new way of life and vision of the world through the use of cultural abstractions and the recognition of "an organic spiritual union" (35–39).

Amid the panoply of academic anthropologists researching pagan cultures at the turn of the century, Harrison stood alone in professing markedly
feminist and heretical positions. Criticism of late has only begun to recuperate her interesting life and avant-garde ideas. She was among the first generation of women to receive a college education in Britain, and over the course
of her fellowship at Newnham, she became known as a true performer at
the podium, fondly remembered for her evocative gestures. In spanning the
period from 1883 to 1924, Harrison's academic career roughly embodies the
historical trajectory of the intellectual, political, and cultural ideas addressed
in this study. The historical reception of Harrison's ideas also exemplifies the
gradual acceptance over time of heresy and heretics that history sometimes
allows, and her development of Nietzsche's idealized sense of pre-Olympian
cults illustrates the anthropological and historical relations between paganism and Christianity of particular interest to Pater, Hardy, and Joyce.

Opening her address to the Heretics with an etymological account of the
word "heresy," Harrison claims that a "zealous pursuit," forever embedded in
the word, continues to radiate from the courage of heretics "who were burnt
at the stake for love of an idea" (27). The pejoration of the word only arises
from "an enemy's mouth" since the value of personal "choice" is also rooted
in the history of the word. In pursuing her driving question as to why heresy
becomes "desirable," Harrison returns to a speculative time when societies
first formed their initial bonds. When "sympathy" and "uniformity" draw
people together, the collective struggle for life cannot abide the heretic. The
modern day "good soldier" is an avatar of the archetypal orthodox person.
The danger of rejecting tradition had previously been akin to abandoning the
safety of the "herd," but Harrison suggests that as a result of the progress of
civilization a self-defining membership in the Heretics is not only obligatory
but desirable. To paraphrase Harrison's perspective, the toleration and viability of the modern heretic derives from the humanist growth of civilization.
In the past, custom enslaved its peoples and wielded a tyranny so powerful
that individual thought was unheard of in a culture mechanically chugging
through time without recognizing a need for improvement. The past, Harrison provocatively states, is embodied by "an oligarchy of old men," "and in
such a society, personal choice, heresy, is impossible" (28–29).

In Harrison's view, this oligarchy perpetuates orthodoxy and blind faith
out of the force of "herd suggestion" that causes traditional views to have
the feel of instinct. These collective suggestions seem ineluctable because as
she states, "they are what Mr. William James would call a priori syntheses of
the most perfect sort." Here Harrison appeals to her audience's vowed rejec-

tion of all "traditional a priori methods of approaching religious questions."
When discussing this topic, Harrison feels that a pious perspective is inher-
ently intense and irrational, so she calls on the Heretics not to "reason with
our opponents," but rather try "to get this immense force of herd-suggestion
on to the side we believe to be right" (31–32). While evincing a desire for
a new synthesis, Harrison not only seems to forget the better intentions of
the Heretics in courting open debate, but she also anticipates Bloomsbury's
self-assured consensus building and G. K. Chesterton's criticism of heresy. As
noted before, in his dealings with the Heretics, he implied that heresy ends
when it begins to think itself "right." It is one of the compelling aspects of the
Heretics that they provided a forum so tolerant that internal dissent never
allowed for a foothold strong enough to begin promulgating its own orthodoxy. While the individual Heretics, and Ogden especially, would begin to
defend the correctness of their own personal schools of thought, for over
twenty years the Heretics enabled the possibility of being oppositional out of
principle.

On many levels, Harrison's address draws on the methodology and perspective of Nietzsche's works. She put forth a vision of humanity that evolves
across time by reconciling contradictory elements and moving beyond the
past. Reason is a useful tool for her, but equally important is the ability to
acknowledge the irrational in life. While Harrison declares an "*impasse*" in
the nineteenth-century struggle between orthodoxy and science, tradition
and individual freedom, she claims that in the Edwardian period "life" began
to feel "its way blindly to a solution, to what was literally a harmony." In this
way, Harrison characterizes the Edwardian period in a manner similar to
Nietzsche's description of the nature of Greek tragedy in the time of Aeschylus. In *The Birth of Tragedy* (1872), he argues that the plays of Aeschylus
represent an aesthetic reconciliation of the old world collectivity of Dionysus and the new world individuating processes of Apollo and the other
Olympian gods. Similarly, Harrison inspires her fellow Edwardians with
thoughts that they have also managed a remarkable synthesis of worldviews.
By progressively liberating the individual within the ties of civilization, the
Edwardians embody a "disparate organism." The modern miraculous harmony lies in the fact that a "Society" can be composed of "Heretics." However, Harrison implies that the future of heresy may see its assimilation by
society: "We live now at the transition moment; we have broken with the
old, we have not quite adjusted ourselves to the new" (35–36). In a sense,
she affirms Arnold's diagnosis of "the want of correspondence" between
"old bottles" and "new wine." Through the cooperation implicit in society,

though, Harrison believes that the Edwardians "at once differentiate and organically unite" and that this "new gospel" saves people "not by science, not by abstraction, but by a new mode of life" (37).

Though Harrison may recast many of Nietzsche's views, her critique of the "oligarchy of old men" and her privileging of the pre-Olympian matriarchal Greek cults distinguish her from his repeated denigration of women. Such sharp feminist perspectives had earlier hindered Harrison's academic career, but by 1909 she was firmly entrenched in her fellowship at Newnham and had already written her influential *Prolegomena to the Study of Greek Religion* (1903). She could then join Chawner in growing more radical with age, and her general reputation and self-confidence helped to defuse the charge of Cambridge's own oligarchy of old men. In fact, when Harrison turned to publishing her address, she told her fellow Cambridge Ritualist, Gilbert Murray, that she wanted to send copies "to lots of young girls who are full of sweetness by nature but who for conscience sake are Militants" (J. Stewart 119). Her militancy was strictly pacifist in its desire for a radical liberation of the human spirit, and she concludes her address with her own view that only "in a civilised anarchy . . . can the individual come to his full right and function" (40).

In his 1962 preface to her later work, *Epilegomena to the Study of Greek Religion, and Themis,* John Wilson suggests that "many of her colleagues were utterly bewildered and angered by her" because she was a "militant agnostic" who "gave no comfort" to the Christian society in which she lived (x). Wilson therefore points to the conservative political and religious leanings of her contemporary publishers as the reason her books went out of print. Shelley Arlen observes that "Harrison's feminism, pacifism, and atheism made her a particular target for the outrage of conservative male colleagues" (165). In addition to these radical ideas, her attack on the primacy of reason in studying the Greeks aligned her too much with Nietzsche for some of her contemporaries. While antagonizing some of her lay peers, Harrison's address also elicited a hostile response from Edward Selwyn, an Anglican priest and fellow at Corpus Christi College. In *Tradition and Reason: being a reply to Miss Harrison's 'Heresy and Humanity'* (1911), Selwyn tried to defame her work as "emotional," "provincial," and an "amazing position," arrived at, not surprisingly "by the irregular tendency of her own logic" (13). However, Selwyn does not address Harrison herself, but those students "who have not yet quite decided that they will 'not reason with their opponents'" (5). In other words, he overemphasizes her one point of questionable rhetoric. In distorting Harrison's desire for free thought and open debate, Selwyn tries to appeal to those Cambridge undergraduates who will have only read his paper. Underscoring her definition of heresy as "personal choice," he wants people to choose to be traditional.

For the title of his inaugural address, "Dare To Be Wise," McTaggart anglicized the motto of the University of New Zealand, and asserted that the Heretics have the "duty" to follow the "injunction"—"Sapere Aude" (3). In discussions of religion and philosophy, McTaggart agreed with James' *The Varieties of Religious Experience* (1902) in recognizing the undeniable lived experience of many people whose happiness fundamentally depends upon a belief in God.[14] However, the "search for truth" about religious questions calls for a unique brand of courage so that the seeker is willing to confront painful and bleak conclusions drawn from independent reasoning. Echoing his formative influence on the laws of the Heretics, McTaggart declares that each potential philosophical or religious question must be approached without any a priori assumptions. Though philosophical investigation may destroy happiness, this possible effect cannot legitimately lead to a denial of an undesired conclusion.

The bulk of McTaggart's quickfire address served as a pointed corrective to both the religious and philosophical communities. Through his dialectical methodology, McTaggart exposed the errors of both sides in order to let the Heretics begin their philosophical quests on a proper footing. In his mind, doomsday prophets mistakenly assert that "if certain views on religious matters were true, all morality would lose its validity" (4). To this perennial perception of the decline of morality, McTaggart retorts that, aside from precluding the need for holy observances, disbelieving in religion does not affect everyday life and its perpetual moral choices. The second error of defenders of the faith is to assume that agnosticism or heresy "would destroy the value, for those who accepted the beliefs, of many of those parts of experience which would otherwise have the highest value" (5). Here McTaggart disagrees with Tennyson's claim in *In Memoriam* that love would suffer without a belief in immortality; instead, the unconditional goodness of love should be valued regardless of duration. Asserting "the practical importance of the problems of religion," McTaggart argues that all moral and metaphysical questions "must be answered one way or the other according to the solution we adopt of religious problems" (4–7). As a metaphysician, McTaggart shares with religious-minded people an interest in what he considers to be the most central concerns of humanity. Religion must be debated.

The chief difference between religion and philosophy, as McTaggart reminds the Heretics, is that the latter does not accept a proposition without sufficient evidence. In turning to philosophical questions, McTaggart demonstrates for his audience the proper methodology to use in following the fourth law of the Heretics, the rejection of "traditional a priori methods of approaching religious questions." Therefore, "test everything," and however painful it may be, dismiss what does not fit, and endure the consequences since there is no certainty beforehand that religion will not be challenged by the implications of the findings. At work here is the Edwardian synthetic agenda, trying to harmonize beliefs, beginning to show signs of the modernist proclivity for exclusion.

In miniature, McTaggart's address replicates many of the arguments from his *Some Dogmas of Religion* (1906). By revisiting his personal idealist positions there, it is easier to understand his incomplete responses to the religious questions he cursorily raises. For in discussing immortality, the existence of God, the general goodness or evilness of the universe, and whether it is progressing or devolving, McTaggart only offers some guidelines for the investigations. In his earlier work, he had suggested the possibility of immortality, and thereby escaped Dante's circle of hell for heretics, while arguing against the belief in a personal God. The questions about the universe affect potential happiness, and this factor taints the objectivity of the pursuit and influences both benevolent and maleficent views of the world. To the Heretics, McTaggart declared that on this matter there "is no intrinsic à priori connection between existence and goodness." Further, he indirectly commands them to reject Kant's idea of a categorical imperative since they should not believe an action to be "truthful" simply because it unilaterally leads to good. Though he would like to prove the world good, it may in fact "be very bad." Assuming that the universe is benign blindly begs the question of "the nature of existence" which McTaggart claims "is the one we are setting out to determine" (12). Interestingly in his major work, *The Nature of Existence* (1921), McTaggart later concluded that time will end and that, in this stage of existence, beings will exult in a pure state of love. Along the path to such potentially wondrous conclusions, he promises nothing else to the Heretics but the glory of the search itself. Quoting some anaphoric lines from William Morris' "Love is Enough," he suggests that, though the search for wisdom may endure repeated suffering, the reward comes from seeking truth for its own sake.

As would be the practice at future meetings, the chairperson, in this case Francis Cornford, opened the floor to questions. Often the ensuing discussion would last two or three hours before the Heretics would close the meeting near midnight. After this first meeting, Harrison prophetically wrote to Ogden over the Christmas vacation: "I thought the discussion that followed McTaggart's paper promised well for the future" (MCMA 107.8). In November, McTaggart had written a letter to Chawner too late to be included in the "Prove All Things" supplement. After his inaugural address, McTaggart might have felt that his prophetic words applied equally to himself: "I am convinced that in twenty years those who remember 1909 will realise how much your action has done to promote in Cambridge not only true learning, but also true religion" (WCL 402–3).

Chapter 2

The Early Years of the
Cambridge Heretics, 1910–14

AFTER THE INAUGURAL lectures at the end of 1909, the Heretics Society indeed enjoyed tremendous growth and notoriety until the First World War drained Cambridge of its men. By 1913, over 200 undergraduates had joined the Heretics, representing between five and ten percent of the student population (CH 226).[1] This period from 1910 to 1914 was one of the two most active and influential times of the Society, the other being 1920–24 when "normalcy" returned to campus after the war and the influenza epidemic, and Ogden finally would finish his twelve-year presidency of the Heretics. In the "Georgian" period, though, a sense of discovery and a remarkable diversity of perspective tempered the Heretics' meetings with a tolerance and joy of religious debate noticeably diminished after the war. For one thing, the voice of orthodoxy, or at least liberal Christianity, maintained a consistent presence in the early years with addresses by the Reverends P. N. Waggett, E. W. Lummis, and R .J. Campbell, a popular Fabian cleric who preached the gospel of social reform at the City Temple.[2] Additionally, the two most resonant debates at the Heretics saw Christians G. K. Chesterton and H .G. Wood respond to the "heresies" of Bernard Shaw and J. M. Robertson, M.P., respectively. In the 1920s, the topics of the meetings became nearly altogether secular, though the speakers still often identified their works as heretical.[3]

By then, Ogden had established himself as a major editor who controlled *The Cambridge Magazine, Psyche,* and the Today and Tomorrow Series. He also had co-written *The Meaning of Meaning* (1923) with I. A. Richards and translated into English Wittgenstein's *Tractatus Logico-Philosophicus* (1922). Ogden's interest in language and specifically Benthamite principles of linguistic reform had earlier carried over into the Heretics Society and, according to Florence, "set the tone of Heretics discussion" (CH 232). From all accounts, Ogden's presence in the social gatherings of the Society was strategically understated, and he often dissembled his personal feelings on matters. Terrence Gordon emphasizes Ogden's fascination with the use of African and other assorted masks in speaking to people and claims that he was "[n]ever satisfied with any vantage point but the panoptic" (3–9).[4] Similarly, Florence explains that Ogden remained out of the spotlight because he "seemed rather to fancy the role of an *éminence grise* acting in secret" (CA 15). Dora Russell reports that he presided with "his usual impish provocation of argument" (*Tamarisk* 43). Perhaps most revealing is Ogden's own description of his interaction with the Heretics. Though the following comment was written in 1929 as part of a grant proposal for language study, it nevertheless suggests that he distanced himself from the Heretics' meetings with a calculating objective in mind: "In 1909 with a view to studying the handling of words in practical discussion I founded a society called 'The Heretics,' which for the next 12 years played a considerable part in University life and thought . . . I was thus able to stage and direct some 300 experiments of three hours each, to study the defects of verbal exposition and argument, under the most favourable conditions" (MCMA 128.10). At the time of the application, Ogden had just started his Orthological Institute (1928–56), and he defines "orthology" as "the term which has been used to cover the new researches into the possibilities of developing the instrument of language (from the Greek *orthos* 'correct' and *logos* 'word')" (MCMA 128.10). In a sense, "heresy" trained Ogden to develop his own orthodoxy of language. In the conclusion, the finer details of his creation of Basic English at the Orthological Institute and the implications of this transformative shift become apparent in discussions of *Finnegans Wake* and *Nineteen Eighty-Four*.

Though Ogden's personal engagement with the Heretics raises many important questions about his motivations and influence, before the war he was still a tyro in his scholastics, and the older intellectuals still championed or confronted the workings of religious heresy. While Ogden was remaining a relatively silent observer, however, two events occurred that would solidify his eventual prominence in the Heretics. In the academic year of 1910–11, the president, C. M. Picciotto, left the Society, and the Emmanuel College governing body silenced Chawner, the Heretics' inspiring voice, shortly before his death. The leadership of the Heretics then clearly fell to Ogden and his detached persona. He would use *The Cambridge Magazine* to make his voice heard and to publish extracts and reports of the Heretics' meetings. In the journal, he often referred to the Heretics as "the ungodly."

Before Chawner died, the Heretics shared the forum for Cambridge free

THE MASTER AND FREDDY.

"FIAT VERITAS, RUAT CŒLUM!"

Figure 3. "Let there be truth, may the heavens fall": cartoon lampooning "The Chawner Affair" at Cambridge. William Chawner, Master of Emmanuel College, hands out pamphlets on freethinking, while the Senior Tutor F. W. Head turns away in horror. (*Source: The Lion,* May 1910)

thought with the Emmanuel College Religious Discussion Society. Often the two organizations held joint meetings, including the pair of inaugural lectures for the Heretics. On March 10, 1910, Chawner presided over one of these meetings in which the Apostle L. H. G. Greenwood discussed "Agnosticism and Conduct"; two months later Chawner's continued dissemination of pamphlets finally precipitated a response from the administration at Emmanuel. On May 18, he circulated an address by the president emeritus of Harvard University, Charles Eliot, entitled "The Religion of the Future." Chawner attached a cover letter in which he stated his hope that the pamphlet would help undergraduates "to discard the ill-founded and superstitious elements which still survive in popular Christianity" (TCA 10). A cartoon in the college paper, *The Lion,* captures the effect of Chawner's renewed readiness to spread free thought (see figure 3). The senior tutor, F. W. Head, here recoils in horror from the sight of another corrupted undergraduate mind, and less than two weeks later he signed the first public opposition to Chawner at Cambridge. After Charles Raven received a letter from a headmaster asking "whether Emmanuel was a fit place for a candidate for

holy orders" (178), he, Head, and five other fellows sent Chawner the following protest: "Fellows of the College whose signatures appear below wish
to represent to the Master their conviction that his recent practice of issuing
to the undergraduates pamphlets and circulars dealing with questions of
religious controversy is detrimental to the general interests of the College
and specifically and gravely embarrassing to other officers of the College
in the discharge of their statutory duties" (TCA 7).[5] While Chawner had an
equivalent number of supporters on the governing body, he nevertheless
sought consul which opined that he had not broken any college statutes, but
had "committed a breach of duty as Master." Caustic and unrepentant, he
only admitted an error in publishing a denunciation of compulsory chapel
and promised to be silent thereafter about that issue (TCA 8–9).

Eighteen months after "Prove All Things," however, Chawner's candid
voice echoed through the halls of Emmanuel once more. In his address to the
E.C.R.D.S., "Truthfulness in Religion," Chawner wanted "to put into practice
the principles [he] advocated" (2). Stridently against those who believe it is
better not "to say what we think" (5), he labeled miracles an embarrassment,
atonement unjust, and openly denied the divinity of Christ. For the most
part, though, Chawner concerned himself here with defending heterodoxy,
calling for a secular educational system, and stressing the idea that religion
evolves. In fact, he mentions the significant work of the Heretics Society in
manifesting this notion, and states that "[p]rogress has been the work of
the dissenter, the non-conformist, the heretic" (19; 9). Chawner would not
see much more of the "progress" made by the Heretics. While on holiday
the next spring, he died in Switzerland on March 19, 1911. According to D.
B. Welbourn, there "were those who alleged he had committed suicide, but
probably he died of a brain tumour" (TCP 19).

The passing of the master, though, was not an irreparable loss to the Heretics since the host of Honorary Members were already in place to assume
mentoring roles. In particular, two fellows of Trinity College, Francis Cornford (1874–1943) and G(eorge) M(acaulay) Trevelyan (1876–1962), took
up Chawner's lead in condemning compulsory chapel. By the time of the
Heretics' arrival on campus, Cornford had already satirized chapel attendance in *Microcosmographia Academica,* and his *Thucydides Mythistoricus*
(1907) established him as one of the Cambridge Ritualists. In that unorthodox work, Cornford had argued for the myth and ritual origins submerged
beneath Thucydides' history. In October of 1911, Cornford addressed the
Heretics on "Religion in the University" and offered a close analysis of Anglicanism on campus in its component parts: Theology, Ritual, and Faith. In

this short speech which Ogden transcribed for publication, Cornford affirms that, though the diversity and ubiquity of religion makes it one of the most important studies, campus life should be free from religious bias which corrupts the intellectual atmosphere. Religious tests for *all* teaching posts should be rigorously abolished because he suspects that possibly "sometimes tests are secretly applied in making College appointments." More importantly for Cornford, compulsory chapel should be eradicated since its oppressive nature abuses the power of ritual to influence impressionable minds, and those forced to attend will compromise the morale of those who do want to worship. Since it is "not the business" of a university "to maintain one form of creed," Cornford suggests that it should "have a mosque, a Hindu temple, a Baptist chapel and so on" if they have an Anglican chapel (3). To some degree this policy is in effect today on university campuses, though Cornford saw a different future for ritual faith, which he felt was dependent on theology. Explaining his definition of a Heretic "as one who thinks that theology can be remodelled," he promises the ambivalent hope to his audience of Heretics that if "they are successful, their heresy [will become] the orthodoxy of the next generation." He foresees the development of heresy as one that will make the Incarnation and the Resurrection dubious and leave only the theology of Christ, who was "the arch-heretic and rebel of his time." However, Cornford suggests that by then "students of comparative religion" will have traced "the continuous history of the representation of the divine back from its present forms to its primitive origin" (5–6). Here Cornford is laying the groundwork for his *From Religion to Philosophy* (1912) and sensing the modernist impulse toward a historical method applied to the life of Jesus. Cornford, though, sides with the paganizers who see Christ as another in a line of "dying" gods.

In October 1913, Trevelyan further questioned the ethics of religious conformity in his address, "De Haeretico Comburendo." Trevelyan, a fellow of Trinity who would become the most widely read historian of his generation, had recently completed a trilogy on Garibaldi, highlighting the Italian patriot's anticlericalism. Trevelyan also was a militant agnostic with a particular anti-Papist strain. His *History of England* elicited the defensive reaction of Hilaire Belloc, who wrote his own Catholic-inflected history of the nation. However, tolerance is the keynote of Trevelyan's address, and he insists that heretics, with whom he identifies himself, must stand up for their beliefs yet still feel the orthodox are approachable for discussion. The title of his address, "De Haeretico Comburendo," refers to the act of Henry IV, which, according to the Eleventh Edition of the *Encyclopedia Britannica*, "enabled the diocesan alone, without the co-operation of a synod, to pronounce the sentence of heresy, and required the sheriff to execute it by burning the offender, without waiting for the consent of the crown" (Garvie 362). As Trevelyan explains, his paper examines "the general conception that underlay that old statute, namely the assumption that every one is morally bound to believe the doctrines of the society in which he lives, and that if he does not really believe them he ought at least to conceal his thoughts" (1). Since he finds this conception to be the prevalent tenor of the Edwardian period, Trevelyan implores his audience, for the humanitarian good, to resist the demands of social convention while refraining from an equivalent reactionary intolerance. Insincere conformity, including chapel attendance, whether for altruistic or conventional reasons, "is disastrous to human progress," and the hypocrisy results in a "decay in moral character" (7). Above all, tolerance is necessary because "an ever increasing variety of religious experience and belief is the rule of the modern world" (2). For Trevelyan, society should mirror the platform of the Heretics in not privileging any religion, thereby eroding intolerant divisions and facilitating the vision of all peoples as "one body" (22). He points out that the Edwardians are already on the road to this universal equality by reaching "the last stages of legal persecution, in the application of the Blasphemy Laws in cases only where the 'Christian doctrines are attacked by poor and more or less uneducated persons in language which may be described as coarse and offensive'" (3). Affirming Marsh's argument that blasphemy laws were a particularly class-based interdiction, Trevelyan did not foresee the turn toward censorship a few years later that such propriety would engender.

Along with the death of their mentor less than two years after their inception, the Heretics endured another fundamental change to their organizational dynamics when Picciotto resigned his presidency and membership. Florence refers to this change as the "disconcerting conversion of Pittiotto [sic] to mysticism" (CA 14). Gordon also reports Ogden's succession to the presidency when Picciotto "converted unaccountably to mysticism" (6). However, Picciotto in fact had tried to account for his experience when he addressed the Heretics for the one and only time on October 23, 1910. His epistolary conceit, "Via Mystica," elaborates on the difficulties and rewards of mysticism by addressing the unreported questions of a friendly correspondent, "Dick." Since he believes "mysticism to be in its essence undefinable and, to all but the sympathetic, meaningless" (ix), Picciotto stresses the conception that the mystical mind is of a different "kind" and not degree. Therefore, those who deny the intuitive and spiritual dimensions of knowledge cannot glimpse the fundamental unity of an intangible world withdrawn from rational thought. Picciotto finds himself in a difficult position, not only because there are unsympathetic gainsayers of mysticism, but he is obliged to account for himself despite the inadequacies of language to communicate such profound experiences. Language is of the rational world, but the joy, sorrow, and primal unity seen when the veil of Maia lifts propels one to struggle against the walls of ineffability. The nature of mystical experience makes it, however, dramatically convincing to Picciotto, in that as William James describes the consciousness of the mystic, "something in you absolutely *knows*" that the result of intuition and meditation "must be truer than any logic-chopping rationalistic talk" because "articulate reasons are cogent for us only when our inarticulate feelings of reality have already been impressed in favor of the same conclusion" (84–85).

During the period in which Picciotto underwent a spiritual transformation, Ogden began a correspondence with Lady Victoria Welby (1837–1912) and then became the leading proponent of her forays into "Significs," a study of language as signs of meaning.[6] Picciotto's address reflects the divergent paths of the two leading undergraduate Heretics. His newfound mysticism was "disconcerting" to Florence because he, like Ogden, was a rationalist. In the opening remarks of his first address to the Heretics on February 9, 1911, Ogden might have had Picciotto's difficulties with expression most clearly in mind: "Since reaching what may better perhaps be called years of indiscretion every successive discussion to which it has been my fortune to listen has left me more convinced of the incalculable confusion produced by our neglect of the clear conceptions of the functions of language" (CUL Add. Ms.8309). This address would become the basis of the historical section of Ogden and Richards' *The Meaning of Meaning*. Picciotto would later enter the bar and become a member of both the Council of the Jewish Historical Society and the Knights of Columbus, an international benevolent organization of Roman Catholic men. In fact, "Via Mystica" already defended Catholicism as the most important religion on the grounds that it perpetuates mysteries and "carries ecstasies into daily life" (18). For Picciotto, the Heretics were enemies of mystical reverence, since in his mind "one is either a born mystic or a born rationalist, and the two can have nothing to say to each other" (34). Finding that empirical minds "are best left alone" (x), he left the Heretics, apparently taking to heart the concluding words of Harrison's inaugural lecture. She ended her talk with an admonition against egotism, and suggested that when it "snarls within us, we should resign our membership of the Society of Heretics, and go back for a season of the 'godly discipline' of the herd" (41). Among Picciotto's few subsequent publications is a history of his London Day School, St. Paul's, in which he extolled its virtue in letting "all things . . . be openly and freely discussed, by word of mouth or in print, and that nothing need ever be regarded as prohibited save the blasphemous or the obscene" (140). Between the interdictions against blasphemy and obscenity discussed earlier, heresy came forth as the means by which Picciotto discovered mysticism. St. Paul's had tolerated heresy, and spawned a host of heretics, but the Heretics Society Picciotto had helped found under the same principles no longer met his needs.

Picciotto's decision to resign from the Heretics did not reflect the tenor of the Society as a whole. He was not as dominant a personality behind the scenes as Ogden, and he felt his voice was being muffled. The public face of the Society, though, allowed room for both the rationalist and the mystic. Indeed, the Society and its journalistic organ, *The Cambridge Magazine,* had committed themselves to "welcome every point of view" (CA 18). By encouraging an embodied form of heteroglossia, the Heretics produced a unique composite of oppositional thought that further attracted a set of earnest intellectuals from across Europe who needed such a forum to expound their ideas.

In his address to the Society, "Mysticism and Logic," shortly before the war, Bertrand Russell encapsulated the conflict of concern to Picciotto and found that these varying perspectives produced the best form of philosophy when put in dialogue with each other. His opening remarks state that, though metaphysics has been developed "by the union and conflict of two very different human impulses," the "greatest" philosophers "have felt the need both of science and of mysticism," and "the attempt to harmonize the two was what made their life" (BR 8:30).[7] It made Russell's too. In this last-minute addition to the Heretics' schedule in March 1914, Russell explained a key transition in his own philosophy in which he denied the mystical position on metaphysical questions, but commended its spirit of reverence. A similar brand of reverence facilitates the ethical neutrality of "true" objective science because that is how "the world is to be understood" (BR 8:49). On the other hand, mysticism "often holds that all Reality is good" (BR 8:45), whereas Russell believes in a subjectivity that can only effectively and legitimately realize good in the individual. Though he was beginning his "religion of science" period, Russell, in miniature, emblematized the Heretics' desire and recognition of the importance of entertaining all sides of a debate.

In fact, the distinguishing characteristic of the Heretics Society before the war rested in a series of debates that secured its respect and notoriety. The brainchild of the two heads, Ogden and Picciotto, did justice to the remarkable if short-lived cooperation of two fundamentally opposed minds. Had Picciotto remained another year he would have witnessed Chesterton, his fellow "Pauline" and future Catholic, respond in dramatic fashion to Bernard Shaw's address, "The Religion of the Future." This extended debate of 1911 is the signature mark of the Heretics in bringing together two of the most famous people in England at the time. Shaw's address is central to the theory of heresy underwriting *Saint Joan,* which is discussed along with the Shaw/Chesterton debate in full in chapter 4. These early years of the Heretics would also, incidentally, see discussions of the same authors whose "pagan" discourses are examined in chapter 5. For example, A. C. Benson, fellow at Magdalene, surveyed the religious and artistic temperaments of Walter Pater, his academic area of specialization,[8] and A. L. Bacharach addressed the Society on "Thomas Hardy, the Poet of Heresy." Classical and "savage" paganism were common enough topics for the Heretics, but paganism and the heresy of syncretism came to a head in the debate over the "Christ-Myth" between H. G. Wood (1879–1963) and J. M. Robertson, MP (1856–1933).

During the Michaelmas term of 1911, Wood initiated the debate by arguing for the historicity of Jesus and against Robertson's theory that Christ was another in a series of solar myths. A few weeks later Robertson defended his position. In drawing the Liberal member of Parliament, the Heretics heightened their notoriety in a term that had just seen the conclusion of the Shaw/Chesterton debate. Scottish and self-educated, Robertson was not only a governmental figure, but also an established Shakespearean scholar and one of the most militant freethinkers of the day. He had worked for the *National Reformer* with Charles Bradlaugh in the 1880s and 90s, and his *Modern Humanists* (1891) had championed the radical, rational defense of liberty and emphasis on morality in human affairs in the work of Carlyle, Ruskin, Mill, and Arnold, among others. During the late 1890s, Robertson went on a well-received lecture tour of the United States before publishing his two-volume *A Short History of Freethought* (1899), tracing heterodoxy from ancient to modern times. Of concern to Wood, though, was Robertson's subsequent companion works, *Christianity and Mythology* (1900) and *Pagan Christs* (1903). Robertson's views had recently gained notoriety and affirmation with the translation into English of Arthur Drews' work of 1910, *The Christ-Myth.* In opposing the mythical view of Christianity, the young, unknown Wood could only offer his sincere faith and a personal study of histories of Jesus' life.

On November 12, Wood addressed the Heretics on "The Christ-Myth" (a criticism)," and his argument chiefly tries to debunk the claims of *Pagan*

Christs. He believes that Robertson's work "contains some good criticism and much good material," but, as "a contribution to the historical problem of Christian origin, it is unscientific in method and irrelevant" (Wood and Robertson 14). Robertson had posited the idea that the Gospel account of Jesus' life from the Last Supper to the Crucifixion was actually just a mystery play based on a sublimated ancient rite. Disputing the claims for a "Palestinian" origin of the Gospels, Wood shortens Robertson's "history" to his claim that "something happened to recall to the mind of some Jews not only the general idea of human sacrifice, but also an old and elaborate ritual of human sacrifice connected with an early and entirely forgotten Jesus-cult" (8). Later, he explained to Ogden that "a hypothesis like Robertson's is out of court from the start," and that "[w]hatever Christianity was, it did not arise from Jews in touch with Hellenism" (MCMA 112). He believed that his opponent was an acute anthropologist, but that Christianity is more than a question of folklore. Three weeks later, with Wood in the audience ready to begin an actual debate, Robertson bluntly replied that he professed merely a "theory," not a "history," based on "things remembered," not forgotten (18). Moreover, he pointed out that his theory traces the origin of such rites to the "Joshua-myth" and even earlier primitive rites surrounding human sacrifice, not simply Jewish culture of the first century B.C. In an approach similar to the Cambridge "Ritualists," Robertson suggests that the Gospels are myths, or "stories," accounting for ancient rites. He concludes his response by noting Wood's dismissal of all that is outside "orthodox tradition" (16), in contrast to his own rejection of the a priori acceptance of orthodoxy. Wood, nevertheless, enjoyed the spirited debate, and wrote to Ogden: "let me congratulate you on the temper of your Society. So long as it is interested in truly scientific questions it is bound to be useful, and I should count myself happy if I were to see more of you" (MCMA 112). He did speak to the Heretics again in October of 1913, and in the 1920s his literal approach to Christianity led him to join the Society of Friends. Robertson continued his literary scholarship, and became the parliamentary secretary to the Board of Trade from 1911 to 1915.

Other provocative issues rousing debates at the Heretics included coeducation, Bergson's theories of consciousness, and the general function of churches in the modern world. Education, along with economics and other social sciences, fit under the rubric of the Society because there were room and scope enough for what Florence calls "practical human heresy" (CH 238). In November of 1913, Mr. C. Reddie, while addressing the Heretics on "Sex in Education and Education in Sex," denounced coeducation for causing an "electric leak" in men. He later stated "the pith" of his lecture to be: "if the British Empire is not to perish, we must fill it up with Britishers. This is women's work. If they cannot marry in England, let them go to the colonies" (CH 238). Responding to Reddie the following February, J. H. Badley of Bedales School defended coeducation and received much support from several Heretics as the debate played out through letters in *The Cambridge Magazine*.

After 1912, when Ogden began functioning dually as president of the Heretics and editor of the magazine, he used his journal to further the discussions of the Heretics and called on his new connections in the publishing world to reproduce the debates. One such instance of this is the pamphlet encapsulating Bertrand Russell's synopsis of the philosophy of Henri Bergson, a reply by H. Wildon Carr, and finally a rejoinder by Russell. Before his discussion of "Mysticism and Logic," Russell had addressed the Heretics on Bergson in March of 1912, and this lecture, which would be reduced slightly for Russell's famous *A History of Western Philosophy* (1945), was, according to Alan Wood, of great significance to Russell in "helping to re-establish him as one of the leading figures in Cambridge" since "it was his first big success as a public speaker" (89). As Russell described his anticipation of the event to Lady Ottoline Morrell, "the whole world seems to be coming tonight." Afterward, he told her: "It had a great success last night—the place was packed and they seemed to enjoy it. Not a soul rose to defend Bergson at the end, so there was no discussion. McTaggart spoke a few graceful words and we all went away" (BR 6:316). No doubt the reason the audience was speechless arose from Russell's intricate and idiosyncratic attack on Bergson's dynamic view of the world. Moreover, he had extensively quoted several of Bergson's works without sufficient explication, and the whole of Russell's synopsis can be seen as the work of a logician making a travesty of an anti-intellectual philosophy. In his biography of Russell, Wood adds that "the reader must imagine it delivered in Russell's dry, precise and ironic voice, and punctuated by laughter and applause which greeted his sallies" (89). The satire, obliquity, and intricacy of Russell's dismissal of Bergson's reasoning stunned the audience into silence. Only when Ogden solicited Carr for a defense of Bergson before the Heretics and a further rebuttal in the *Cambridge Magazine* did Russell hear a challenge to his views. To be fair and provocative, Ogden allowed Russell to respond in a later issue of the journal, and eventually in 1914 the Heretics printed all three sorties as a pamphlet.

To begin his lecture, Russell supposes that Bergson writes out of a "love of action" since his singularly distinct philosophy precludes classification by methods or results. Russell commits this intentional fallacy in order to categorize Bergson and avoid having to address the overall effect of seeing the world as constantly in flux. The British empiricist cannot abide a "becoming" view of the world which thwarts the static positings of discrete logic. Instead, Russell focuses on defending the intellect versus instinct and space versus time. Along similar grounds, Wyndham Lewis would attack Bergson and Joyce in *Time and Western Man* (1927). While Lewis reflects the modernist desire to impose order on the world through a "right-minded" exclusivity, Russell would later allow a place for instinct in the world in "Mysticism and Logic." The difficulties he had had with Bergson's thought suggest that he felt compelled to revisit the role of instinct and mysticism in his subsequent address to the Heretics. For instance, in trying to defend contemplation against action and Bergson's idea of duration, "the time which is of the essence of life," Russell admitted: "I do not fully understand it myself" (BR 6:323).

As few as nine days before his address to the Society, Russell had not started writing, and in working out Bergson's philosophy for himself and the Heretics, he utilizes familiar concepts to ground his understanding. He describes Bergson's ideas "as synthetic rather than analytic" (BR 6:326), and his opening image likens Bergson's philosophy to the Manichean heresy. Russell believed that the Heretics will recognize dismissively the similarity of the conception of the "whole universe" as "the clash and conflict of two opposite emotions" to the Manichean dualistic battle between spirit and matter (BR 6:320). Furthering this sardonic portrayal, Russell turns Bergson's associations between matter, space, and the intellect into the evil forces at work in the world. In a crucial move, he makes Bergson's philosophical condemnation of the certainties of the intellect hinge on his use of space, and the English logician could not have disagreed more with the idea that "the whole of the intellect depends upon a supposed habit of picturing things side by side" (BR 6:330). (Virginia Woolf would seem to have been aware of this debate in her caricature of Mr. Ramsey when he ponders what comes next in his "alphabetic" philosophy: "If Q then is Q—R—".[9]) Since the intellect separates matter in Bergson's view, only instinct and memory adhere to the workings of duration, the closest intimation we have of the spirit world. Poetic visions such as these charmed Russell, and he realized that Bergson might best be judged on aesthetic grounds. To conclude, however, that "there is no reason to think it [Bergson's philosophy] true" (BR 6:337) suggests that he had missed the point that there may be an intuition to feel it true.

In June 1912, Wildon Carr defended Bergson in his address to the Heretics entitled "Life and Logic." As the secretary of the Aristotelian Society in

London, Carr had hosted a dinner party in October of 1911 when Russell first met Bergson. Bernard Shaw was also present, and Russell reported that the playwright "made an amusing speech explaining how glad he was that Bergson had adopted his (Shaw's) views" (BR 6:318). Shaw was jokingly claiming that Bergson's "creative evolution" affirmed Shaw's "original" idea of a "Life-Force" that he had extolled in *Man and Superman* (1903) and in his speech to the Heretics the previous May. (Certainly, Shaw well understood his and Bergson's mutual debt to Nietzsche's concept of the Will to Power.) As a host and admirer of Bergson, Carr then felt compelled to defend his former guest when Ogden asked for a rebuttal to Russell. Carr's simple and careful reply qualifies Russell's perspective in two important ways. He points out that Russell focuses on details while ignoring the luminous clarity of the whole idea of duration, and he states: "Mr. Russell is perfectly entitled to question or deny that we can have knowledge by intuition, but if there is such knowledge it is characterised by just this fact that it is consciousness of life in living" (BR 6:459). Indeed, in Russell's rejoinder, he had to "admit that there is an element of question begging in all refutations of Bergson" (BR 6:346). Not only did he recognize that he could not use intellect against instinct, but Russell further acknowledged that, though he still finds Bergson's reasoning to be wrong, his philosophy is not necessarily false. Russell's desire to become more "synthetic" and later incorporate mysticism into a philosophical system testifies to the provocative influence and atmosphere of the Heretics Society during these early years. By its very existence, the Society promoted the possibilities of alternative yet totalizing worldviews.

Finally, perhaps the most emotionally charged debate at the Society occurred in February 1914. This unrecorded formal debate between the Heretics and the X Club of Oxford found the Heretics arguing in favor of a motion proposed by Hubert Henderson, "That in the opinion of this House the Churches today are doing more harm than good." Though this debate is now mostly lost to history, Florence believes that the motion carried "by a small majority" (CH 230).

The "victory" over the X Club must have been bittersweet to the Heretics who had watched the Oxford branch of their Society fail to sustain itself in 1911. During the same academic year that Ogden took control of the Heretics, the new president sojourned in Oxford with R. F. Rattray of Manchester who later reminded Ogden of how he "helped us to start the Heretics" (MCMA 113.37). By May of 1911, Rattray and the Oxford Heretics had organized sufficiently to have a full schedule of meetings for the Easter and Trinity terms. They adopted wholesale the laws of the Cambridge Heretics and admitted thirty-five members and five Honorary Members including Russell and F. C. Conybeare. McTaggart also came to give a talk on "Optimism," and E. S. P. Haynes' address, "Religion and Modern Morality," was published in association with the Cambridge branch. However, the ensuing fall found the Oxford Heretics dissatisfied with their progress, and in December, the secretary, H. H. Bellot, put forth the motion that "this Society has failed in its object, and that it be herewith dissolved." The motion carried, although it included B. H. Wilsdon's suggestion that they possibly be reconstituted "at some future date" (MCMA 114.7). Heresy was more decidedly a "Cambridge Movement." Despite the permanent hiatus of their brothers in heresy, the Cambridge Heretics still advertised the existence of the Oxford branch in their 1912–13 prospectus and noted that "efforts [were] being made to found similar Societies at other universities" (MCMA 114.4). The printing of three thousand copies of this prospectus registered their confidence, and Harrison's quotation, "To be a heretic to-day is almost a human obligation," served as an epigraph to the document. The First World War certainly must have dampened the efforts to establish other Societies of Heretics. Yet in September of 1918, Jean Foley, the president of The Women's Art Society of Montreal, wrote to Harrison seeking information about the nature and object of the Heretics. Foley explained that a "few adventurous spirits of our city would like to found a 'Heretic Club'" (MCMA 107.8).

The growth and proliferation of the Cambridge Heretics, on the other hand, does indeed owe much to the tremendous skill in solicitation and recruitment of Ogden. Doubtless, the elder dons at Cambridge had been especially receptive to heresy due to the cultural contexts discussed earlier, but Ogden's persistence in his pursuits enabled the Cambridge Heretics to avoid the sophomore jinx that befell the Oxford branch. He was relentless in feeling out potential members amongst the faculty and student body through casual conversation. Ogden would then follow up on these first encounters by sending out gracious letters requesting someone's membership. As a result, in the first few years of the Society, he had systematically enlisted those undergraduates and dons at least friendly to heresy. H(erbert) A(llen) Giles (1845–1935), professor of Chinese, typified the encouragement Ogden would receive in his response that "it will give me much pleasure to become an Hon. Member of 'The Heretics'" (MCMA 113.36). In Giles, the Heretics added the English authority on Chinese language and culture, who also fanatically took sides on other intellectual issues. With the passing of each academic year, Ogden would recuperate lost membership by approaching the new arrivals on campus. For instance, George Santayana became a member while spending the First World War in Cambridge. To facilitate signing up members, the Heretics printed cards which stated that the bearer had been selected as a potential Heretic. The new recruit only had to fill in the date, his or her name and college, and then pay dues.

Perhaps the most significant addition to the Heretics after the immediate rush of Honorary Members came after Ogden sent the following letter to G. E. Moore upon his return to Cambridge in October of 1910:

> Dear Sir,   October 17th, 1910
> I am writing on behalf of the above Society to express the hope that you will permit us to include your name in our list of Hon. members. This does not necessarily imply liability to read papers or otherwise actively support the Society.
> Hoping that we shall have your approval.
> I am yours truly
> C. K. Ogden
> (CUL Add.Ms.8330 80/1/1)

With Moore's prompt acceptance, the Heretics further solidified their discursive exchange with Bloomsbury and the Apostles. His "ethical religion" became one of their multifarious heresies, and it informs Bell's *Art* (1913), Woolf's *The Voyage Out* (1915), and Strachey's address to the Heretics, "Art and Indecency" (1920). Even though Ogden assured Moore that he need not undertake additional obligation, Moore grew to be the Heretics' most prolific speaker as he addressed the Society no less than five times between 1914 and 1925, including one talk on "The Value of Religion." Six months after Moore joined, the Heretics extended their influence most flamboyantly outside the pale of Cambridge when Shaw accepted an invitation to become an Honorary Member after his irreverent, progressive speech on "The Religion of the Future." The striking nature of Shaw's vision compelled Chesterton to respond, and Forster would also take issue with Shaw's apotheosis of "work" in *Arctic Summer*.

To entertain their distinguished guests from outside the university, the Heretics would depend upon the good graces of their members who might happen to know the visiting lecturer. Usually, an Honorary Member would provide lodging and hospitality to the invited speaker so that the Heretics did not incur further costs, for the budget of the Society functioned solely on dues and the occasional sale of tickets for major lectures. In most academic years, the Heretics collected between £40 and £50 of income, and most of these funds went toward operational costs. Tickets sold for Chesterton's response to Shaw suggest that this debate was the economic as well as popular highpoint of the Society. Receipts from Chesterton's meeting brought in nearly £35 and put the Heretics income over £100 for the academic year. With their surplus, the Heretics could afford to pay some expenses of the lecturers. Mostly, such expenses were one pound or less, but Chesterton and Georg Brandes did receive speaker's fees of five to ten pounds.[10] The limitations of the Heretics' budget occasionally hindered their goals. Indeed, amid all Ogden's solicitory successes, there were some grand failures.

In the immediate aftermath of Chesterton's popular triumph, Ogden wrote to Chesterton's cohort in defending Catholicism, Hilaire Belloc (1870–1953). However, this other member of the twin-headed orthodoxy Shaw characterized as "Chesterbelloc" would not stoop to refute heresy without sufficient financial payment. Belloc wrote to Ogden on November 23, 1911: "You do not say whether I should receive a fee from the receipts of such a Meeting or not. I certainly should not be prepared to address a Meeting at less than my usual fee of ten guineas, and if, as I presume, this is not what you had in mind, I fear my engagements are far too numerous to leave me time for the discussion of Agnostic, Protestant, Judaic, and other religions" (MCMA 113.36). Whether or not the Heretics could meet his price, Belloc's tone suggests that he had little interest in participating in open debate with a potentially hostile audience. In fact, he never addressed the Heretics, but his view of the agnostic rationalists in the Society can be seen in his polemical discussion of "The Modern Attack" in *The Great Heresies* (1938).[11]

In addition to Belloc, Ogden, despite his best efforts, also failed to secure the affiliation or appearance of W. B. Yeats and Thomas Hardy. When Ogden wrote to Yeats in January of 1913, the poet had recently decided to publicize his fear about the potential dangers of anti-Protestant bigotry if Ireland were granted Home Rule, and Ogden tried to appeal to Yeats' thoughts on Catholic intolerance. However, Yeats was also busy championing Rabindranath Tagore and campaigning for a Dublin Modern Art Gallery. Yeats had recently met with Ezra Pound, and together they extolled the virtues of noble patronage of the arts in Renaissance Italy. Amid this influence, one of Yeats' contributions to the Irish Home Rule movement at the time was to write a poem noting Guidobaldo's patronage and suggesting that public demand should not determine funding for the arts. The day before Yeats replied to Ogden on January 9, 1913, he had written to Lady Gregory about his satisfaction with the poem and the brewing thoughts he had for new ones concerning Aubrey Beardsley's dying sister, Mabel. With so many preoccupations, it is easy to understand Yeats' polite refusal of Ogden's offer to address the Heretics. Yeats explained that "at any other time" he "would have accepted with pleasure but at the moment" he was "so deep in a new book of verse" that he could not "turn aside to prepare a lecture" (MCMA 113.37).

In November of 1913, Ogden set his sights on Thomas Hardy, "The Poet of Heresy." The timing would seem to have been perfect, except for the fact that Hardy had begun to think about how posterity would receive him. In June, Hardy had been granted an honorary Litterarum Doctor degree from Cambridge, and earlier in November Magdalene College, with A. E. Housman among other guests, had made Hardy an Honorary Fellow during a formal ceremony in chapel. Ogden asked the newfound affiliate of his own college to become a member of the Heretics. Little would Ogden have expected the following unpublished letter of November 20:

> Max Gate
> Dorchester
>
> Dear Sir:
>
> My thanks for the pamphlets of 'The Heretics,' and for your interesting note, to which I cannot reply adequately offhand. I have of late been withdrawing from societies, etc., that I formerly belonged to, and I fear that instead of joining the Heretics even as an Honorary Member I must stand and be merely a sympathetic spectator of their doings in the cause of truth. I will read the papers with great pleasure.
>
> Believe me.
>
> Yours truly
>
> Thomas Hardy
>
> (MCMA 113.36)

Indeed, Hardy would be an especially sympathetic supporter when Ogden began receiving abuse during the war for printing articles from the foreign press in the *Cambridge Magazine*. Heresy was a different matter. In 1913, Hardy's health began to falter, he often wrote to churchmen about church architecture, and he had started to think of an "autobiography" after the death of his first wife. A month before his polite refusal of Ogden's request, Hardy had published one of his last returns to prose, the suggestively entitled short story "A Changed Man." In the strange autobiography, *The Life and Work of Thomas Hardy*, written in the third person with the collaboration of his second wife, the narrative voice explains the bestowal of the fellowship at Magdalene in rather pious terms. Even though early in life he had decided he could not enter the church conscientiously, it states "Hardy had read the lessons in church in his young-manhood, besides having had much to do with churches in other ways, and the experience may have recalled the old ecclesiastical times" (391). In projecting himself for future generations, the narrative also notes a sketch-painting of Hardy to be hung in the hall of Magdalene. After the scornful reviews of *Tess*, Hardy had identified himself with heretics being beaten by the "hammers" of the Inquisition, and he did not want that to continue. Ogden might have asked himself, as Jude did of Sue after her turn to piety, if this could be the same person "who brought the Pagan deities into this most Christian city," who "quoted Gibbon, and Shelley, and Mill" (276).

Hardy and Yeats were not Cambridge figures; however, E. M. Forster was not only a Cambridge Apostle and member of the Bloomsbury Group, but after the publication of *Howards End* (1910) his string of eloquent and successful novels also had made him one of the most respected artists in England. He initially presents a conspicuous absence from the Heretics Society. From 1909 to 1911, he had been mostly out of the country, ruminating over what to do after his recent masterpiece. The Heretics would seem to have been far from his mind and of little relevance to his own aesthetic experiments and philosophizing about the ways of the world—that is, until he began to pursue a new variant of his stylized narrative "antithesis" upon returning to Cambridge in November 1911, the month that can be considered the high watermark of the Society. The Oxford Heretics were still active, Robertson and Wood were in the midst of their debate, Cornford addressed the Society, and Chesterton delivered his rebuttal to the "dogmas" of Shaw. While Forster sojourned at Rupert Brooke's lodgings in Cambridge, a new idea for a novel blossomed. He would explore the dynamic between a heroic man and Brooke figure, Cyril Marsh, and Martin Whitby, a Quaker aesthete and fellow at Cambridge, using Roger Fry as a model. Through this antithetical complement, Forster sought a synthetic reconciliation of two "outdated" types of men—Marsh needs reeducation, Whitby revitalization.

In addition to the dichotomy between the chivalric and the civilized man, Forster also poses Brooke's and Fry's recent discussions of art against each other in an attempt to see if they can "connect." As Forster wrote on November 24 to Brooke, "I have this moment decided to put all I can remember of your paper on art into a novel—and as I remember it. You have not to mind. 'It will never get written unless'" (*Letters* 1:126). While here he is referring to Brooke's "Democracy and the Arts," a paper delivered to the Fabians in December 1910 calling for state subsidies for literature, Brooke's later address to the Heretics in February 1913 better illustrates the chivalric code Forster found in Brooke. In this defense of August Strindberg's passionate realism, Brooke identifies with the Swedish playwright's disgust toward feminism and wants "to declare that men are men and women women" (Hassall 378). In contrast, Forster wrote in his "Locked" diary, the same day as his letter to Brooke, about how he was inspired by Fry's desire "to clear Art of reminiscences," such as an idealized chivalric past, and to "paint the position of things in space" (AS xviii).[12]

Amid this tension, the debate between Shaw and Chesterton filters into the first draft of *Arctic Summer* known as the Tripoli Fragment. The title comes from the theater of the Italo-Turkish War in September 1911, and Marsh plans to go to Tripoli because supporting the Turks is a "clear issue" on behalf of which he can demonstrate his chivalric code (AS 193). In championing war, Marsh represents the type of man Shaw hopes will fight for the "religion of the future," "men with some belief in the purpose of the universe, with determination to identify themselves with it and the courage that comes from that" (RF 5). As Forster also notes in his diary, he had also been in Cambridge in May at the time of Shaw's address, and he was either in the audience for Chesterton's reply on November 17 or heard of it from his mentor and great friend "Goldie" Dickinson, who had questioned Chesterton about reason and liberty in relation to Christianity. The defender of orthodoxy responded that only the nonrational mystic can confuse the terms, forget about free will, and believe that "God could at the same time keep men bound and prevent their going wrong" (18). While this phrasing also is important to Forster's novel, Chesterton's critique of the belief in creative evolution underwriting Shaw's "religion of the future" more explicitly informs Forster's discussion of ethics and progress. Chesterton attacks the mystic, as Shaw identified himself, who does not hold a necessary "fixed ideal" and instead believes in something which is only "trying to exist" (10–11). Shaw's heresy postulated that God works through humanity, and "it is ours to work for something better, to talk less about the religion of love (love is an improper subject) and more about the religion of life, and of work." Heretics must apply the driving Life-Force and "work towards that ideal" of making God until they "get to be supermen" (RF 6–7). In Forster's novel, Whitby distances himself from such ideals and "what 'being right' means today," working for social justice for the underprivileged in a progress "lumbering slowly forward." He laments the passing of the Crusades whose "reward of fighting" was "pleasure" rather than "comfort," and he defends the use of the "spiritual life" against "*Work the religion of the future*" (AS 194–95, emphasis mine).

In this emotion, Whitby has been infected by Marsh, who feels "saved by the war" and describes the chance circumstances that prevented him from "going wrong" as "conversion" and "a sort of miracle" (AS 192–93). In war, he can avoid the fate of his brother, Robin, who had planned to take holy orders at Cambridge before he went "wrong." In its vagueness, the novel constructs this taboo misdeed as either heresy or homosexuality, perhaps united in the euphemism "sexual heretic." Marsh, rather, wants to be "worthy" of women "or the whole thing goes." Whitby, who is attracted to Marsh in another fragment of the novel, tries to console him by noting: "we must be worthy of them in the way they wish, not in the way we wish. That is the new chivalry" (AS 193). Here Forster openly begins to question the gentlemanly code which he had previously defended in a paper read before both the Apostles and the Bloomsbury Friday Club, "The Feminine Note in Literature" (1910). Reflecting on *Arctic Summer* in 1951, Forster felt he had "got my antithesis all right"; however, he could not finish the novel because he "had not settled what was going to happen." He added that the two men could never be reconciled except as "companions in defeat," but "such an ending doesn't interest me" (AS 162). Perhaps in leaving for India in October 1912, he discovered the exile that could grant triumph to the male lovers in *Maurice*.

Chapter 3

Aesthetics
and the Modern Heretics

THE FIRST WORLD WAR AND
THE BLOOMSBURY HERESIES

The blunder we know as the First World War eventually brought a drastic decrease in enrollment at university. By 1916, male enrollment had dropped well over 80 percent.[1] Ogden stayed in Cambridge after receiving a medical exemption from service. The lack of a significant student body makes it remarkable that he was able not only to keep the Heretics functioning, but also to help them thrive. Increased dependence on elderly dons, female students, and refugee scholars enabled the Society to continue their meetings without abatement. Major events subsided, but Harrison, Moore, George Santayana, Vernon Lee, Rebecca West and others ensured that flair and cutting-edge thought still shone in the city of learning. G. H. Hardy continued to assist mentoring the Heretics, spoke on "The Value of Knowledge," and persuaded the self-taught phenomenal mathematician Srinivasa Ramanujan (1887–1920) to loosen his Brahmin orthodoxy and accept an exhibition from Trinity for the duration of the war. The illustrious *Cambridge Magazine* disseminated the ideas of the Heretics beyond the university town. The history of the serial is fascinating and beyond the pale of concern here, but it did maintain its practice of publishing and discussing parts of addresses to the Society. Of more lasting effect, the magazine brought Ogden fame, notoriety, and respect. For out of all the British press, the *Cambridge Magazine* was the only one to print foreign news coverage of the war. As copy man, marketing agent, and editor, Ogden had no external accountability, and he received enough faculty support to prevent being threatened or shut down.

Bertrand Russell, Thomas Hardy, and Arnold Bennett were among the more vocal supporters of his practice that allowed people to read a more objective account of the war. With such a controversial publishing policy, though, the *Cambridge Magazine* became as notorious as the Heretics, all to Ogden's glee.

From his position of power, Ogden turned directly to practical concerns, secure in both an economic base and an outlet for his ideas. His interests in pacifism, syndicalism, worker's rights, and universal and women's suffrage provide a more complete and mainstream progressive portrait of him than his more idiosyncratic adventures in linguistics. Among his more provocative intellectual output during the war, *Militarism versus Feminism* (1915) and *Fecundity versus Civilisation* (1917) synthesized his interests in pacifism and feminism. Each of these was first published serially in the *Cambridge Magazine* under the pseudonym Adelyne More. In fact, many of the magazine's editorials and columns were written under this nom-de-plume, or others Ogden donned such as T. L. for "The Limit," or C. M. for the *Cambridge Magazine*. While *Militarism versus Feminism* developed the idea that a military state necessarily implied the subjection of women, *Fecundity versus Civilisation* argued that over-population was "the cause of war and the chief obstacle to the emancipation of women" (1). Bennett wrote the introduction to the latter when it was published in book form, in which he dismisses the hygienic, religious, political, and economic arguments against birth control as wrong, elitist, or warmongering. Since he finds that intelligent people no longer find these arguments valid, he points to a "false shame" that keeps the topic of birth control hushed (5). When Marie Stopes addressed the Heretics after the war on the topic and her practice, some of the more fastidious members of the Society wished to keep their ears shut and quietly resigned their membership.

Despite Ogden's resourceful maintenance of the Heretics Society during the First World War, Dora Black (Russell), the secretary from 1917–19, had fundamental doubts about the future legitimacy and function of the Heretics. Ogden's growing association with Bloomsbury furthered her opinion that the important issues for a post-war Britain concerned either politics or art. A few weeks after the Armistice, Black addressed the Society on "How to be Happy" by valorizing eighteenth-century hedonism over medieval asceticism, but her feelings over the viability of the Society were better captured by J. C. Squire's discussion of "The Limitations of Heresy" the following May. In the summer of 1919, she wrote to Ogden expressing her doubts: "As to Heretics I am really rather worried about the whole business, because I cannot see any basis for going on with the Society. When I look around for people to give papers I only see political people and purely literary people. . . . It seems impossible to keep free of politics without being ineffective. It is like the latter period before the French revolution, when the religious battle had been fought, they all went into politics." The Russian Revolution had inspired her with hope for a socialist future, and the Heretics did not seem to her to be working effectively toward that end. However, the birth control controversy surrounding Marie Stopes later caused Black to think she had been "quite wrong about the need for anti-religion." Still, she facilitated the aesthetic turn of the Heretics by suggesting that they solicit Lytton Strachey, Clive Bell, and Virginia Woolf to address the Society. All of these figures would travel to Cambridge in the next few years and address the Heretics before Ogden moved to London. Prior to committing to this reorientation, Black went to Paris in the fall of 1919 to study while the Heretics took a "sabbatical" term to regroup.[2] As the influenza epidemic plagued Europe that fall, Ogden, Black suggests, thought of "temporarily dropping the Society" ("Friend" 89–90). The new face of peace forced Ogden on several levels to redraw his battle lines.

On Armistice Day, Ogden's publication of foreign press during the war came back to haunt him as rioters, celebrating the peace, ransacked his Cambridge Magazine Book Shop and Art Gallery, smashing the establishment and throwing paintings by Duncan Grant, Vanessa Bell, and Roger Fry into the street. The reactionary rabble, reportedly medical students, were angry at Ogden's pacifism and publication of varying viewpoints on the war. As a witness to this tumult, I. A. Richards reports a mythologizing account of meeting Ogden across the street trying to identify the culprits before embarking on a philosophical discussion that would eventually lead to their collaboration in *The Meaning of Meaning*. According to Richards, the treatise exemplified Ogden's interest in ridding language of "word-magic," sought to improve communication, and discouraged "received and approved practice in the conduct of the word *meaning*" ("Co-Author" 101). Basic English would follow this same agenda. A week after the riot, F. C. Bartlett's address to the Heretics, "In Praise of Intolerance," must have reverberated in Ogden's ears. In effect, as Florence states, the riot "did in fact uproot him from Cambridge" (CA 41). Though his Cambridge establishments rebounded with great financial success, Ogden became more and more centered in Bloomsbury over the next few years where he came to live in Gordon Square next door to J. Maynard Keynes and near James and Alix Strachey. In London, after transforming the *Cambridge Magazine* into a quarterly, he launched

Psyche, the Soho-based journal which would become his vehicle for an early form of psycholinguistics and later his Orthological Institute.

In this immediate post-war period, Ogden began gradually to use the Heretics as a staging ground for explorations into aesthetics and linguistics. In April of 1920, Ogden and Richards spoke to the Society on "The New Symbolist Movement" and shared some of their forays into verbal signification. While the Heretics lost some of their visibility as the *Cambridge Magazine* no longer reported their weekly meetings, Ogden started the Today and Tomorrow Series in 1924 and provided a public outlet for many addresses to the Heretics by publishing over a hundred volumes of unconventional thought over the course of the next ten years.[3] Perhaps Ogden's most lasting work, his translation of Wittgenstein's *Tractatus,* further echoed the interest in semantics growing in the discursive exchange between Cambridge and Bloomsbury. As Florence states, one of the more remarkable facts about Ogden was the "topicality in the application of his thinking, turning from international affairs to the peace-time discussions that were exercising Bloomsbury at that time on art and philosophy" (CA 49).

During the academic year 1920–21, Bloomsbury began to exert an even greater influence on the Heretics when Lytton Strachey addressed the Society on "Art and Indecency." On the tails of his widely acclaimed *Eminent Victorians* (1918), he delivered what S. P. Rosenbaum calls his "best paper on literary theory," a critical approach which "bears directly on his verse and other writings" (*Edwardian* 308). His essay also reflects the culture of censorship beginning to grow around the obscenity trials of Lawrence and Joyce. Strachey's discussion of the relationship between ethics and aesthetics bears the direct imprint of the evaluative method outlined in Moore's *Principia Ethica.* Since Strachey believes that works of art are examples of Moore's complex "wholes," he stresses the importance of observation and reception within the "organic unity." However, in a defense of "art for art's sake," he admits that art has ethical elements and produces ethical effects, but he does not relinquish belief in the idea that "the aesthetic whole must be judged by purely aesthetic standards" (84). As a result of these conclusions, art, in his view, can possess indecent qualities and still be beautiful, depending on taste. In an inversion of Judge Biron's later statement during *The Well of Loneliness* trial, Strachey declares that a "work of art which is indecent may be of the highest merit" (89). Like Moore, Strachey leaves others to decide the ethical effects produced by an "aesthetic whole." The underlying assumption of his argument suggests that the "right" aesthetic relations can be determined, and further implies that a coterie of critics such as the Bloomsbury Group will decide them. Though his address therefore has utility for censoring literature (i.e., indecent art can have deleterious effects), Strachey principally defends art potentially seen as obscene, because as a whole the overall greatness of a work of art can withstand the effects of indecent elements. In a paraphrased application of Moore's theory, he states that "the values of these wholes cannot be determined merely by a *sum* of the values of the parts, but depends on their *combination*" (89).

In the same masterful style that characterizes his unique study of Victoriana, Strachey blends a sardonic irreverence with vivid illustration to show the possible ludicrous results of confusing ethics and aesthetics. For example, he jokes that "the Kaiser's delinquencies have really nothing to do with his moustaches," and that "many clergymen who have read Catullus with impunity, have been, it is reported, completely demoralized by Mrs. Humphry Ward" (83–84). To pursue the topic of the relations between the artistic and the indecent, Strachey offers three categories of people whose views are "pronounced and completely incompatible" (84). In each case, the Prudes, the Naturalists, and the Bawdy do not account for the "whole" complexity of art in Strachey's mind. The Prudes, "who seem never to have recovered from the loss which they sustained on the death of Victoria," abandoned bowdlerization and compromised to allow some indecencies such as those in Shakespeare (85). Similarly, blasphemy law allowed for irreverent religious discussion and produced a horde of heresies that eventually broached the realm of modernism. Once on this slope, Strachey argues, the Prudes lost the strength of their foothold on moral propriety—rigidity. Consequently, moral principles may vary "according to individual taste" and illustrate that "there is no criterion for deciding which are the orthodox" (85).

Even though Strachey's method functions under the same principles of difference, he wants to impose an aesthetic criterion. One of his premises implies an aesthetic orthodoxy will decide taste. For instance, the Naturalists, Strachey's second category, react against prudery and instead promote the liberation of the body. Since "acts of reproduction, of excretion, and so forth" are "indistinguishable from other bodily acts," the Naturalists believe that the "very notion of 'indecency' was a fallacious one" (86–87). Strachey finds in favor of the advanced Naturalist position over the Prudish one, but noted that the basis of the Bawdy perspective, which places value on the indecent, exposes the flaw in the Naturalist argument. The works of Aristophanes, Rabelais, and Voltaire rely upon the existence of indecency.[4] If, as Strachey feels, indecency is a state of mind resulting from feelings and not a state of body coded by acts, then his conclusion fails in calling for an altogether different perspective that sees art as complex wholes. Feelings or, in Moore's word, "contemplation" are parts of the luminous "whole" and the *reception* of the work of art. Though Strachey's conclusion might explain the "conflicting views that obtain on the subject" and defend the place of indecency in art, it does not admit the importance of readers' changing ethical and aesthetic values over time, a salient point implicit in its own rhetoric.

Several months later in November of 1921, Clive Bell arrived in Cambridge to further Strachey's point that people of good judgment (read Bloomsbury again) would agree upon the nature of aesthetic qualities. In this particular case before the Heretics, jazz is the victim of Bell's authoritative taste. Addressing only the full members of the Society on "Jazz Art," Bell declares that "Jazz is dead" and that he, "someone who likes to fancy himself wider awake than his fellows," will "write its obituary notice." Such elitism informs his rambling, racist account from his disparagement of the shallow, trendy "*bonne compagnie*" who support jazz, to its influence on "riff-raff" such as Italian Futurists, to its origins in a "troupe of niggers" who "can be admired artists without any gifts more singular than high spirits." Jazz itself, no less, consists only of an "impudence" full of a "determination to surprise" and "to make fun." By denigrating even the techniques of jazz syncopation and brevity, Bell grants no quarter to music, "the art that is always behind the times" ("Jazz" 214–17). Indirectly, his discussion of jazz becomes a tribute to the glories of modern painting.

For Bell, painting such as the work of Cezanne reflects a deliberate thought process on the part of its practitioners, whereas jazz opposes "the products of the cultivated intellect" and is merely "a ripple" on "the wave" of modernism. He finds that post-Impressionist painters "firmly settled on their own lines of development," as if artists do not evolve and instead foresee the full scope and trajectory of their careers (214–16). In this rhetorical move, Bell both imposes a strategic perspective on the part of his subjects and reveals himself as a critic who is trying to do the very same thing and steer the direction of aesthetic taste. His perspective considers the egalitarianism of jazz repugnant since "it encourages thousands of the stupid and vulgar to fancy that they can understand art, and hundreds of the conceited to imagine that they can create it" (227). In Bell's view, one must be discriminating in order to appreciate art, and the populace is not trained enough. As the thrust of his argument in *Art* (1913) put it, the critic's role is to guide an audience's interpretation of art and create *the* aesthetic experience of it. Here Bell's critic functions like a tube to Pound's artist who is the "antennae of the race" (58). One elite group will be attuned to the world, and another will interpret their message clearly.

In *Art,* Bell had first posited the existence of a common aesthetic emotion that manifested itself internally when appreciating "good" art, and he suggested that a powerful literati could decide what defined "good" and hence impose that view on the masses. Such a dogmatic view is ubiquitous in incipient modernism as seen in Pound's Vorticism and H. D.'s *Notes on Thought and Vision* (1919).[5] For purposes of the Bloomsbury/Cambridge nexus, Bell's view of the ministry of culture reflects the direct application to aesthetics of the theories of Moore's *Principia Ethica.* Both Moore's ethics and Bell's aesthetics stress the importance of envisioning the whole and predetermining a course of action or creation, and hold that the philosopher or critic can declare something to be good or beautiful and convince others that it was not an arbitrary decision. In particular, Bell's idea of "significant form" depends, like Moore's belief in the "good," on the illumination of the entirety of a set of relations in art or in conduct. In *Art,* Bell pursued the "central problem of aesthetics," the cause of the aesthetic emotion, which all "sensible people agree is a peculiar emotion provoked by works of art." He adduces this cause to the essential quality of "significant form," and finds that "lines and colours combined in a certain particular way, certain forms and relations of forms, stir our aesthetic emotions" (16–17). While this reductive theory of art has been handily debunked, it nevertheless exerted considerable influence in drawing attention to form over subject matter, and represents one of the first ahistorical modernist turns in art.

Ogden himself was one of the first, along with I. A. Richards and James Woods, to critique the essentialism of Bell's theory. In the self-mockingly entitled *The Foundations of Aesthetics* (1922), these writers collaborated in exposing the fallacious "meaningless" of significant form by asking "logically 'significant of what?'" (n61). Richards adds that the book "has pages of undermining fun at the expense of the Bloomsbury aestheticians" (CA 47). Later, in a letter to Thomas Bodkin regarding his book *The Approach to Painting* (1927), Ogden not only continued to attack the idea of significant form, but also speaks of the theory as heresy. Writing under the guise of a "housewife," Ogden states that "she" just wants to offer an opinion before returning to "her cooking and parenting" (UCLA 1/2). Under another in his long line of assumed identities, Ogden expressed "surprise" in reading Bodkin's book "to find no reference to the standard refutation of Clive Bell's heresy, 'significant form' which is based on a purely verbal confusion, as documented in [Ogden's] article on Aesthetics . . . in the 13th Edition of the *Encyclopedia Britannica.*" Ogden also questions Bodkin's implication that he "accepted Clive Bell's other heresy," the existence of an aesthetic emotion, and inserts "her" view that "standard analyses" render "otiose" Bell's "assumption that there is *an* aesthetic *emotion* (unknown to modern psychology), as distinguished from an aesthetic *experience* or *state* (which though in part 'emotional,' is surely not *one* of the 'emotions')" (UCLA 1/2). Though Bell's idea of "significant form" had become the basis of an established aesthetic school, it is a heresy to Ogden because the standard of Benthamite linguistic analysis, "verbal fictions," deconstructs its validity. While courting Bloomsbury aesthetes and living among them, Ogden did not relent in his general critique of received interpretations. By the late 1920s, though, Ogden had deployed Bentham's ideas in his creation of Basic English. As many of the modernists did in refining a school of thought, he eventually created his own orthodoxy and tried to control the "fictions" inherent in the psychological dimension of language.

Bell's own discriminating orthodoxy centered on the belief that painting is *the* avant-garde form of art, one that was beyond the influence of others such as jazz. On the other hand, though "so shallow a current," jazz could still claim musicians such as Stravinsky and writers such as Eliot whose forms broke the rules. Jazz can appear in literature in versions of its chief formal element, syncopation, and this fact suggests that while Bell denigrated the jazz movement as a whole, he can respect individual manifestations of its form. For example, he notes how syncopation informs Virginia Woolf's style as she "developed a taste for playing tricks with traditional constructions" and "'leaves out' with the boldest of them." However, he carefully qualifies his view in stating that his sister-in-law does not "properly" belong to the jazz movement, and does not "jeer at accepted ideas of what prose and verse should be and what they should be about." More importantly, she discriminates and strikes "no note of protest against the notion that one idea or emotion can be more important or significant than another" ("Jazz" 224). When Woolf spoke to the Heretics on the nature of character in modern fiction, her own view of the proper response of modernity to tradition, shuttling between intolerance and egalitarianism, would alternately problematize and affirm his account.

Virginia Woolf among the Heretics

For the next few years, the Bloomsbury Group continued to take the train up to Cambridge with increasing regularity. Edith Sitwell spoke in the same term as Bell on "Modern Criticism"; the Russells together indicted "Industrialism and Religion" in March, 1922; then during the Lent term of 1923 Margery Fry discussed reforming "Prisons and Punishment" before her brother, Roger, shared his ideas on "Composition." Leonard Woolf spoke of "Hunting the Highbrow" in 1926. Undoubtedly, though, one of the most resonant historical moments of the Heretics Society occurred on May 18, 1924, when Virginia Woolf developed her treatise on modernist aesthetics, "Character in Fiction." Woolf spoke while, as legend would have it, the British track team trained for the Paris Olympics by racing the stroke of bells around the Great Court at Trinity. The role of the Heretics in the evolution of her famous essay, better known as "Mr. Bennett and Mrs. Brown," remains overlooked.[6] Before and after addressing the Heretics, Woolf substantially changed the tenor, economy, and charge of her essay. Of further literary import, within days of her address, Woolf wrote in her diary, "my mind is full of The Hours," the working title for the novel that would become *Mrs. Dalloway* (301).

The centrality of "Mr. Bennett and Mrs. Brown" to British modernism need not be reaffirmed extensively here. It is a touchstone of modernist aesthetics. Serving several critical purposes, biographers, aestheticians, and literary historians have used the essay to explain the modernist or "Georgian," in Woolf's terminology, epistemic break from their Edwardian predecessors, the testy episode over character development between Woolf and Arnold Bennett, and the indirect dialogue between Woolf and Joyce, *Mrs. Dalloway* and *Ulysses*. The essay has become a modernist aesthetic manifesto appropriated by formalists and feminists alike. Prior to this final, canonized version, Woolf had expanded her initial "Mr. Bennett and Mrs. Brown" from the previous fall for presentation to the Heretics. In Cambridge, Woolf chiefly took issue with Bennett's claim that she and the modernist generation could not create "real; true; and convincing" characters.[7] To discredit his point and demonstrate the beginnings of character formation, Woolf inserts herself in the scene of a railway carriage. One Mrs. Brown and a Mr. Smith converse, stiffly trying to keep up respectable appearances, when Mrs. Brown suddenly starts crying. Mr. Smith's gruff British-male response and quick abandonment of her causes Woolf to want "to realise her character" and to note that here was a common inspiration to write fiction (CF1 508–9). To rebuff Bennett's perspective, she claims that no "generation since the world began has known quite so much about character as our generation" (CF1 504) and that the Georgians/modernists such as Strachey, Forster, and she herself had to create characters anew because their predecessors provided no appropriate example of how to package content into form.

In the lecture version alone, Woolf explained to the Heretics that, if "you read Freud," you will understand the "scientific reasons" why modernist writers "dive deeper in to the real emotions and motives of their fellow creatures" (CF1 504). In contrast, the Edwardians were too focused on a superficial materialism of objects rather than the self and its psychology. When Woolf revised "Character in Fiction" for T. S. Eliot's *Criterion,* she added the epoch-making lines explaining that "on or about December 1910 human character changed" and "when human relations change there is at the same time a change in religion, conduct, politics, and literature" (CF2 420–22). An extensive amount of criticism has discussed the reasoning behind the periodization, but the fact remains that she inserted the date after, in her words, a "good hard headed argument" with the Heretics who underwent severe turmoil during that month in 1910 and who were founded on rejecting the a priori perpetuation of the conclusions of tradition (*Letters* 115). The history of the Heretics, with whom she had just become familiar, perhaps instantiated further the historical transition she had in mind for many other significant reasons.

Beth Daugherty has discussed the importance of the audience to an understanding of Woolf's lecture in causing the "foremost effect on her mind, the primary impetus for reworking the essay, and the major influence over the essay's final shape" (278). However, Daugherty unfortunately hinges her argument that "Bennett's sexism and Woolf's feminism lie at the bottom of their public wrangling" (269) on erroneous statements common to glosses on the Heretics Society. Since Daugherty reports that Woolf spoke solely to an "audience of women" at the "Heretics Club, a group in Girton College," she concludes that "the sex of the audience" encouraged Woolf "to confront Bennett" and persuaded her "to incorporate her feminism within the essay and was thus the decisive factor in Woolf's development of the essay" and "her career" (279).[8] On the contrary, a mixed-gender hall of heretics became the crucial lever Woolf used to launch her principles on the proper, self-contained function of literature. The Heretics served both as an arena in which Bloomsbury could build an aesthetic consensus and as a straw man in Woolf's argument that fiction should not drive you "to join a society," but rather to read the book again. She would invert her belief that "everything [could be] inside the book, nothing outside" (CF2 427–28), in her famous statement from "A Sketch of the Past" that "the whole world is a work of art; that we are parts of the work of art" (72).

Woolf's theory of aesthetic "wholes" owes much to the philosophy of the Heretic who in all likelihood was a member of her audience, G. E. Moore. Gabriel Franks contends that "the student of *Principia Ethica* will find its ideas echoed again and again in her work and her convictions" (230). The philosophical echoes resound throughout Woolf's first novel, *The Voyage Out* (1915), a novel preoccupied with the idea that human society is an organic whole plagued by the inefficacy of communication. As Woolf struggles to find her fey, distinct narrative voice still caught in the inheritance of Edwardian forms, Richard Dalloway appears as a rakish gentleman who had his best thoughts at Trinity College where he concluded that his ideal was "Unity" (64). When he seduces young Rachel Vinrace and kisses her "passionately" telling her she has "beauty," it is as if Moore's two highest ideals consummate in this enjoyment of a beautiful object and pleasure of human intercourse (76). Dalloway has just read the dictum from *Principia Ethica,* "Good, then, is indefinable," and draws the same conclusion that, in discussing ethics, "it's the arguing that counts" (74). St. John Hirst, another Cambridge man, echoes Moore's belief that persuasion alone enables ethical propositions to be held true: "He said that he thought one could make a great deal of difference by one's point of view, books and so on, and added that few things at the present time mattered more than the enlightenment of women" (164). The polemics of the novel anticipate Woolf's later sustained critique of the objectification of women, while still deliberating the social function of art. Evelyn M. embodies this tension. She is a member of a "Saturday Club" designed "to talk about art," but she wants to be more politically active and "form ourselves into a society" to fight for causes that constitute "[b]eing real" (248–49). In one of her last appearances in the novel, Evelyn explains that "she was going to found a club . . . in Bloomsbury preferably, where they could meet once a week." She feels certain that "if once twenty people—no, ten would be enough if they were keen—set about doing things instead of talking about them, they could abolish every evil that exists" (321). A pursuit of this idea of the "real world" behind the visible world pervades the novel, which sometimes suggests it is a mystical conception of love.[9]

In these instances from *The Voyage Out,* Woolf introduces four themes that preoccupied her throughout her literary career. Her address to the Heretics bears directly on these issues: philosophical mysticism, the influence of a coterie of intellectuals, the value of art versus political engagement, and the tension between aesthetic "wholes" and "leaving things out." The paradoxical tenet that an oblique, fragmented aesthetic work can still point toward an organic unity derives in part from her self-described mysticism. Andrew McNeillie refers to the epiphany in "A Sketch of the Past" of the flower's relation to the earth, "That is the whole," as the "clearest critical expression" of her "hybrid, emphatically secular, yet also mystical" view of "transcendental reality" (17–18). Mrs. Brown is an early personification of this flower. Through such microcosmic character expositions as Mrs. Brown on the train, Woolf believes that novelists can provide "us at the same time a complete view of human life." In reading great novels such as *Jane Eyre, War and Peace,* and *Jude the Obscure,* she explains that "you do at once think of some character who has seemed so real that it has the power not merely to make you think of it in itself," but also "of religion, of landscape, of love, of the immortality of the soul" (CF1 509).[10] To achieve such aesthetic wholes, Woolf's repeated intimations imply the necessity of a synthetic view.

Throughout her oeuvre, Woolf worked to develop a narrative technique both rich in perspective and mystically suggestive. Ann Banfield's *The Phantom Table* (2000) considers her fiction, in part, a metaphysics of unseen spaces: "The universe of Virginia Woolf's novels is a monadology whose plurality of possible worlds includes private points of space and time unobserved, unoccupied by any subject. Its principle of unity is not a pre-established harmony conferred ahead of time by authorial intention. It is constructed *ex post facto* via a style and an art" (1). Psychology and philosophy provided fiction not only with a new understanding of character motivation, but also access to a spatial dimension shared with religion and literature, what Woolf called "moments of being." Since people subsequently look closer at reality, in Woolf's view, modernist "literature must be different" (CF1 504). If art could achieve a flickering sense of unity through a formal construct, then the artist had not only the liberty but the duty to "leave things out."

Woolf's formal principles, then, operate under a different conception of synthesis. McNeillie suggests that her "synthesis of forms and genres" owes something to the Bloomsbury fascination with the post-Impressionists, of whom Fry's famous 1910–11 exhibit marks one of the main reasons for Woolf declaring the opening year the dawning of a new age (19). Another Bloomsbury figure, Desmond MacCarthy, as noted earlier, characterized the painters as "Synthesists" who "find completer self-expression" in their work "than is possible to those who have committed themselves to representing objects more literally" (97). MacCarthy, who spoke to the Heretics on "Heroic Poetry" in 1915, further claims that the artist tries "to unload, to simplify the drawing and painting, by which natural objects are evoked, in order to recover the lost expressiveness and life." Aiming "at *synthesis* in design," the artist prepares "to subordinate consciously his power of representing the parts of his picture as plausibly as possible, to the expressiveness of his whole design" (101). Rather than a coherent text woven of disparate discourses, synthesis here means artifice. Woolf's fictions reflect the change in currency of the term "heresy" from 1883–1924, from Edwardian syncretism to discrete "choices." Synthesis becomes synthetic.

In the published version of "Character in Fiction," Woolf states that various aesthetic artifices make a novel such as *Tristram Shandy* or *Pride and Prejudice* "complete in itself" and "self-contained," leaving "one with no desire to do anything, except indeed to read the book again, and to understand it better." In this fetishization of the text, she believes that readers will concomitantly be able to understand the world better, and inserts the previously mentioned contrast that in order "to complete" Edwardian novels "it seems necessary to do something—to join a society, or, more desperately, to write a cheque" (CF2 427). While the premise of *Three Guineas* implies that Woolf revisited the importance of subsidizing social justice, the revisions added to the published "Character in Fiction" also suggest that the address to the Heretics, who would solicit her to join, caused her to rethink the role of audience and public readership in relation to the principles of her treatise. To the Heretics, she described Edwardian novels as leaving her with a "strong feeling of disappointment" (CF1 510). In changing this to a "strange feeling of incompleteness and dissatisfaction," Woolf emphasizes the importance of an aesthetic "whole" (CF2 427). However, as if she remembers the readerly component in Moore's ideal of the contemplation of beautiful objects, Woolf accentuates the role of public readership in the published essay. Clearly she is against didacticism in art, but not in determining how the public should appreciate it. She wants to overcome the "division between reader and writer," and believes that books "should be the healthy offspring of a close and equal alliance between [them]." As part of this agreement, readers must "insist that writers shall come down off their plinths and pedestals, and describe beautifully if possible, truthfully at any rate, our Mrs Brown." Mrs. Brown can become one of those substitute artifices tapped into unity; once manifest, she will be "life itself" (CF2 436).

Before the manifestation of the emblematic Mrs. Brown can signal "one of the great ages of English literature," Woolf believes that the need to break from the Edwardian legacy causes fragmentary forms and the "prevailing sound of the Georgian age"—"crashing and destruction." Though she confesses that she too cries out "for the old decorums," she admonishes the readerly public to be patient and "[t]olerate the spasmodic, the obscure, the fragmentary, the failure" (CF2 434–36). In making choices of omission in narrative, the writer must convince the reader of their validity. In directing the public on principles of literary taste, again "it's the arguing that counts." Bloomsbury was in place not only to help determine rhetorically how art should be received, but also to make its associates find the Heretics Society superfluous.

Toward the end of both versions of "Character in Fiction," Woolf's famous dismissal of Joyce's *Ulysses* on grounds of indecency illustrates the creation of Bloomsbury taste at work. She uses the same aesthetic principles as those in Strachey's address on "Art and Indecency." Joyce's unnamed "indecencies" reflect her idea that the "Georgians" have not yet discovered their technique, yet such works can still be judged on their overall merit. Indecency is not one of the literary experiments to be tolerated if it is deleterious to the aesthetic whole. Woolf states: "Mr Joyce's indecency in *Ulysses* seems to me the conscious and calculated indecency of a desperate man who feels that in order to breathe he must break the windows. At moments, when the window is broken, he is magnificent. But what a waste of energy! And, after all, how dull indecency is, when it is not the overflowing of a superabundant energy or savagery, but the determined and public-spirited act of a man who needs fresh air!" (CF2 434). Joyce's overexertion makes "[m]uch of the book . . . very poor stuff in consequence" (CF1 516), and, since the indecency is "not the overflowing of a superabundant energy," Strachey's thesis that the "whole" can abide indecent asides does not apply. Bloomsbury's decorous taste refrained from supporting the sexuality of Lawrence's and Joyce's work, possibly out of class bias, and this unintentionally facilitated the conventional wisdom of the censorious legislation declaring that a "book may be a fine piece of literature and yet obscene."

Examined with more than a formalist lens, "Character in Fiction" may appear naive. To Woolf's grand credit, though, both her literary style and vision of the political dimension of art evolved. She would write two formal masterpieces, *Mrs. Dalloway* and *To the Lighthouse,* fight against the censorship of literature, and even more actively work for feminist and other radical causes. In this light, Moore's work fails to account for her complex ideas regarding ethical and social order. Banfield points to the "dominant role of Russell's thought for [her] reading of Woolf" (40), and McNeillie nods to the influence of Harrison in reminding us not to lock Woolf's "intellectual seriousness" in the "wooden embrace of G. E. Moore" (13). Several studies of *Between the Acts* argue that Woolf's novel uses Harrison's theories on Greek ritual to structure her narrative.[11] When Woolf took the podium before the Heretics, she certainly felt the presence of the "famous scholar" "J—H—," as she refers to Harrison in *A Room of One's Own* (18). Woolf recently had read Harrison's *Epilegomena to the Study of Greek Religion* (1921), whose third section, "The Religion of To-Day," derives from her February 1921 address to the Heretics.

In this capstone to her scholarly career, Harrison diagnoses and recom-

mends several changes in contemporary views of religion which also illustrate a historical current informing the ideology of modernist aesthetics.
From 1890 to 1920, she grew to believe that religion needs to be seen in context, that god is an important but not essential by-product of pagan rites, and
that religion promotes life, though this can be "hindered by the idea of a god"
(xxii). Revised over the course of her thirty years of research, these points
are Harrison's final conclusions in her brief *Epilegomena,* in which she also
stresses the point that "it is possible to have a living and vigorous religion
without a theology" (xliii). In her studies of the origins of Greek religion,
she welcomes the emendations she had to make over time in order to reflect
the implications of new thought, primarily that of Durkheim and Freud. To
paraphrase, God is a social construct created out of our desires. Her methodology is consistent with her central point that religion evolves in accord
with culture, but, as Shaw suggests in his preface to *Saint Joan,* thought that
is ahead of its time generally is decried as heresy. And Harrison sees her own
work in such a light. In the preface to the second edition of *Themis* (1912),
she expresses her "joy that most of my own old heresies that had seemed to
my contemporaries so 'rash' were accepted by the new school, almost as postulates" (539). Central among these postulates are the ideas that pre-Hellenic
society was matriarchal and that dance and *daimon* were primordial rituals
corrupted by the construction of the Olympian gods.

   In "The Religion of To-Day," Harrison argues that the First World War
had made asceticism the core of modern religion. Gabriel Murray wrote to
her soon after the publication of *Epilegomena;* he found that the third chapter "explains and justifies asceticism, which is almost the most important
piece of teaching that the world needs nowadays" (J. Stewart 182). Though
Harrison believes that the impetus of all religion seeks "*the conservation and
promotion of life*" (xvii), she feels that the Catholic modernist doctrine of
vital immanence affirms her idea that modern religion "aims at the bettering
of life, by the exercise of the function of *choice* and the practice of asceticism"
(lii, emphasis added). What Pius X had decried as the heretical essence of
modernism, Harrison gladly embraces, and she adds the stipulation that
God can only be found in the human "self" where people decide values.
After associating value in general with religious questions, Harrison told
the Heretics that asceticism looks toward higher values because "you and I
are good but . . . we can and need to be better" (liv). For example, she claims
that the flesh is shameful because the spirit is better. Her interest in the
psyche explains both points crucial to her argument, i.e., that human beings
rank values based on their desires and that the doctrine of vital immanence

implies that the "best in you, is one with God, *is* God, your work *is* the divine activity" (liv). This internal, experiential view of the Kingdom of God, however, does not solely make asceticism a function of negation. Art and science better society and "rank as of the highest religious value" (lv). Asceticism, or the function of choice, attunes the aesthetic "instrument" and provides the "discipline that is necessary for eminence in art" (lv). Art and science uplift the human soul and make the question of God's objective existence irrelevant.

When Harrison ends her *Epilegomena* with the epigram "*Via Crucis, Via Lucis*" (lvi), it would appear that she has had a seachange in her religious thought. Mute is the Dionysian revelry, muffled the cry to separate from the herd. However, the function of heresy ("choice") rings clear in providing what she had earlier asked the Heretics to find, the "new mode of life" in the "transition moment" of Edwardian syncretism. The tension of synthetic heresies facilitated the making of hard "choices" by bringing forth a variety of ways of thinking. Often modernism would make hierarchies of them in closed, determinate forms. The trajectory of Harrison's discursive career emblematizes this shift, and her emphasis on the value of asceticism may inform Woolf's critique of indecency. The change in Harrison's interests from pre-Olympian cults to asceticism parallels the turn from orgiastic collectivity to rational propriety that Nietzsche finds in the literary history of Greek tragedy. Similarly, the rich, flowering, productive character of modernism from 1890 to 1940 owes much to the fluctuation between the bounty of uncertain discovery and the brilliance of formal conceptions. Synthesis in tension with discriminatory thought indeed makes modernism, like Classical Greece and the Renaissance, in Woolf's words, "one of the great ages of literature."

THE DISSOLUTION OF THE HERETICS

Several factors, including the passing of a generation of elderly dons and the growth of substitute humanist societies, led to the dissolution of the Heretics Society. None, however, was quite so important as Ogden's permanent relocation to Bloomsbury. On January 3, 1925, Harrison wrote to Ogden: "I am sorry that you have left Cambridge for Cambridge needed you. Well—thru the Heretics you put up a good fight just when most needed" (MCMA 107). Two weeks later McTaggart died. The Executive Committee of the Heretics quickly tried to recoup their losses. On a postcard crucial to the enduring preeminence of the Heretics, the Society disseminated the announcement of

G. E. Moore's influential address, "A Defence of Common Sense," above the following list of proposed new Honorary Members: E. M. Forster, Roger Fry, Virginia Woolf, Lytton Strachey, C. K. Ogden, I. A. Richards, and J. B. S. Haldane (MCMA 114 env.6). Though Ogden would be an Honorary Member until 1927, the four members of the Bloomsbury Group refrained from joining the Society. From 1924 to 1932, the cache of the Heretics slowly petered out, punctuated on occasion by a dramatic episode. In dissolving into a vague humanism, though, the principles of the Heretics diffused into other disciplines and eventually transmuted into orthodoxies of economics, philosophy, liberal humanism, and literary criticism. Spawned out of the pool of heresy, various schools of thought of continuing influence tried to offer a humanistic vision of the world which excluded the religious, but remained implicitly heretical. For instance, there is Keynesian economics.

While Bloomsbury was not brought into the heretic fold in one fell swoop, the rogue economist already was an Honorary Member. The outcry surrounding his *Economic Consequences of the Peace* (1919), highly critical of the Treaty of Versailles, the heavy reparations imposed on Germany, and the overall negative impact on free markets, inspired the Heretics to found an Economics Section of the Society. Sargant Florence states that the section was "heretical in criticizing theory based entirely on the assumption of a rational economic man" (CH 237). They would meet in Florence's house until 1927 when it merged, in another instance of the Heretics' gradual loss of currency, with the newly formed Marshall Society. Though Keynes was not as active as other Honorary Members, he identifies himself as a heretic and consistently refers to his economic theories in his writings as "heretical" and opposed to the "orthodox" economies of Marxism and laissez-faire capitalism.[12] He considered himself a "free-thinking heretic,"[13] and professed his belief in 1930 that the "heretic money reformers" have "flourished in undiminished vigor for two hundred years," and that this proves that "the orthodox arguments cannot be entirely satisfactory" (6: 190–93). Keynes believed in the power of intuition in economic planning, denounced the importance of the Gold Standard, and stressed the idea that banks only imposed costs for profit and instead could supply all the production and trade necessary without anyone incurring any "real costs." As he worked toward his highly influential, now unread *General Theory of Employment, Interest and Money* (1936), he sought as a "heretic" who is an "honest intellectualist" to "reconcile heretics and bankers in a common understanding" (6: 194).[14] The General Theory has become a standard economic principle of the G8, and in it Keynes believed that he discovered the "fatal flaw" in the "orthodox reasoning" of economics to be that there was no "satisfactory theory of the rate of interest" (13: 489).

In order to even out the drastic market cycles between boon and slump, Keynes proposed to change the rate of interest accordingly in order to stimulate consumption or investment. Now when Wall Street muzzles itself to hear the Federal Reserve Board make a decree, it hears Keynes' distant, heretical voice determining its trade.

As Keynes grew in national prominence, his presence in Cambridge concomitantly diminished. He emblematizes a trend throughout the 1920s, which saw the first generation of Honorary Members of the Heretics gradually fade away. Harrison and McTaggart died; several others retired; Moore lost some of his cutting-edge appeal. By 1929, Florence had taken a post in Birmingham and Ogden had withdrawn his Honorary Membership since he found it no longer necessary to maintain contacts at university. In pursuit of funding for Basic English, however, he highlighted the possibility and importance of reestablishing his Cambridge connections in the same successful application to the Rockefeller Foundation in which he touted the Heretics as teaching him about the "verbal defects" of language.[15] To stress the urgency of an endowment for Basic English in 1929, Ogden claimed that now at hand was a "great opportunity which may not occur again" because "[n]ot only is the older generation, the leaders of 19th Century thought, by whose advice and experience we should like to profit, rapidly passing away, but for some years we have kept in view certain brilliant young students at Cambridge and elsewhere whose services should be secured without delay" (MCMA 128.10). For the next fifteen years, Ogden would call on many of these dormant and burgeoning connections to drum up support for Basic English.

Ogden certainly had William Empson in mind as an example of one of these "brilliant young students." The flamboyant, precocious scholar was working under the tutelage of the Heretic I. A. Richards in 1929, and the influence of his thesis, *Seven Types of Ambiguity* (1930), needs little elucidation here. Empson's career at Cambridge from 1925 to 1929 was, in short, stellar. He excelled in math during his first year, wrote a large body of poems, edited *Granta*, and, in debates, defended modern literature against the charge that it was degenerate and oversexed. He also joined the Heretics upon entering Magdalene College and became the president for his final year while writing a large section of *Seven Types* in a furious few weeks.[16] Christopher Norris believes this undergraduate past infuses Empson's entire literary career with "the workings of a rationalised 'heretic' outlook" (*Philosophy* 4). In this light, the influence of the Heretics not only informs the controversy surrounding Empson's interpretation of *Paradise Lost* in *Milton's God* (1961),[17] but also suggests possible heretical implications veiled in his first critical book, which inspired New Criticism and close attention to the verbal ambiguities enriching a text. In *Milton's God,* Empson confesses that he thinks "the traditional God of Christianity very wicked" and that he had done so since he "was at school" (10). John Constable points out to neo-Christian formalists who "dodge the implications of [Empson's] linguistic theory for their theology" that "'ambiguity' destabilizes the word of God by suggesting it has human origin," and that it is not "possible for a Christian to believe that God's mind contains unresolved conflicts" (5). Such critiques of *logos* and apologistic interpretations of God's paradoxical will became more manifest throughout Empson's career, but they are also evident in *Seven Types* and his early poems. For instance, one of his best poems, "Camping Out," published while President of the Heretics, uses the parentheses to comment subversively on "(God's grace)" as something subservient to nature and as a "glass of the divine (that will could break)" (*Poems* 29).

From the viscera, Empson recoiled from Christian doctrines regarding sin and sacrifice that he believed constituted a brutal, primitive ideology. In *Seven Types of Ambiguity,* this barbarous conception of Christianity permeates his illustration of the last, most ambiguous type. The seventh type "occurs when the two meanings of the word, the two values of the ambiguity, are like two opposite meanings defined by the context, so that the total effect is to show a fundamental division in the writer's mind" (192). Empson ends this chapter by explicating passages from Crashaw, Dryden, Hopkins, and Herbert which all reveal "[s]omething weird and lurid in this apprehension of the sacrificial system" (222). Here is an example of Empson's critique of the primitive in Christianity drawn from the relationship between Christ and Mary in Crashaw's "Blessed be the paps which Thou hast sucked" (1670): "a wide variety of sexual perversions can be included in the notion of sucking a long bloody teat which is also a bloody wound. The sacrificial idea is aligned with incest, the infantile pleasures, and cannibalism; we contemplate the god with a sort of savage chuckle; he is made to flower, a monstrous hermaphrodite deity, in the glare of a short-circuiting of the human order" (221). To make grave this critical joviality a few pages later, Empson points to Jupiter's "magnificent obscenity" in Pope's *Dunciad* (1728) that "makes the indifference of God disgusting and the subservience of man unendurable" (223). Immediately, though, Empson returns to his sardonic irreverence in his riff on the moment in Crashaw's translation of "Dies Irae" (1652) when "discharge" ambiguously relates to both "soft bowels" and God's judgment. Empson stresses the capital importance of a poem that "defines God and dung as opposites," and, in one of his sliest jibes, he states that "it is proper that they should have been brought into this chapter" (224). It is proper for

Empson and also insulting to God, because he had earlier stated that the ambiguous mind of seventeenth-century poets "draws its strength from a primitive system of ideas in which the unity of opposites . . . is of peculiar importance" (222–23). To conclude with "a more controlled and intelligible example," Empson turns to George Herbert.

Empson's crowning analysis of Herbert's "The Sacrifice" (1633) had initially been published in the May 1929 edition of *Experiment* during Empson's presidency of the Heretics. He views Herbert as pious and the poem merely a "mouthpiece" for the "theological system" which it addresses, but Empson's play with verbal ambiguities works to put the contradictions the poem holds in equilibrium, or synthesis,[18] in a dissonant if "luminous juxtaposition" (224). That is, orthodox doctrine becomes profanely illuminated. Though Herbert may have had a reverent intent, and is able to balance perfectly the doctrine of Christ's sacrifice, Empson exposes the doctrine itself as ambiguously constructed and intolerably savage. To make his case, Empson focuses on the following lines in the poem attributed to Christ on the cross: "Only let others say, when I am dead, / Never was grief like mine" (31). One interpretation may say Christ wants humanity never to have to suffer as he did, but Empson adds the view that "he may mean *mine* as a quotation from the *others*" (228). From this perspective, Christ asks for retribution and wants his persecutors to suffer eternal damnation. Though Empson questions the acceptance of this double meaning, he insists that readers will always think this interpretation is a possibility, and turns to doctrine as evidence of how this contradiction can be reconciled. Christ atoned for our sins, but we must still toil and have faith out of fear of hell. To conclude, Empson argues that it is not important whether Herbert was conscious of these implications, that the interpretation is not blasphemous but "merely orthodox," for orthodoxy is savage in its desire to inflict pain and deny life (229).[19]

This, then, is an example of a division in the writer's mind, conscious or not, whose ambiguity is reconciled by a formal unity and a "false identity" provided by doctrine. However, the reconciliation is inevitably false in its construction, something religious New Critics tended to obscure in appropriating Empson's methods. In 1930, Allen Tate, R. P. Blackmur, Kenneth Burke, and Yvor Winters all contributed to the symposium, *The Critique of Humanism*,[20] and the battle lines were drawn between historical, humanist-minded textual criticism and its conservative, veiled-religious counterpart. Toward the end of his career, Empson would accentuate historical context and biographical material to fight what he considered the Christianization of secular and skeptical authors.[21] Empson's own biography includes a notorious end to his affiliation with Cambridge. A month after the appearance of his heretical analysis of "The Sacrifice," Empson won the Charles Kingsley Bye Fellowship at Magdalene for the following year. His zest for life made him careless and his fellowship short-lived when a college servant found condoms in his room. Empson lost the fellowship and had his name stripped from the college books. It is uncertain how his continuing presence in Cambridge might have affected the Heretics, but his influence on literary criticism during this time when English emerged as a discipline is not as ambiguous.

Cleanth Brooks, one of the influential critics Empson believed inserted a neo-Christianity into literary analysis, appropriated Empson's methodology for his own ends while denying all political, religious, and social implications of his interpretations. In *The Well Wrought Urn* (1947), Brooks outlines this view in the concluding chapter, "The Heresy of Paraphrase." In this staple of New Criticism, he argues for the inseparability of form and content in any proper study of poetry, and his emphasis on the formal constructs of irony and paradox illustrate the inheritance that orthodox modernist aesthetics in the Eliotic school bequeathed to New Criticism. Questions of form predominate. The critical terminology, the heresy of paraphrase, represented a taboo for New Criticism in the vein of the Affective or Intentional Fallacies. For Brooks, any interpretation of verse that goes beyond formal close reading is "heretical," and, in this denunciation, he implicitly indicts one of the most salient characteristics of Empson's mode of analysis.

Certainly, Empson's common method is to paraphrase several interpretations of a kernel of verse in order to illustrate the ambiguities created by poetic technique and language. Brooks declares that "most of our difficulties in criticism are rooted in the heresy of paraphrase" because, in splitting the "poem between its 'form' and its 'content,'" the "paraphrastic heresy" brings "the statement to be conveyed into an unreal competition with science or philosophy or theology" (183–84). In Brooks' mind, "most of the common heresies about poetry derive" from the belief that a "poem constitutes a 'statement' of some sort" (179). For Brooks, paraphrase does a disservice to the complexities enriching a poem, and symptomatizes the "distempers of criticism," which mostly derive, as Richards had argued, from making propositions "*about* the poem" (182). Instead, he works to establish a mode of analysis of poems in the "tradition" which share a "common goodness" in terms of "structure," not "content" or "subject matter" (177). This approach is what initially attracted him to Empson, whose criticism he described in an earlier review as "an attempt to deal with what the poem 'means' in terms of its structure *as a poem.*" However, Brooks also notes a common objection to Empson's criticism which "forces upon the poem his own personal associations," and often appears in interpretive paraphrase ("Empson's" 125; 128).[22] By the time of *The Well Wrought Urn,* Brooks seems to have sensed Empson's "heretic outlook," for he indirectly summarizes Empson's methodology in describing the "most subtle" manifestation of the heresy of paraphrase. This "error" of criticism is "most stubbornly rooted in the ambiguities of language," begins with the "'paraphrasable' elements of the poem," and subordinates the "other elements" (183). In effect, Empson's interpretive riffs unpacked the synthetic "wholes" theorized by High Modernist aesthetic manifestoes, orthodoxies of the organic, closed craftwork. Brooks tried to stifle this critical "heresy" which might raise questions about theology in Herbert's "The Sacrifice," and his use of the term "heresy" reveals not only his own biases, but also its residual currency.

Empson was the dynamic force in a cluster of bohemians at Cambridge who were engaged in avant-garde aesthetics and radical politics. They continued the use of the Heretics Society as a forum for cutting-edge thought, and they entertained Marxism. They dabbled in surrealism. They published in *Granta, Venture,* and *Experiment,* an extreme left-wing journal whose submissions emanated mostly from Magdalene College. The Woolfs' Hogarth Press published the voices of several Heretics in the famous volume *Cambridge Poetry, 1929.* The poems of Heretics (Empson, Christopher "Kit" Saltmarshe, Hugh Sykes Davies, and Julian Bell) were gathered together with those of John Lehmann, Michael Redgrave, and Jacob Bronowski to express the voice of a new generation. Later the Woolfs sounded them off the Oxford contingent of Auden, Spender, and Day Lewis in another landmark collection, *New Signatures* (1932). A sense of promise was trying to mitigate the economic slump plaguing Britain at the time. In Empson's inner circle, Julian Trevelyan and Kathleen Raine began their respective careers in painting and poesy as radical Heretics.[23] Among this generation at Cambridge, Julian Bell and John Cornford exemplified the growing appeal of Marxism, and their commitment to social justice eventually led them to volunteer in the Spanish Civil War, where they died fighting for the Republic. Bell was the son of Clive and Vanessa Bell, nephew to the Woolfs, and Cornford's father was the classical scholar and mentor of the Heretics. The Society was passing on its legacy within families. Bell became one of the last treasurers, and Trevelyan, the nephew of the Heretic historian, took over the secretarial duties for a year and a half after Empson's dismissal.

When Empson was sent down from Cambridge in 1929, the Heretics still had a host of talented members, but they had lost their president and his magnetic presence. He realized the precarious situation of the Society and immediately set out to advise Trevelyan, his new recruit. In telling the story of his expulsion, Empson cautioned him: "What happened (since you ask) was the porters found a French letter in my rooms, and the bedmaker had also been very industrious at reading letters and so forth; let it be a warning to you, young man, I had no idea one was so officially spied on. It was high time I got away from the place; I shall do journalism now if I can." He passed down Ogden's standard recruiting technique: "The great thing is to get somebody who will do for the first or second Sunday, and get out some sort of card. Then you can pick up the locals" (*Letters* 10–11). Empson suggested specific faculty to solicit, and he leveled with the sophomore secretary on the state of the Society's affairs: "I'm afraid I've let you in for a difficult job rather; I have just been kicked out of Cambridge, so probably the President next year will be Professor Piccoli, a dear thing who doesn't know a bit what the Heretics like, and wants watching about Croce. I have got a promise from Wittgenstein to speak next term but that is absolutely all" (*Letters* 9). Piccoli too would be gone by the fall of 1931, leaving Cambridge amid vague hints of distress. Empson regretted handing over the reins to Piccoli, though everyone called him "the dear," especially since the latter's passivity would replace Empson and Trevelyan having their "year of feeding the lions together" (*Letters* 12). From Empson's other notes, it is clear that the Heretics are the prideful beasts for him, so that the gladiatorial image is one of the Society donning the image of the Cambridge mascot to eat Christians.

From the summer of 1929 through the fall of 1930, Julian Trevelyan and Elisabeth Wiskemann sent out a flurry of solicitous letters in a struggle for the survival of the Society. The Heretics had kept the correspondence with artists and intellectuals who had previously accepted, postponed, or declined invitations to address the discussion group, and now the Society came calling again. The Heretics renewed these dormant acquaintances with some success, and Arthur Waley, Sturge Moore, and C. E. M. Joad all returned to address the Society. The family Sitwell was willing to speak again, but illness and travel kept them away. Foreshadowing his work in *Milton's God*, Empson himself offered to "read a paper, or read from notes, about whether poems ought to be annotated, whether it is important, and why it is hard." He suggested the "bright caption," evocative of ambiguity, "Sphinx, or the future of exegesis," and said he "could give examples from the Bentley edition of Milton, and the answers to Bentley, which I have been very excited about" (*Letters* 20). On the other hand, Richard Aldington and Leonard Woolf politely declined, citing preoccupations with other affairs, while Aldous Huxley was more brusque in his refusal. In June of 1930, he responded to Trevelyan: "Your telegram was forwarded to me by post, after some delay. Thank you for asking me to read a paper to the Heretics on Sunday: but I'm afraid I can't accept your invitation. I am returning you the virgin half of your telegram, which will be of more use to you than me" (TCL JOT 1/48). Though Empson told Trevelyan that "certainly Virginia Woolf had better come again" (*Letters* 10), she wrote the following poignant response to Trevelyan's invitation:

> 22nd, August 1929
> Monks House
>
> Dear Julian,
> (If I may call you so)
>
> It is awfully nice of you to ask me to come and speak to the Heretics. I have the greatest respect for them, and if I could speak to anybody it would be to them.
>
> But I find thinking more and more impossible—it takes up so much time and I can't ever say what I want—so that I brought my life as a speaker to an end last October, and shall never open my mouth in public again:—I hope.
>
> But many thanks to you and the Heretics for inviting me.
>
> Yours sincerely,
> Virginia Woolf
>
> Please remember me to your mother and father.
> (TCL JOT 1/63)

Woolf is referring to her delivery of sections of what became *A Room of One's Own* to the Arts Society at Newnham and Odtaa at Girton. Amid the sadness of her inner struggles, she still found the grace to cast favor on the Heretics. Her newfound difficulties with public expression brought a significant loss to the Heretics, one more than recovered with her focus on fiction and social commentary in the 1930s.

Perhaps news of debauchery and the growing debt of the Heretics eventually influenced others to distance themselves carefully from the Heretics. On October 29, 1929, Black Tuesday, Kit Saltmarshe complimented Trevelyan on the "full and excellent programme . . . produced for the fall term," and cherished Julian's letter which "came like a breath of heretical Cambridge air." At the same time, "horrified by the revelations of extravagance," he ominously admonished his fellow Heretic: "if you only knew how Bill and I denied ourselves . . . and now you are destroying the sound financial position we made for you, alack and woe. Let me tell you that we made it a rule to pay for ourselves except upon one occasion a term" (TCL JOT 2/16). In November 1930, Rex Warner regretted that his "paper did not provoke more discussion," but suggested that, "possibly, the vodka is to blame" since "[m]ore sober," he "should have been more argumentative" (TCL JOT 2/7). The following March, Saltmarshe informed Trevelyan of a bizarre "Sidney Sussex 'accident.'" He claimed that "by all accounts [it] should have been treated as manslaughter," and added "[s]uffice it to say that a book was found describing an Eskimo rite for getting to Heaven and entailing exactly the same tying-up as that of the deceased student" (TCL JOT 2/17). By the spring of 1931, Trevelyan had left Cambridge without a degree and ventured off to Paris to paint on the Seine with Max Ernst and others. As treasurer of the Heretics, Julian Bell wrote to him: "The Heretics have just avoided bankruptcy, so here's your cheque. Thank goodness I'm free of the job" (TCL JOT 30/106). In the last few years of the Society, a general economic slump combined with a sudden profligate tendency on the part of the Executive Committee broke the economic stability the Heretics had secured for twenty years from Ogden to Empson.

The major intellectual blast of the last four years of the Society came in the Michaelmas term of 1929 when Wittgenstein returned to Cambridge, fulfilled his promise to the Heretics, and delivered to them his famous lecture on "Ethics." Wittgenstein's discussion of ethics was his only popular lecture, and it marks the transition in his thinking from the study of logical propositions and the "picture theory" in *Tractatus* to the rejection of this approach in the posthumous *Philosophical Investigations*. He came to believe that language performed many more functions than those that could be described in terms of truth or falsity, and, in order to show the limitations of language, his focus shifted toward the language of everyday life and the context surrounding an utterance. The subject of ethics is an example of this latter set of expressions which consists of "meaningless" language, and, though he greatly respects ethical issues, he concludes his address by stating that "to write or talk Ethics or Religion [is] to run against the boundaries of language," which is "perfectly, absolutely hopeless" (12). In all ethical or religious propositions, Wittgenstein discerns a characteristic use of similes or allegories. Though he claims it is impossible to drop metaphor and express the same statement without speaking nonsense, he believes that there are other ways of looking at the world than through a scientific lens because people do experience ineffable, pleasurable moments. For example, he points to the way people explain miracles, for the first case, and wonder at the world's existence, for the latter.

Such a view nears mysticism, and Wittgenstein states at one point that "Ethics, if it is anything, is supernatural" (7). In fact, he acknowledges that one can always add "God" to declare absolute values of judgment, and, in his contemporaneous discussion with Friedrich Waismann, he noted that "[i]f any proposition expresses just what I mean, it is: Good is what God orders" (15). However, he has allowed that to invoke God is a case of using metaphor, and that such expressions are essentially nonsense. Wittgenstein's heretical view allows for God while explaining that to speak of divine good is to babble. It is the paradoxical view that enables faith by radical theologians and other Christian intellectuals who sincerely engage modern thought. It also deconstructs *logos*. The implications of his address on ethics thus underwrite both religious humanism and the poststructuralist onslaught on humanist value-formation.

Within a year of the dissolution of the Heretics, the collaborative "Humanist Manifesto" (1933) provided a theoretical platform that would be adopted, at least tacitly, by a growing number of liberal humanist societies. The sixth statute of the manifesto declares: "We are convinced that the time has passed for theism, deism, modernism, and the several varieties of 'new thought'" (Wilson 36). Rather than the modernist attempt to synthesize sacred and secular impulses, humanism often sought to replace religion in name or principle, and take command of all aspects of social life. The manifesto itself is another example of the modernist production of manifestoes designed to decide what is right. In 1941 the American Humanist Association appeared, and Dora Russell probably mistook another Cambridge humanist organization for a new branch of Heretics in a 1967 letter to Ogden's brother, Frank. She writes: "There must have been some attempt to revive the Heretics at the end of the Second War, for I went to Cambridge to deliver a paper to them, 1946 or 47 or even later. Two of the former pupils of my own school Jeremy Pritchard and Donald Alcock were then at Cambridge as undergraduates, and were at this meeting. The paper was called the 'Fundamental Heresy of Women' ie [*sic*] of women as the natural heretics to the Machine Age Religion" (MCMA 65). Probably the title of her talk led her to confuse the Heretics with another humanist society, though the history is unclear. During the 1960s, E. M. Forster was president of the Cambridge Humanist Society, founded in 1955, but in that year he initially asked G. E. Moore to take this helm. The aging don and former Heretic "declined because he did not think the name strong enough" and asked, 'Is not the main point of it to be anti-religious, i.e. to believe very confidently, as I do, that there is no God,' or, at least 'that it is extremely doubtful whether there is any?'" (WCL 406). Between heresy and humanity, Moore chose the one more striking.

In 1963, Julian Huxley as president inaugurated the British Humanist Association during a dinner held in the House of Commons. Forster was on the advisory council during the 1960s. The BHA was designed as the unifying heir apparent for such "humanist" groups as the Rationalist Press Association, the National Secular Society, the Heretics, and the Ethical Union. The BHA is still active and runs its own press, publishing a variety of humanist texts including Forster's *What I Believe and Other Essays*. One of the first volumes off its press, *The Humanist Outlook* (1968) includes Florence's memoir essay on the Heretics. At the end of the memoir, he states that the "moral of the story is that senior members of universities should take some responsibility for the stability of humanist societies from one fleeting generation of undergraduates to another" (CH 239). Another "moral" of the history of the Heretics Society is the neglected fact that heresy was a prevalent methodological approach and discursive trope of modernism. Now that this recuperative sketch of its influence is before us, the following chapters turn to analyses of textual instances and the reception of heresy, in part to explain this neglect, but largely to examine the heretical modernists' subtle, synthetic vision.

PART II

Modernist Literary Heresies

Chapter 4

Canonical Transformations

IN ALDOUS HUXLEY'S *Brave New World* (1932), when Mustapha Mond explains to the Savage why people in their *soma*-induced stupor no longer need religious books such as William James' *The Varieties of Religious Experience,* the benevolent megalomaniac states that the books on his secret shelf are "about God hundreds of years ago" and "[n]ot about God now." Though the Savage objects that "God doesn't change," Mond ends the discussion with the sharp retort: "Men do, though" (157). As Gladstone's discussion of heresy illustrates, authoritative discourses also will shift to account for the changing worldviews implicit in much of modern thought. Vatican II (1962–65) accepted many propositions of the clerical modernists in its ecumenical movement to renew the Catholic Church. More recently, Pope John Paul II apologized for the Inquisition in 1992, and he suggested thinking of hell as more of a state of mind than an actual place. Oftentimes heretics themselves have been the subject of revisionist histories, and this chapter examines how works by Shaw and Joyce engage the cultural movements from 1883 to 1924 to rehabilitate the burnt heretics, Joan of Arc and Giordano Bruno. The biblical and literary canons undergo similar transformations, for example, in revisiting neglected works, the ideology of the Apocrypha, and the portrayal of religion in works by such authors as Boethius, Milton, and Joyce.

The cry of heresy depends upon the estranged reception of readers, historians, and inquisitors. But the same heresy often will also advance thought and social justice before being received as orthodoxy in subsequent generations. To achieve its subversive ends between 1883 and 1924, heterodox literature often subtly inserts a recusant voice amid its competing discourses, a voice that privileges being "other" out of "choice." While a syncretic heretical gesture works to make contradictory ideologies cohere, disparate textual elements may not be reconcilable and thereby will create a gaping chasm in the reader's mind. The most suppressed type of heretical discourses in litera- ture, and therefore the most susceptible to orthodox appropriation, occurs in the ideological construction embedded in a text's linguistics, competing doctrines, or implied genealogy of religion. The ensuing analyses over the next three chapters examine these issues in the synthetic vision of heretical discourses in works by Shaw, Joyce, Pater, Hardy, and Lawrence. Hereti- cal inclinations in literature often become interpreted for orthodox ends by focusing solely on the accepted religious elements. The subversive discourse of a text, however, can luminously come forth both within the constraints of an unfolding narrative and over the course of history with the widening horizons of its readership. The process of reading, in its very nature, pro- duces an engagement with a constructed world dependent on evaluation, broadens the possibilities for living, and brings the capacity for changing cul- tural values into the domain of the human will. Heretics and literature itself participate in the process of transforming the canon and making orthodoxy seem strange, and on this note Shaw's address to the Heretics, "The Religion of the Future," champions the function of heresy and reception in changing cultural values over time.

"THE RELIGION OF THE FUTURE"

As I mentioned in chapter 2, the "debate" between Shaw and Chesterton dur- ing 1911 was the signature mark of the Heretics before the First World War. At no other time did the Society enjoy as much financial clout or as large a national audience. In fact, the prolonged battle of ideas between Shaw and Chesterton known as the "Great Debate," officially began in Cambridge, and the friendly rivals quickly launched a series of debates in Memorial Hall, London, to follow on the heels of their successes at the Heretics. As was the case with most of the famous disputes initiated by the Society, their debate was not a debate in the traditional sense since Chesterton responded six months later and neither was in attendance for the other's address. The so- called debate nevertheless finally brought the two dynamic speakers in direct conflict and a widespread notoriety to the Heretics.

The contrast between the six-foot-four, gray-bearded mystical drama- tist and the rotund, beer-loving rational Christian dogmatist continued to have national public appeal until a final debate of 1927, "Do We Agree?"[1] As Alzina Stone Dale notes, after "most of their debates, as contemporaries admit, the question of 'who won' depended upon the political or religious views of the onlooker" (153). Often Shaw and Chesterton would quibble over the definition of a word such as "miracle" or "heresy." The victory would depend on reception, for instance, whether a person could be convinced either to embrace or repulse heresy. Before the Heretics, Shaw and Chesterton fought over the nature of what happens to heresy over time, while in effect they both agreed that the interdicted discourse, if properly defended and promulgated, becomes orthodoxy. However, while Shaw saw heresy as an aspect of the Life-Force consistently evolving and driving humanity toward progress, Chesterton wanted people to exercise their free will, defend their opinions and yet always consider them "orthodox." In each perspective, received acceptance tolls the death knell of heresy—it becomes orthodoxy.

Though Shaw's and Chesterton's separate addresses to the Heretics comprised their first critical engagement covered extensively by the national media and published in pamphlet form, for several years these men of letters had been lampooning and critiquing each other in the press. In *Heretics* (1905), his denigration of Edwardian religious inclinations, Chesterton initiated the battle of ideas by including Shaw among other "heretics" such as Wells, Kipling, and Goldie Dickinson. Shaw's *Man and Superman* (1903) had clearly enough delineated the principles of the Life-Force, and its protagonist, John Tanner, declares in the addendum, "The Revolutionist's Handbook," that "[e]very genuine religious person is a heretic and therefore a revolutionist" (214). Indeed, the resonance of this play led Chesterton to say that he was "not concerned" with Shaw "as one of the most brilliant and one of the most honest men alive," but "as a Heretic—that is to say, a man whose philosophy is quite solid, quite coherent, and quite wrong" (*Heretics* 15). The rhetorical appeals of this position would characterize all of Chesterton's comments on Shaw and heresy. Chesterton would flatter his opponent, and he would note the coherence heresy holds while forever refraining that this is due to orthodoxy and simply a "wrong" interpretation.

Chesterton could not abide the changes in modern thought that find people willingly identifying themselves in opposition to orthodoxy. Ignoring the earlier etymological meanings of "heresy" such as "personal choice" or "school of thought," he condemned the Edwardian world in which the following is permissible: "The word 'heresy' not only means no longer being wrong; it practically means being clear-headed and courageous," and the "word 'orthodoxy' not only no longer means being right; it practically means being wrong." Somehow this change in connotation only signifies for Chesterton "that people care less for whether they are philosophically right"

(*Heretics* 4). On the other hand, rather than illustrating a culture that has forsaken philosophy or the desire to be "right," people, as the Heretics most flamboyantly displayed, had usurped the charged power of the word in order to confront orthodoxy head on.

In the February 1908 issue of *The New Age,* Shaw responded to Chesterton's intransigent dogma with the grotesque and lasting caricature, the "Chesterbelloc." In this portrayal of two divided conservatives bumblingly trying to work together, Shaw satirizes the allure of "the Chesterton-Belloc chimera," which "can produce the quadrupedal illusion" of a "pantomime beast" (77). At the front end, the rabid attack-dog of orthodoxy, Hilaire Belloc, bites while the jovial and consoling Chesterton pulls up the rear to digest Belloc's bilious critique for a popular audience. Later in the year within the same pages of *The New Age,* Shaw more seriously responded to Chesterton's charge that he denied miracles. This was a controversial topic in the air since Pius X had recently condemned the modernist tendency to deny the veracity of miracles. To be sure, Shaw affirms, he has always believed in miracles because the world is full of undeniable miraculous events such as birth, life, and consciousness. The person who denies miracles "is simply wrong in his definition of a miracle" in thinking it "something that he is not accustomed to and did not expect" ("Miracles" 43). The *sine qua non* nature of miracles for canonization by the Church later caused Shaw to revisit his theory of miracles for *Saint Joan.* In the play, the degree of credulity becomes of lesser importance than the personal or official reception of miracles, which he has a cleric define as the process that creates faith.

Two years before the official "Great Debate" began in Cambridge, Chesterton offered a final preparatory sortie with his book-length literary and biographical study, *George Bernard Shaw* (1909). Labeling Shaw a "heathen mystic" (7), Chesterton finds that he has too many individual opinions and that a "man must be orthodox upon most things, or he will never even have time to preach his own heresy" (8). As a result, Chesterton argues that Shaw's plays have become more philosophy than drama, and their successes further promote a Shavian heresy. Nevertheless, Chesterton claims that Shaw's attempt "to offer some key to all creation" by "rallying his synthetic power" will only preach a "vast and universal religion" of which "he is the only member" (127).

On May 25, 1911, Shaw and the Heretics said otherwise. Not only did the Irish playwright accept, upon finishing his address, an invitation to become an Honorary Member of the Society, but over a thousand people packed a Cambridge lecture hall and nearly two hundred others were turned away

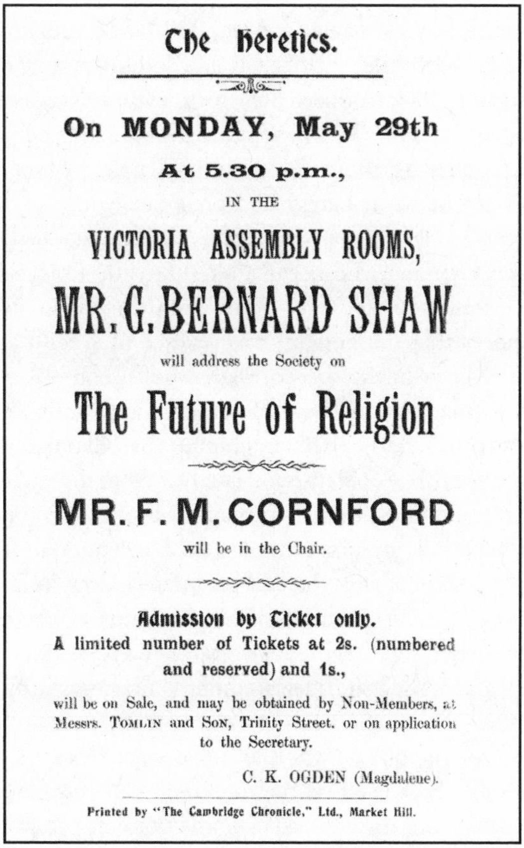

The Heretics.

On MONDAY, May 29th

At 5.30 p.m.,

IN THE

VICTORIA ASSEMBLY ROOMS,

MR. G. BERNARD SHAW

will address the Society on

The Future of Religion

MR. F. M. CORNFORD

will be in the Chair.

Admission by Ticket only.

A limited number of Tickets at 2s. (numbered
and reserved) and 1s.,

will be on Sale, and may be obtained by Non-Members, at
Messrs. TOMLIN and SON, Trinity Street, or on application
to the Secretary.

C. K. OGDEN (Magdalene).

Printed by "The Cambridge Chronicle," Ltd., Market Hill.

Figure 4. Announcement of Bernard Shaw's address to
the Heretics Society. (*Source:* C. K. Ogden fonds, McMaster University Library, MCMA 114.29)

from the door. Writing for the *Gownsman* in the year before the *Cambridge Magazine* appeared, Ogden rejoiced that the "enthusiastic audience which crowded to the Victoria Assembly Rooms on Monday is a striking example of the recent triumphs of heresy in Cambridge" ("Shaw" 669). Most Honorary Members of the Heretics were in attendance, and for the event the Society initiated the practice of disseminating advertising broadsides for their more renowned public lectures (see figure 4). Proceeds from ticket sales amounted to eleven pounds nine shillings, and hiring the Victoria Assembly Rooms cost only two pounds five shillings (MCMA 113.38). This surplus combined with the fact that Shaw, as was his practice, did not request a speaker's fee made the event the first major financial success for the Heretics.

For the addresses by both Shaw and Chesterton, Cornford took the chair, and Ogden copied down their words. Cornford, though, let his biases shine through and specifically introduced Shaw with enthusiasm "as a protagonist of the Heretical movement" (RF 1).[2] When Shaw began his hour-long speech on a stifling Monday late afternoon, he immediately set forth a definition of the relationship between heresy and orthodoxy that would eventually undergird his theory of heresy in *Saint Joan*. In likening a heretic to "a man with a mechanical genius who began tinkering with a bicycle or a motor car and made it something different from what the manufacturer had made it," Shaw considers that the heretic "was really a man with a home-made religion" (RF 1).[3] Later in the speech, Shaw would echo this description of the heretic in stating that the "man of genius" must "amuse and frighten" the laity because they fail to understand him or the "vital truths of religion." Such elitism, though, drew applause and laughter from the audience when he said, "with a smile," "I know this . . . for I am by profession a man of genius" (RF 3–4). However, in a premise crucial to his conception of the Life-Force and its role in historical change, he deflects interest away from the heretical genius who molds religion "to suit himself," and onto the "orthodox people," the "people who really mattered." Shaw grants his privileged audience the historical agency to propagate ideals amongst the masses by stating that what "the Heretics had to do was to prepare a ready-made religion for the next generation for the people who had to accept religion as it came" (RF 1). Shaw's speech founds itself on the *élan vital* of Bergson and the will to power of Nietzsche, and his view reflects this shared attempt to synthesize spirituality and evolution. To affirm his belief in progress, Shaw assumes that just and visionary heresy becomes the religion of the future as the changing horizon of readerly expectations reflects on history and changes its reception. The Life-Force below progressive heresy, however, consistently evolves and never satisfies itself with becoming a static set of tenets. As a member of the orthodoxy of posterity, the heretic thinks he or she is "right" as a heretic, but this "correctness" changes relatively over time.

Confronting his audience with such an unstable cosmos, Shaw is acutely aware that he might alienate some of his listeners; consequently, he alludes to natural selection which had made "evolution" familiar, and he interchangeably uses the concepts of "God" and the "Life-Force." In the question-and-answer session, one unnamed Heretic objected that "Shaw ought to endeavor to avoid the unpleasant word God, with its unsatisfactory associations"; to which Shaw "admitted the word was somewhat fatuous, yet 'Life-Force' did not please people, and he could find nothing better" (Ogden, "Shaw" 670).

Shaw believes that people want a "God whom they could understand," so he offers some guidelines stressing the need to rid religion of idolatry and borrowed, archaic legends. Additionally, he feels that natural selection created "a horrible void" that left us in a world without "purpose or design." To fill this chasm, the Life-Force presents the goal of the superman. If the Heretics used "what they called their will," Shaw argues that society could return to "some belief in the purpose of the universe" by establishing "laws and morality which they supposed to be the will of God." He underscores the point that this will is not God, while still finding that the idea of being possessed by God or the devil is a "conception of enormous value." Not only does it illustrate the similarities between temptation and inspiration, but conceiving God as needing to work through human hands and brains in order to "struggle with a great, whirling mass of matter . . . meant our moulding this mass to our own purposes and will, and in doing that really moulding to the will of God" (RF 2–6). Such slippery spirituality begets the superman. This user-friendly theory of the Life-Force also accounts for the origin of evil because through trial and error humanity was "liable to make some mistakes." Replete, however, with the majestic possibility characteristic of the Edwardian period, Shaw demands belief in the "Will to Good" and the idea that people are "all experiments in the direction of making God." He even concludes with an optimistic Edwardian vision of synthesis: "when the different races of the earth had worked out their own conceptions of religion, those religions might meet and criticise each other, and end, perhaps, in only one religion." The First World War had not yet made common what he finds impossible, "to regard man as willing his own destruction" (RF 6–8). As French soldiers in the trenches of the Western Front would pray to Joan of Arc for morale, Shaw in *Saint Joan* would call on her "vitalism" and recent canonization in order to counter the Thanatos drive.

Joan's trial and the war were examples of "error," and overcoming them suggested to Shaw, as he had told the Heretics, that a sober, courageous humanity still could be "super-supermen" and "a world of organisms who had achieved and realised God" (RF 7). Willaim Furlong evocatively reports that, in communicating ideas such as the Life-Force or the superman, Shaw worked for crescendo effect, the "Shavian head was thrown back, his eyes seemed to pierce through and beyond his auditors, and his voice deepened into a more pronounced Irish accent as his tone became prophetic" (82). Shaw certainly did have his audience of Heretics enraptured, and even a review in *The Christian Commonwealth* described his performance as "gloriously irreverent, transparently sincere, divinely prophetic, and inspiring—

the very thing for our older universities" (RF 12). Indeed, the mystic, as Shaw identified himself, immediately accepted the invitation to become an Honorary Member of the Heretics.

Orthodoxy would have to wait six months before Chesterton arrived in Cambridge to respond to what *The Academy* called "A Detestable Outrage" in protest "against the dissemination of poisonous theories amongst young persons" (RF 13). The Heretics remembered a similar conservative reaction to Chawner and the "Prove All Things" controversy, and actually seemed to revel in it by printing this news clipping at the end of Shaw's speech and as an introduction to Chesterton's. Another excised quotation from *The Fortnightly Review* mandated that "it is surely time for a chivalrous revolt against this conventional unconventionality" (qtd. in Chesterton, "Future" 2). Ogden knew that outrage only brought more notoriety to the Heretics, and he even knew how to spin Chesterton's fame and rebuttal to serve the needs of the Society. For instance, the Heretics' prospectus for 1912–13 stated that "the most important outcome of the event [Shaw's address] was the great meeting the following term, when Mr. G. K. Chesterton defended orthodoxy against the attack of Mr. Shaw" and resulted in "a remarkable accession of strength to the Heretics" (MCMA 114 env.4). Publicity of any sort brought timorous and blossoming heterodox thinkers into the fold.

In facing the Heretics with all the hopes of orthodoxy behind him, Chesterton could have imagined himself in the role of Gabriel Syme, the protagonist in his most popular novel, *The Man Who Was Thursday* (1908). Syme had been recruited as a "philosophical policeman" who will fight "The Last Crusade" and wage the "battle of Armageddon" against the anarchy of the modern world created by "the most dangerous criminal now . . . the entirely lawless modern philosopher" (43–47). Easily disguised as an anarchist called "Thursday," Syme is perfect for this mod squad and its "heresy hunt" since he is a poet at heart and can "discover from a book of sonnets that a crime will be committed" (43). Once accepted into the cell of elite anarchists in this chase novel, Thursday pursues every other modern rebel named after a day of the week until they each literally pull off masks and reveal themselves to be undercover thought police. Each philosophical policeman personifies an element of the creation of the world, and immense, mysterious Sunday represents "the peace of God" (178) and the "mystery of the world," of which we know only "the back" (167–68). In its allegory of creation which emphasizes the need to defend the faith and learn from the power of anarchy, the novel clearly shows the influence of the recent condemnation of the Catholic modernists. At one point, Syme jokingly declares, "we are all Catholics now" (16), and later he elucidates his position by stating: "The moderns say we must not punish heretics. My only doubt is whether we have a right to punish anybody else" (44). Punish he would not, but Chesterton saw the opportunity at Cambridge as a chance to subdue the "modern" Heretics.

After arriving fifteen minutes late to the Guildhall, the City Council building, where an audience of eight to nine hundred waited to hear him on a Friday night, Chesterton spoke for over an hour and answered questions for another one. A magnificent pipe organ rose behind him, and the room was strewn with heraldic emblems of English kings and paintings of mayors and Queen Victoria. Tradition was on his side. He received ovations at beginning and end, and he "dealt with hecklers in a prompt and ready manner." His first heckler was Cornford who introduced him as "the only living man who had ever written two books, one entitled 'Orthodoxy' and the other 'Heretics.'" Though he had read *Heretics* the previous day, Cornford refrained from *Orthodoxy,* "having, he supposed, been repelled by the title." Upon rising to the platform, Chesterton first explained that his tardiness "was due to the fact that he came there in a Cambridge cab, and constantly encouraged the horse and driver to go slower and slower so that he might see the beauties of the town, and also begin to make up what he was going to say" ("Future" 3–4). The trip from Petty Cury to Market Hill had inspired him. Later in January 1912, Ogden printed a sketch of Chesterton taking these notes in the first issue of *The Cambridge Magazine.* Chesterton inadvertently had launched the reciprocal relationship between the Heretics and Ogden's first journal. He later wrote to Ogden: "My best notes were made, not just before the lecture, but just after it. . . . But these were also made in a cab; so that your picture will do quite as well for the baffled and remorseful lecturer as for the expectant and provocative one" (MCMA 113.36). Among Chesterton's last-minute notes, which were written on the pamphlet of Shaw's address Ogden had sent to him, Joseph Pearce reports that he outlined his main points and psychologically prepared himself with the declaration: "It has taken about 1800 years to build up my religion. It will not take 18 minutes to destroy Mr. Shaw's" (168).

After noting the weight of history behind Christianity, Chesterton immediately defended Shaw against the writer of the review in *The Academy* who was merely "an idiot" with "no belief in Christianity" (4). Chesterton claims there are two mistakes that have been made by both Shaw and orthodox reviewers; the first was "to suppose that the commonwealth was Christian" (a diagnosis which received applause), and the second was to believe "they were living in an age in which the Christian religion had been eclipsed" (6).

Because Christianity has always triumphed before, Chesterton has faith in its power to rise once again to the challenge of heresy and apostasy. From his Roman Catholic–friendly perspective, Chesterton defends Christianity in terms of a pragmatic battle in which England should be seen as a "heathen country to be conquered and redeemed" (6). In his mind, Christianity can and will be resurrected.

In particular, Chesterton focuses on Shaw's use of the word "God," and claims that he had to choose the traditional signifier of divinity because "Christianity had been born again" after the onslaught of the French Revolution and Nietzsche (7). When one Heretic in the audience objected that Chesterton "was making rather a caricature of Mr. Shaw," the defender of orthodoxy ignored the point of order that in speaking of God, Shaw "had to speak in human terms to a human audience" (15–16). In his review for *The Gownsman*, Ogden also underscored the idea that Chesterton, while skillful at debate, did not "fully appreciate the position of Mr. Shaw" and misunderstood the proposition that people can advance the purpose of "God" or the "Life-Force" (196). Chesterton refused to consider Shaw blasphemous since he was "a very sincere religious man," and "it was absurd to talk about blasphemy" in "a state profoundly divided about what is sacred" (8–9). Heresy, instead, was the discursive mode at work.

Though he considers Shaw a "Pagan," Chesterton tries to redirect his position by stating that "nobody as alert, alive and vigorous as Mr. Shaw could do without a God in the modern world" (7). What Shaw considers a divinity not yet mature, Chesterton redefines as a paganism blind to the imminent return of Christianity. He therefore turns to Shaw's ideas of the Life-Force and questions "the good of a God which was gradually trying to exist" (11). Ignoring Nietzsche's philosophy and other developments in modernist thought, Chesterton declares that "when men had talked about a God, they had meant a large number of ideas, but they certainly had not meant something produced by the people who were thinking about it" (10). Chesterton abhors change in the definition of theological dogma, which is a fundamental characteristic of many heresies. In making God an aim rather than a cause or principle, Shaw had presented a belief system that had no "good" because "a God which was gradually trying to exist" offered no fixed ideals "by which we regulated ourselves" (11). In stating that people must have preset ideals and "must be absolutely certain that that object was right and the thing to be attained," Chesterton begs the question in assuming knowledge of value before it has been confirmed. His appeal fell on deaf ears, since the Heretics under law 4 rejected all traditional a priori modes of thought. They were more inclined to Shaw's view, which avoids the logical fallacy by not having fixed ideals and allowing for trial and error. To account for human foibles and provide an alternative to Shaw, Chesterton calls on the concept of free will from "the historic creed of Christianity," which is based on "the ideas of Reason and Liberty" (13). Since God gave people the right to create and then be responsible for their actions, Chesterton believes this condition explains not only how the world changes, but also why God might want to make the world.

In the question-and-answer session, Brimley Johnson argued that Chesterton's view implied that Christianity evolved and that both he and Shaw were trying to adapt God to the modern world. Chesterton responded that he "regarded that as an answer to Mr. Shaw and not to him" (19). In general, the defender of orthodoxy avoided the implications of the questions and instead would steer his response toward the haven of dogma. For instance, an unnamed person asked his position on the recent excommunication of the modernist cleric George Tyrrell; to which Chesterton defended Pius X's actions by invoking the beneficent past practice of Popes. Bradlaugh Bonner asked if Chesterton thought his grandfather, Charles Bradlaugh, "denied God"; to which Chesterton made a joke about the Greek root of "atheism." Goldie Dickinson took issue with Chesterton's comments on reason and liberty and wondered if he "believed that nothing else was essential" to Christianity (17). Chesterton simply referred to his original point. Even the *Christian Commonwealth* adduced this elusivity and chastised Chesterton for his "enigmatic" remarks and for not providing clear answers to meet "the difficulties of those who are looking for light in these matters" (Chesterton, "Future" 20–21). In his review, Ogden pointedly encapsulated the effects of the divergent speeches; he believed that Shaw's position needs to be explained more and "urged," while Chesterton's "does not appear to call for further comment" (196).

THE RECEPTION OF HERESY AND SHAW'S *SAINT JOAN*

By 1913, Shaw himself "urged" his theory of heresy forward when he first began to ponder writing a play about Joan of Arc. In September of that year, Shaw wrote to Mrs. Patrick Campbell explaining that he would "do a Joan play some day, beginning with the sweeping of the cinders and orange peel *after* her martyrdom, and going on with Joan's arrival in heaven." He wanted to condemn the English for their part in her execution, but "save" English literature with his representation of the English soldier who gave her a makeshift crucifix as she was tied to the stake. For Shaw, the soldier is "the only redeeming figure in the whole business." Consequently, Shaw wanted to provide a British account of Joan that would correct the "puffing libel" of Shakespeare's *Henry VI*. As part of his desire to emphasize the posthumous legacy of Joan's power, Shaw joked that one of his "scenes will be Voltaire and Shakepear [*sic*] running down bye streets in heaven to avoid meeting Joan" (SJ 123). While this scene never made it into his drama, *Saint Joan*, his wish to conflate characters anachronistically points to the epilogue of the play in which the canonization of Joan simultaneously canonizes heresy. As an overt and didactic estrangement effect, the fantastic *mise-en-scène* during the epilogue works to elicit responses that privilege progressive politics and produce a self-critical awareness of the possibility of modern cases of intolerance.

In accord with Huxley's presentation of the idea that the perceived nature of divinity shifts with the unfolding of history, Shaw also claims that religion must eventually respond to an evolving world since, as he says in the preface to *Saint Joan*, "the law of God is a law of change" (38). Whereas Huxley's modernist view of a dystopic world has its values dictated for it by an elite few, Shaw's chronicle play sees "the law of change" as underwritten by the gradual reception of forward-minded thinkers and doers. By characterizing Joan's decided presumption as "miraculous" and "unbearable" (4), Shaw underscores two qualities of his definition of heresy that make it unacceptably ahead of its time. Institutional forces may work to thwart the upstart heretic, but the energetic struggles of a martyr for a heretical cause eventually effect a mystical and "miraculous" change in the course of history.

On several levels, *Saint Joan* is a play about reception. As Shaw states in the preface, compelling historical "theocrats" such as Joan, who claim to profess God's will, "need never fear a lukewarm reception." The marked stridency of their declarations mandates that they are received as either "messengers of God" or "blasphemous impostors" (44). Indeed, the figure of Joan of Arc further presents a unique composite illustrative of how values can change over time. Joan is a hero, then a heretic, then a saint. From 1429 when she captured Orleans, to 1431 when she was burnt at the stake, to 1920 when she was canonized, Joan demonstrates that an individual can participate in and affect historical processes and historiography. Nevertheless, Shaw stresses the idea that history usually drags behind the individual visionary, and the value of the avant-garde vision can only be recognized with hindsight and much delayed approbation.

The plot of the drama excludes battle scenes and focuses on Joan's rise to power and her subsequent trial and execution. Of more compelling critical interest, the form of *Saint Joan* presents a metacommentary about reception, and the reviews of the play capture in one historical moment the way popular and critical success can be met with a reactionary backlash from an orthodox and established few. Joan's canonization was "in the air" when Shaw's play was produced first in New York in December of 1923 and then in London the following March. *Saint Joan* generally met with a captive audience for 213 performances in the States and 244 in England; the success of the play suggests that the cultural context of the early twenties found something particularly fascinating about Joan. The appeals made to its audience are manifold: Joan is a medieval suffragette, a "super-flapper," a forerunner of Protestantism, the perennial French national heroine, and, in a peculiar Shavian twist, Brigid or the "poor old woman" who will save Ireland. In addition to her sainthood and rebellious, pious view of God, Joan also addresses the worldly concerns of feminism and nationalism. The women's movements of the time of the staging certainly accentuated the reception of the play. Joan embodies a plurality of identities and offers a unique answer to the anxieties of the First World War and its aftermath. Here was a woman who believed in defending her nation in the name of God.

However, Shaw, as usual, has his own overt didactic purposes to promote and deftly inserts them into the momentum launched by the popular and religious cult which had recently effected Joan's full recuperation. In addition to his quirky endeavor to purify the English language and strike "Foul Mouthed Frank dead for swearing" (76), Shaw calls for a truce in the war within the Church over modernism and asks for the clergy not to see themselves in a struggle with science. Most importantly, Shaw usurps the occasion of Joan's canonization to canonize heresy in principle and in deed. In fashioning Joan anew, he sees himself as Joan's canon, the filter of all that has been said of her before and the "measuring rod" of what should be valued in and remembered about her. Often in the play, he puns on the word "canon" and points to the word's etymological origins in the Greek for "rule," reed," or "measuring device." The Church *"canons, the doctors of law and theology,"* will "mark" Joan's character, while Joan herself "can make" her own "mark" (121; 140). Joan's self-canonization also appears in her critique of official military strategy when explaining that only she knows "how to use your cannons" (114). As Joan's trial comes to a close in Scene VI, the Inquisitor delivers a diatribe against the contagion of heresy and orders his fellow judges to "Mark what I say." Despite the Inquisitor's slippery slope argument warning against the future effects of heresy that "at first seems innocent and even laudable" (128), the audience can still feel the influence of Shaw's words from the preface in which he casts himself in the role of the new Inquisitor. There he says that we must privilege heresy "on the simple ground that all evolution in thought and conduct must at first appear as heresy and misconduct" (38). To appear fair, Shaw repeatedly claims that his portrait of Joan is both the first to treat her realistically and the first not to vilify the Church. He congratulates himself on his historical accuracy and his careful perusal of the trial records.

Certainly, T. Douglas Murray's 1902 translation into English of Joan's trial records and her subsequent canonization were both historical developments necessary for Shaw's conception of The Maid. The trial records were first published by Quicherat in 1841, and for the next eighty years grew the cult of Joan, the movement for her canonization, and the literature surrounding her. In a section of the preface to his play, Shaw rhetorically summarizes the representations of "The Maid in Literature" as either scurrilous or romanticized portraits. *He* will be the one to offer an objective account that also welcomes Joan's mysticism. Discussing Shaw's attraction to the figure of Joan, Louis Crompton finds that, through her, he could put forth a dramatized treatise on Creative Evolution and "combine the free critical spirit of a skeptical age with the coherent convictions and fervor of an age of 'organic' faith." In the figure of Shaw's Joan, readers acutely perceive this synthesis that indicts orthodoxy while embracing a knowledge beyond reason, because her dramatized reception illustrates a historical process that alternates between ages of doubt and faith (32).

Both Shaw's positioning of himself as respondent to all of the literature on Joan, and the multivalence of the expansive reviews of the play, make *Saint Joan* a valid and troublesome text to place vis-à-vis reception theory. In his seminal essay, "Literary History as a Challenge to Literary Theory" (1970), Hans Robert Jauss claims that literary history can synthesize Marxist and aesthetic approaches by discovering the "socially formative function" of literature (37), a function that "necessarily also includes the criticizing and even forgetting of tradition" (23). Still, Jauss is no nihilist; rather he wants to understand the mechanisms by which literature helps its readers escape or supersede tradition on an everyday level. Through both diachronic and synchronic analyses, readers will reconstruct their horizons of expectations in response to the aesthetic distance generated by a new work. Consequently, Jauss invests the reading public, as a Joan of their own, with "history-making energy" (8).

The role of the readers in literary history draws on not only what has already been read but also what has been lived, and Jauss acknowledges the import of the idea that "the scholarly forming of theories [lies] in the pre-scholarly experience of life" ("Literary" 32). In this light and by remembering Shaw's belief in an ethereal Life-Force driving the world, *Saint Joan* can be read as an anticipatory treatise on reception theory. Jauss' work directs us toward a synchronic analysis of the reception of Shaw's diachronic view of Joan. What results is a focus on a historical moment explosive with questions of power.

The most obvious power-monger in relation to *Saint Joan* is Shaw, who claims that the play "contains all that need be known about her" (57). While he is here referring to the two-year part Joan played in history, Shaw also sees himself as supplanting four centuries of myth and literature erected around her. Shaw is now the expert in a literary subject that has been treated by such lesser writers as William Shakespeare, Voltaire, Friedrich von Schiller, Robert Southey, Samuel Taylor Coleridge, Thomas De Quincey, Gioacchino Rossini, George Eliot, Margaret Oliphant, Mark Twain, Anatole France, and Arthur Conan Doyle. In summarizing the previous accounts of Joan, Shaw points out how the historical context informs their portrayal of her and illustrates "the too little considered truth that the fashion in which we think changes like the fashion of our clothes" (46). His diagnosis functions self-reflexively too. In staging a play, actors and directors will interpret the drama differently over time, and the effects of the performance as a whole will change. While a stage director in the 1920s, for instance, might have chosen to stage Joan in flapper dress, of more importance is the fact that the period in which Shaw wrote was rife with variant valorizations of heresy.

Despite any reluctance we might have in acknowledging Shaw's self-promotion of his own influence, his 1934 words are rather prophetic: "It is quite likely that sixty years hence, every great English and American actress will have a shot at 'St. Joan,' just as every great actor will have a shot at 'Hamlet'" (qtd. in Tyson 114). With the first performance in mind, though, Shaw had written the play for Sybil Thorndike, the British star of the stage. Thorndike later recalled: "I simply lived in that part. I have never had anything in the theatre which has given me as much as *Saint Joan* did. Something more than just theatre. It confirmed my faith . . . all the things I had to say were things I wanted to say" (Gibbs, *Interviews* 310). The heresies within the play are what Thorndike could not quite explicitly state in another recollection of how the play appealed to her sense of Christianity: "One felt in *Saint Joan* that here was something Shaw wanted most passionately to say about the Christian who was a true Catholic and a true Protestant in one—two opposing qualities existent at the same time, which is the balance—the hard, but the true thing in Christianity." In her wish for a Church tolerant of free thought, Thorndike refrains from using the term for the interdicted discourse, yet still points to a synthetic heresy which would make her follow Joan "without question" if "she lived to-day" (Trewin 59–60). The list of actresses subsequently playing Shaw's Joan runs from another prominent star of the 1920s, Winifred Lenihan, to Jean Seberg, Sarah Miles, Joan Plowright, Judi Dench, Jane Alexander, Lee Grant, and Lynn Redgrave.[4]

Joan's canonization can be read as a move on the part of the Catholic Church to assert its place in the world after the First World War and win hegemony by adapting to the times. There are several moments in the play when Shaw suggests this has been a long-held stratagem on the part of the Church. The Archbishop says "a miracle, my friend, is an event which creates faith" (79), and the Inquisitor anticipates changes in the future reception of Joan and believes that a "flaw in the procedure" of her trial "may be useful later on" (145). These statements are in accord with Shaw's points that the Life-Force is subject to human error, and that, in the Church, "there is no wrong without a remedy" (32). He characterizes the Vatican as highly cognizant of the processes of maintaining hegemony. The end, which is Church authority, justifies the means. Though Joan's canonization resolves the question of her relationship to the Church, Shaw's play engenders a new definition of saintliness, one far from orthodox tenets.

By defining a miracle as "an event which creates faith," Shaw strips the act of its supernatural and inexplicable qualities. Though Monseigneur de la Trémouille finds such a definition "a bit fishy," the Archbishop stresses the idea that an "event which creates faith does not deceive," and that these miracles "are not frauds because they are often . . . very simple and innocent contrivances by which the priest fortifies the faith of his flock" (79–80). More importantly, faith is now built upon reception, not immanence, and the First World War did much to instill faith in soldiers and evoke prayers to Joan. In his 1919 biography of Joan, Denis Lynch, a Jesuit, reports that, in the immediate aftermath of the war, people would praise and march in procession for Joan "as if victory even now were due to her" (344). Lynch also suggests a significant power lies in prayer and commends her direct canonization since "Joan has been much invoked during . . . these dark and fateful days" and "[e]xplain it how we may, the tide of invasion rolled no further than that battle line traced by Joan on the Meuse, Marne, and Oise" (344–45). Two years earlier, Cecil B. DeMille's first historical epic, *Joan the Woman* (1917), had framed her biography within a story about heroism and martyrdom in the ongoing trench warfare. The preamble to the film declares: "Joan of Arc is not dead. She can never die—and in the war-torn land she loved so well, her Spirit fights today." Joan then appears as a vision to the English soldier holding Joan's sword he had exhumed and deliberating whether to volunteer for a suicidal mission, and she tells him that the "time has come for thee to expiate thy sin against me." The English soldier assumes the debt of his nation, and the film further promotes the penitent air surrounding the movement for Joan's canonization in having her condemners pray at the end, "God forgive us—we have burned a Saint" (*Joan*). In this context, we can venture an answer for Joan's case to the following general question used, as Kenneth Woodward notes, in the formal procedure for making saints: "What particular message or example would canonization of the candidate bring to the church?" (78). While this question of timeliness incorporated into the Code of Canon Law in 1917 might elicit an acknowledgment of Joan's popularity and the importance of prayer, canonizing Joan would also send a message that the Church was tolerant and able to admit mistakes.

With these issues in mind, the Catholic Church could fortify its position on the contemporary modernist movement within its own clergy. The Church was not unilaterally intolerant, and the acceptance of Joan's miracles offered an appealing rebuke to the modernists' desire to embrace science. Pope Pius X's denunciation of the modernist trend to disbelieve in miracles became, in fact, a move acutely crucial to his own subsequent canonization. Shaw's play offers an alternative solution to the battle between religious modernism and the Church. He calls for a humble Church that allows free thought; otherwise, he claims it is "guilty of the heresy that theology and science are two different and opposite impulses." On the contrary, he feels "[w]e must accept the tension" (36), and he even posits that a synthesis of science and religion is possible through a faith which some people create through miracles and others through "commonsense and simple fact" (30). While Shaw has a different view of the relationship between the Church and evolution, the canonization of Joan suggests that the Church designed its own strategy to create the impression that it could evolve too. Though Shaw would state that the desire for progress and the willful drive of a heretic cause this change in policy, Joan's heresy and the modernist one can be read together to inform an understanding of Church politics. In a three-week period from 1903 to 1904, Pius X took the first steps both to declare modernism a heresy and Joan a saint. He placed Alfred Loisy's books on the Index of Forbidden Books, and declared Joan Venerable. From 1907 to 1908, further steps were taken: he officially condemned "modernism" to be a heresy, and beatified Joan. Eventually, in 1920, Pope Benedict XV canonized her. Witnessing the Church turn to the medieval while ferreting out the modernist, a careful observer might begin to question the Church's relation to modernist heresies and the veiled politics behind canonization.

Since 1234, the papacy alone has assumed the right to canonize, though the extant thousands of saints canonized under more informal procedures have been retained. In 1642, Pope Urban VIII drew on the work of the 1588 Congregation of Rites and formalized the threefold process by which a person becomes a saint, and his stipulations generally continue to underwrite the methodology for making saints today. Currently, the Congregation for the Causes of Saints is the Church office that most often invokes the doctrine of papal infallibility. Canonization declares with certainty that the person is in communion with God, and the pope declares this *ex cathedra*. Under current Church ideology, burning a heretic is a mistake; canonizing a saint never can be. Usually after a local following popularizes the holy qualities of a person, the pope confirms this movement and allows for the "introduction of the cause" for sainthood, thereby terming the person "Venerable." In order to be beatified or declared "Blessed," the Venerable person under examination must be proven to have established a reputation for sanctity, to have possessed a heroic nature to his or her virtues, and to have worked four miracles. After the ceremonial mass of beatification, canonization comes if two further miracles happen as a result of prayers to the Blessed to intercede on behalf of the indirect object of the prayers. Generally, the miracles involve the healing of the sick, and in Joan's case that is exactly what they were. For her beatification, Pius X authenticated three miraculous cures of diseases afflicting three separate French nuns. They had beseeched Joan, and the miracles were attributed to her. The pope can dispense with the fourth miracle if the person had founded a religious order, and Joan was allowed this dispensation because she had "saved" France. The miracles enabling her canonization also involved the healing of French women.

In *Saint Joan,* Shaw instead emphasizes the "miraculous" nature of Joan's engagement in secular affairs. As a result, her miracles become more of a series of actions that changed history, and they assume a less supernatural air since they all can be attributed to coincidence or her presumptuous will. The possibility of the supernatural persists, though, not only in the form of a mystical will to power, but, through reception, in that creating faith out of the *perception* of miracles confirms above all the *belief* in the supernatural. When Robert de Baudricourt concedes to Joan's will and the hens immediately begin to lay eggs, it is seen as a miracle on her part (71); when Joan discerns a disguised Charles VII and "knows the blood royal," the play inscribes this as a miracle and Charles knows he will have his "saint" too; Charles sees another miracle of hers when Foul Mouthed Frank is struck "dead for swearing" (76); and Joan arrives and the wind changes just as Jean Dunois, the military commander, needed this "miracle" to enable the crossing of the Loire and the eventual "miraculous" victory at Orleans (78). In terms of the power Shaw grants the evolutionary heretic, perhaps the most important comment on the nature of miracles is Bertrand de Poulengey's belief that "the girl herself is a bit of a miracle" (66). The remarkable feats of a teenage working-class woman confronting the medieval patriarchal church and state do indeed make her extraordinary, a "miracle" if you like.

They also make her a heretic. In noting the two prevalent opinions of her, that she was "miraculous" and "unbearable" (4), Shaw combines these two views in his definition of a heretic as someone whose "headstrong presumption" challenges, exceeds, and must suffer the suppression of the authorities of the time (118). Shaw, in fact, states that Joan was burnt for her "unwomanly and insufferable presumption" (3–4), and his repeated use of the word "presumption" to describe her heresy points to his idea of forward thinking. Etymologically, "presumption" means "something taken ahead of its time," and its Indo-European root *em- ("to take") inflects other such words as "prompt," "example," and "redeem." For Shaw, then, Joan's heresy was to dare to take liberties before they are granted by authorities, but in the process she anticipated future values. As Joan states, her presumptuous voices are "always right" (118).

Throughout the play, Shaw's address to the Heretics underwrites his portrayal of Joan's supernatural and progressive qualities. While the play jumps on the bandwagon that had led to Joan's canonization, this appropriation of her cause lets him be the first legitimately to write a literary work entitled *Saint Joan,* and then collapse the boundary between saintliness and heretical beliefs. Though Shaw again declares Joan a heretic, heresy has a positive valence for him. He plays with his definition of heresy as he fiddles with the doctrine of miracles. Joan's desire for harmony with God and social progress is what Shaw calls in the preface "an appetite for evolution, and therefore a superpersonal need" (14). He finds Joan exceptional for the "intensity of her vital energy" (21), and the clerical and lay authorities in his dramatization find her "so positive" and "very hard to resist" (61–62). Here is Shaw's belief in Creative Evolution and the will to power, which he mentions and capitalizes in the play. Shaw even has Pierre Cauchon, bishop of Beauvais, say, "I know well that there is a Will to Power in the world" (106).

In his address to the Heretics, Shaw had implied that God's will works through the bodies of inspired people, and Joan indeed states that "it is the will of God that you are to do what He has put into my mind" (62). In the preface to the play, Shaw reminds us of his belief that "there are forces at work which use individuals . . . in the pursuit of knowledge and of social read-justments" (13). God's will becomes inseparable from human will, except through reception. If a character such as de Baudricourt believes that the voices she hears come from her "imagination," another may concur with Joan that that "is how the messages of God come to us" (68). In the preface, Shaw defends people who hear voices and see visions because they have an imagination "so vivid that when they have an idea it comes to them as an audible voice, sometimes uttered by a visual figure." He adds that a "visionary method" of making a scientific discovery "would not be a whit more miracu-lous than the normal method." Results, reception, and in Shaw's words, the "test of sanity" and the "reasonableness of the discovery" matter more than the method (11–12). The overwhelming successes of Joan enable Shaw to dismiss the question of the objective veracity of her voices.

Though he does deride the voices as "illusory" since they often failed her, notably during her incarceration, he finds that she had a "reasonable" expec-tation of rescue according to the logic of her own imagination (17).[5] More importantly, he militates against suppositions that Joan was insane or sui-cidal, and he defends her mindset by comparing it to modern scientific and psychological practices that are equally incredible or suspect. As he states, "modern science has convinced us that nothing that is obvious is true, and that everything that is magical, improbable, extraordinary, gigantic, micro-scopic, heartless, or outrageous is scientific" (47). Shaw's point that historical context influences reception, and that this changes, becomes clearer for his scientific analogy in comparing Joan's history to the debt modern chemistry owes alchemy. Only in Joan's case, the Church tried to determine the mod-ernist context by canonizing her and changing her reception itself.

As a form of the will to power, heresy brings newness into the world by modifying extant traditions, and Shaw calls on the Church to welcome freethinking. He even makes a disingenuous appeal that if freethinking were encouraged he might convert. Since Shaw claims that the "Churches must learn humility as well as teach it" (36), he finds nothing objectionable when Joan "acts as if she herself were the Church" (103). Through the inspiration of her voices, Joan believes that she has special access to God's will, and Shaw claims that "her notion of a Catholic Church was one in which the Pope was Pope Joan" (30). In the phraseology of his speech to the Heretics, Joan is the perfect example of a heretic, that is, someone who has devised a "home-made religion." Additionally, she illustrates his point that God works through specific people, and that these "chosen people" perform God's will. In refusing to deny her voices and accept the clergy as the sole arbiter of divine will, Joan becomes in Shaw's eyes "one of the first Protestant martyrs" (3). After noting the "heresies" of John Wycliffe and Jan Huss, Cauchon compares Joan's "arch heresy" of "Protestantism" to their way of thought, which "sets up the private judgment of the simple erring mortal against the considered wisdom and experience of the Church." Indeed, many subsequent "Protestant" heresies founded their thought on a leader perceived as a "chosen one" or on the belief that the faithful can, in the Inquisitor's description of the origins of heresy, promote "their own judgment against the Church," and take "it upon themselves to be the interpreters of God's will" (128–30).

For these types of heresy, assuming the power of interpretation determines how God will be received, and this presumption has further repercussions at the level of audience because *it* decides whether to sanctify or scandalize the original interpretation. The interpretation of her voices, as with her miracles, is central in determining whether to consider Joan a heretic or a saint. The Inquisitor realizes the difficulties in persecuting heretics who "believe honestly and sincerely that their diabolical inspiration is divine" (129), but he will not relinquish the power of interpretation and the authority of the Church to cut off "an obstinate heretic as a dead branch from the tree of life" (101). When Joan later implies that the Church could be "contrary to God," she commits "[f]lat heresy" and has said "enough to burn ten heretics" (135). However, in then handing Joan over to the English army, the Church enables itself to have a future "remedy" for her execution since it then could deny responsibility and blame these secular authorities for her punishment.

By highlighting the putative possibility that the Church deliberately allowed for subsequent reevaluation of Joan's heresies, Shaw foregrounds the "wilfulness" of heresy to affect future generations. In the logic of the play, the eventual acceptance of forms of nationalism, Protestantism, and feminism depends in part on Joan's various subversions of orthodoxy, an acceptance which in turn causes a reconsideration of her values and social position. As a result, Shaw invests heresy with enormous power, and though Joan's voices may only be "echoes" of her own "wilfulness," they clearly have more lasting effect than the "voice of the Church Militant." When she glories in the "rightness" of her course of action, Joan becomes perceived as tragically proud and one who will not recant her belief that "everyone else is wrong." However, she dismisses the question of her pride, and reminds her prosecutors that her military strategy proved "true" and simple "commonsense"; moreover, she plays down the miraculous nature of her voices in stating: "even if they are only echoes of my own commonsense, are they not always right" (116–18).

Once again the received effect of an action is worth more than its intrinsic value.

By working within tradition and allowing a role for the Church in the modern world, Shaw's play evinced enough conservatism to please his mainstream audience. Perhaps the established academy sought to validate this turn away from the more controversial and subversive subjects of his earlier plays. Shaw had his own form of canonization when he received the Nobel Prize in 1925 in response to *Saint Joan*. The play also became popular with audiences and met critical acclaim on both sides of the Atlantic, particularly in New York. An unsigned review in the *Observer* found the play "brilliant" for its weaving of tragedy and burlesque and the "strangest possible compound of the modern and the medieval" (SJ 126–27). In *The New Statesman*, Desmond MacCarthy underscored the experience of religious emotion as a desideratum for an understanding of the play, yet still found that "[o]nly a languid mind could fail to find in it intellectual excitement, only a very carefully protected sensibility could escape being touched and disturbed" (Weintraub 31). Luigi Pirandello attended the New York premiere and became poignantly moved. He praised the range of "poetic emotion" displayed by Shaw, and hilariously compares the American audience with a hypothetical Italian one. Italian audiences would applaud the moments when Shaw would have them crying (Evans 279–84). In her review entitled "A Super-Flapper," Jeanne Foster critiqued the same production, yet only found that Joan does not wear men's clothing but "a rather modest Coney Island bathing suit." The rest of her review draws an extended, unfavorable comparison of Shaw's play to Chesterton's orthodox treatment of St. Francis (Weintraub 29–30).

In London, the reviews were even more mixed. Many of the regular drama critics found the play entertaining and intellectually stimulating; often the phrase "the greatest of Shaw's plays" was used. Criticisms raised usually objected to the playfulness of dialogue, the anachronisms, and the didacticism and staging of the epilogue. T. S. Eliot led the backlash. He objected to the reform-minded nature of Joan and calls Shaw's portrayal the "greatest sacrilege of all Joans" (SJ 145). In 1925 a former friend of Shaw's, J. M. Robertson, the former M.P. and speaker to the Heretics, objected to the playwright's reverent attitude toward Joan and wrote a *whole book* critiquing the lack of realism and historical veracity in the play. Robertson's *Mr. Shaw and "The Maid"* calls for those curious about "truth" to disregard "Mr. Shaw's assurance that *Saint Joan* tells him all he needs to know" about her and to study history on their own "in the spirit of science" (114–15). In a second review, Eliot championed Robertson's book and claimed the play deludes the

minds of religious people. Though he would distance himself from Robertson's pure rationalism, Eliot found the latter's book "of equal value to people
who approach the problem from an orthodox Christian standpoint." Eliot
feared that "the numberless crowd of sentimentally religious people who
are incapable of following any argument to a conclusion" will be duped into
believing in "the potent ju-ju of the Life Force," Shaw's Joan (SJ 146). On the
other hand, Louis Crompton more recently argued that Shaw's view of Joan
as an agent in Creative Evolution "was calculated to provoke dissent from
rationalists and orthodox Christians" (37). An unsigned review of the world
premier in New York anticipates such a reaction due to Shaw's evident criticism of the Church. No doubt the "indignation" that the reviewer suggests
will be felt "in some circles" (Evans 278) arises mostly from the epilogue
when all the characters in the drama, including her condemners, come back
on stage together to praise and then forsake Joan once more.

In terms of both form and content, the epilogue estranges its audiences
by collapsing historical progression and implying that Joan would still be
burnt in modern times. Even reviews that generally praise the play often
took exception to the epilogue. Because "that final scene says the same thing
several times," Alexander Woolcott believed that "Shaw will cut" the epilogue
"when he sees the play" himself (Evans 276). Yet Woolcott still stressed the
importance of an implicated audience that would condemn her now. Though
G. H. Mair found that Saint Joan "remains a very great play," he believed that
the epilogue is better read, and he objects to the deliberate estrangement
and compromise of the unities of time and place (SJ 135–36). James Agate,
writing for The Sunday Times, dismissed the epilogue as "wholly unneces-
sary" since it "is implicit in all that has gone before" (Evans 289). In his
review for The Times, A. B. Walkley declared the epilogue "an artistic failure"
and "an incongruity" "to the eye," and he finds it "a nuisance that [Shaw] is
so obsessed with the present period as to drag it into every period" (Evans
286). These critiques offer a pointed illustration of the "aesthetic distance"
and "horizon change" that Jauss finds can be measured by the reviews of a
new work that "confronts the expectations of its first readers" ("Literary"
14–15).

When Shaw champions heresy and forward thinking, he does this, in
Jauss' words, by predisposing "readers to a very definite type of reception
by textual strategies" ("Literary" 12). In this way, Shaw practices what he
preaches and tries to shift the horizon of values adventitiously. In the preface,
he emphasizes above all the importance of historical perspective, and the fact
that he did not want to stultify himself "by implying that Joan's history in the

world ended unhappily with her execution, instead of beginning there." Consequently, his positivist nature finds that "the epilogue must stand" because it "was necessary by hook or crook to shew the canonized Joan as well as the incinerated one" (53). Pirandello did find the epilogue "noble poetry" which uses "irony and satire" to create a "second climax" after Joan's burning and adds to this "first crisis of exquisite anguish another not less potent and overwhelming" (Evans 283). Similarly, in a review for *The New Republic*, Edmund Wilson defended the epilogue by arguing that it is necessary to understand that the play concerns "human history," not "individual tragedy," and shows Shaw's growing, "longer view of human affairs." In finding that the play condemns modern intolerance which would forsake Joan again, Wilson suggested that *Saint Joan* reflects a turn in Shaw's plays away from those "before the war" in which "there were no insoluble problems" and they "almost invariably ended cheerfully enough with a precise indication of the solution" (Weintraub 39–42). In miniature, Wilson here diagnosed the change from an Edwardian positivist, synthetic agenda toward a modernism intolerant of divergent heresies.

As a classic case of 1920s defamiliarization or estrangement effects, the formal properties of the epilogue work to expose the recurrent susceptibility of societies to intolerance. In the preface, Shaw states that "as far as toleration is concerned the trial and execution in Rouen in 1431 might have been an event of today" and that "we may charge our consciences accordingly" (29). In the epilogue, Shaw implicates his audience by placing a representative of modern times alongside Joan and her executioners. The mixing of historical periods functions as the interwoven narratives in D. W. Griffith's *Intolerance* (1916) to show not only, as Shaw argues, "that society is founded on intolerance," but also its ugly continuing legacy (40). The epilogue, then, exemplifies Viktor Shklovsky's thesis in "Art as Technique" (1917) that the function of art is to invigorate quotidian existence by making "the familiar seem strange" (265). As he argues, the "technique of art is to make objects 'unfamiliar,' to make forms difficult, and to increase the difficulty and length of perception because the process of perception is an aesthetic end in itself and must be prolonged" (264). When Shaw addresses critics in the preface to *Saint Joan,* he emphasizes the issue of relative value tied to this perspective in ridiculing the critics and "fashionable" people who believe that "the sooner it is over, the better," and defends the length of his play by pointing to the "paying playgoer, from whose point of view the longer the play, the more entertainment he gets for his money" (54). Shaw believes that he is attuned to the popular spirit of the times, and the epilogue does reflect a modernist experimentation with forms.

Though the ingenuity of the epilogue by some standards may not be considered radical, it nevertheless acutely estranged its orthodox audience. Raymond Williams and Terry Eagleton seem to have overlooked both this documented effect of the play and the structure of the epilogue when they each critique Shaw for not departing far enough from traditional forms. Williams claims that Shaw's "whole drama is certainly a case of 'new wine in old bottles,'" since it only adds "the discussion" and accepts "almost all the devices of the old romantic drama" (272). Affirming Williams' critique, Eagleton further suggests that Shaw's traditional, "naturalistic" forms undermine the radicalness of the content. He contrasts the formal properties of Shaw's plays with Bertolt Brecht's use of estrangement effects, and believes that the Irish playwright's work exemplifies the fact that the "discourse of the play may be urging change, criticism, rebellion; but the dramatic forms . . . inevitably force upon us a sense of the unalterable solidity of the social world" (187). While these critiques do have merit for the bulk of Shaw's plays, *Saint Joan* represents a case in which the "old bottle" itself has been cast off with her canonization. As the first literary text to dramatize her life in the wake of sainthood, Shaw's play portrays its subject matter in the light and form of a mystical, evolving Life-Force.

The unusual aesthetic form of the epilogue is a series of *dei ex machina* in which all the dead and dreaming characters and even a modern priest sequentially and fantastically appear on stage. By conflating history formally, the epilogue makes traditional meanings of heresy "seem strange." The ideological construction of the epilogue collates irreconcilable historical moments and views of history, so that to condemn heresy is to condemn not only progress, but also something misunderstood. Drawing off the cliché that one always condemns what is misunderstood, *Saint Joan* therefore implies that Joan's radical and mysterious desire for progress always will suffer persecution. Joan's canonization suggests progress and optimism for the future, and her crowned king, Charles, believes that "Joan would not have fussed about it if it came all right in the end" (151). However, Shaw urges further progress and tries to shock his audience into the recognition that the fight for "progress" is an ongoing process, and he works against the Church's attempt to end the debate over the issues at hand by canonizing Joan. Instead, he puts forth, in the vein of his address at Cambridge, the idea that heretics and heretical literature of the future consistently modify those of previous generations in an incremental, Fabian fashion. When the modern priest announces that Joan has finally been canonized, Shaw steals his thunder and offers a new vision of heresy. Cauchon, the cleric in charge of her trial, states that "mortal eyes cannot distinguish the saint from the heretic" (163). In an argument akin to the conceit in Donne's "The Canonization" that lovers are saints, Shaw formulates his own paradox: heretics are saints. By collapsing the opposition between heresy and saintliness, Shaw effects a *tabula rasa* on a stage now clear to redefine values. Avant-garde thinking, women's rights, tolerance, and a medieval sense of public responsibility would certainly be valued in Shaw's "Religion of the Future."

THE RECUPERATION OF BRUNO AND
THE CANONIZATION OF "CLAY"

In addition to the canonization of Joan of Arc, the period 1883–1924 witnessed the diverse recuperation of another burnt heretic, the Italian philosopher Giordano Bruno. A wide variety of thinkers had discovered inspiration in his metaphysics and martyrdom. In the preface to *Saint Joan,* Shaw nods to this cultural movement and compares the persecution of Bruno with that of Joan:

> When the Church Militant behaves as if it were already the Church Triumphant, it makes these appalling blunders about Joan and Bruno and Galileo and the rest which make it so difficult for a Freethinker to join it; and a Church which has no place for Freethinkers: nay, which does not inculcate and encourage freethinking with a complete belief that thought, when really free, must by its own law take the path that leads to the Church's bosom, not only has no future in modern culture, but obviously has no faith in the valid science of its own tenets, and is guilty of the heresy that theology and science are two different and opposite impulses, rivals for human allegiance. (36)

Of these three victims of orthodoxy, Bruno most clearly emblematizes the variety of free thought which seeks to synthesize science and theology. Of late, the Catholic Church has continued the tolerant, evolving gesture of Vatican II and tried to make ecumenical appeals and engage modern developments in science. The Church has also sought forgiveness for the past practices of the Inquisition. As part of this conciliation, the Vatican admitted in 1992 that Galileo had been right in defending a Copernican view of the universe. Bruno from all accounts will not receive such a formal rehabilitation. However, during the late Victorian and modernist periods, Swinburne,

Pater, Shaw, Joyce, and Annie Besant, among others, found Bruno a heroic figure, championed his philosophy, and used it as a bulwark in their literature.[6] For an illustration of this literary recuperation, the end of this chapter analyzes how Bruno's pantheistic heresy underwrites the canonical transformations in and synthetic form of the short story "Clay" in Joyce's *Dubliners* (1914).

Bruno lived during the late Italian Renaissance and the Inquisition, and the branding of Bruno as a heretic and his subsequent burning at the stake can be seen as the inevitable fate of one who demonstrated a flowering of thought in an atmosphere that viciously suppressed independent minds. Born in the shadow of Mount Vesuvius near the town of Nola, Bruno entered the Dominican order at age fifteen. For ten years, he practiced the faith and developed his views on transubstantiation and other doctrines within the framework of orthodoxy, before cries of impiety forced him into exile. He became an itinerant scholar who graced the courts of France, England, and various German cities throughout the 1580s. He apparently endeared himself to Sir Philip Sidney, and his idea of the divine unity of all things may have inspired Hamlet's riddle on the circulation of essential matter: "A man may fish with the worm that hath eat of a king, and eat of the fish that hath fed of that worm" (IV.iii.27–28). Prior to his apprehension by The Holy Office in 1592, Bruno wrote over sixty books, of which the most influential are *The Expulsion of the Triumphant Beast* (1584) and *Cause, Principle and Unity* (1584). In the latter, Bruno expounds on his theories of the infinite universe, the coincidence of contraries, and the *anima del mondo* (It. "soul of the world"). Part and parcel of divinity, the "soul of the world" is immanent in all things. In the dialogic form of *Cause, Principle and Unity*, Bruno professes a belief that the "universe is . . . infinite and indeterminable" (135). Such a belief is a heresy in the eyes of the Church, for the idea of an infinite universe precludes the possibility of God's exteriority to his Creation. Rather than concluding that there then is an absence of God, Bruno finds an omnipresent immanence of divinity through his heretical, pantheistic belief in "the obscure soul of the world," as Joyce phrases it in *Ulysses* (23).

In *Cause, Principle and Unity*, Bruno uses Aristotelian terms to explicate his paradigmatic coincidence of contraries, and finds that the ubiquitous "soul of the world" is the substance present in both cause and principle and their respective associations of form and matter. Thus, Bruno's theory becomes a paradox that attempts to show the ultimate unity of apparent oppositions. His heresy was synthesis, and therefore his appeal to protomodernists and modernists was both as an avatar of their thought and as a martyr for their cause. The logical conclusion of his synthetic theory effected both Bruno's rejection of the fundamental Church doctrine of the Trinity and his burning as a heretic. Though he never openly denounced the doctrine of the Trinity, Bruno could not uphold the doctrinaire distinction of "persons" in the Trinity. During his interrogation, Bruno told the Holy Office that he believed there is "a God distinguished into the Father, the Word and Love, which is Divine Spirit, and that all three of these are one God in essence" (Imerti 55).

The year 2000 marked both the 400th anniversary of Bruno's martyrdom and a Jubilee Year for the Catholic Church. If the Vatican were to rehabilitate Bruno, it would have happened during the millennium. Pope John Paul II planned a "Day of Pardon" in which he asked God's forgiveness for the past sins of the Church. On February 17, the day of Bruno's execution, people held a celebration in the piazza where Bruno had been burnt, and the Pontifical Theological Faculty of Southern Italy held a conference on Bruno in order to recognize him formally. The hope for rehabilitation and a specific reference to Bruno in the Pope's penitent liturgy did not last long. The Catholic Church could apologize for the Inquisition, but it continued to maintain that Bruno's "intellectual *choices*" (read heresy) remained incompatible with orthodoxy.[7] The reception of Bruno by orthodoxy has not changed because now as in the past his thought threatens to subsume orthodoxy with synthesis.

With the proliferation of discourses surrounding heresy in the late nineteenth century, however, Bruno became a heroic figure during the wave of anticlericalism which swept the Risorgimento. His Latin and Italian works had been collected in separate volumes in the 1830s. Domenico Berti's 1867 biography further enabled scholars to revisit his life and martyrdom, and brief expositions of Bruno's life and thought populated journals on both sides of the Atlantic in the 1870s. Depending on the inclination of the author, Bruno became an exemplar of free thought, heroic virtue, religious belief, or scientific insight. In 1885, the English National Committee was established in order to cooperate with the international movement to rehabilitate Bruno and commemorate him in statue. Swinburne became a member of this organization, and on June 9, 1889, an imposing statue was unveiled in Rome at the site of Bruno's burning (see figure 5).

Swinburne's poem, "The Monument of Giordano Bruno" (1889), responds to this occasion in the Campo de' Fiori. The poem consists of two English sonnets which laud the Italian heretic who possessed the "light / [w]hereby the soul keeps ever truth in sight." Though "the fate required / [a] sacrifice to hate and hell," the poetic voice implies that martyrdom eventually triumphs

Figure 5. The monument of Giordano Bruno, Rome.

and "[a]cclaims the grave bright face that smiled of yore / [e]ven on the fire that caught it round." In effect, the poem affirms Bruno's philosophy in that this "light" comes "[n]ot from without us, only from within," and makes him, as is every element of the universe, "godlike." Bruno can smile at his pyre because the light which "[b]urns in the soul" and "quickens thought" is consubstantial with the fire (6: 176–77).

Swinburne wrote several other poems in which he extols Bruno, but perhaps the closest expression of Bruno's thought in Swinburne's verse occurs in "Hertha," the poem he considered his most polished craftwork. Swinburne wrote "Hertha" in the fall of 1869 in full sympathy with both the anticlericalism reacting to Vatican I (1869–70) and the patriotism which was soon to unify Italy as a nation. He had fallen under the sway of the exiled Italian patriot Giuseppe Mazzini, who believed that humanity had the best access to God. These influences find their most direct expression in Swinburne's

"Hymn of Man" (1871), but they are also present in "Hertha." As the poem declares, the thinking, giving "soul" which is in "man" provides the "[g]reen leaves of thy labor, white flowers of thy thought, and red fruit of thy death" (a reference to the Italian flag), and "[e]ven love, the beloved Republic, that feeds upon freedom and lives." Of more importance, however, the poem rhapsodizes a metaphysics of an evolving world-soul, represented by Hertha, whom Swinburne described as "the vital principle of matter" (Lafourcade 176). She unifies contradictions and finds that "truth only is living, / [t]ruth only is whole." For the poem, Swinburne lets Hertha, the Germanic goddess of the earth, speak about the origins of the world and the nature of beings. Hertha declares her divine primacy: "before God was, I am." In this subversion of God's words to Moses, Swinburne implies, as he often did, that the "twilight" of the Christian god has passed, and that through the world-soul a spirituality centered on the earth and beings can be renewed. Hertha explains that "God changes, and man, and the form of them bodily; I am the soul." The "soul of the world" is an evolving, self-contained "Being," in which the following contraries coincide and unite: "soul" and "body"; "the seeker" and "the sought"; "I" and "thou"; "deed" and "doer"; "seed" and "sower"; "reigns" and "ruins"; and "life" and "death." Throughout Swinburne uses rhetorical questions, like Blake and the author of Job, to tell humanity not to look for God other than in itself. Hertha bids us "but be" and ends on the note that "man" is "equal and one" with her (2: 137–45). In this egalitarian relationship, no homage is needed.

Joyce's interest in the Italian philosopher can be traced to as early as 1901, when Joyce alludes to him in "The Day of the Rabblement." In this attack on parochialism in the Irish Literary Theatre, Joyce refers to Bruno of Nola as "the Nolan" and commends him for his steadfast love of the true and the good (69). Later, in his review of J. Lewis McIntyre's *Giordano Bruno* (1903), Joyce declared: "More than Bacon or Descartes must he [Bruno] be considered the father of what is called modern philosophy. His system by turns rationalistic and mystic, theistic and pantheistic is everywhere impressed with his noble mind and critical intellect, and is full of that ardent sympathy with nature as it is" ("Bruno" 133). For the entry on Bruno, the Eleventh Edition of the *Encyclopedia Britannica* captures the spirit of synthesis and the heretic in the air: "To Bruno, as to all great thinkers, philosophy is the search for unity. Amid all the varying and contradictory phenomena of the universe there is something which gives coherence and intelligibility to them. Nor can this unity be something apart from things; it must contain in itself the universe, which develops from it; it must be at once all and one" (Adamson and Mitchell 687a). Finding divine unity in every "cause" and "principle" of the universe is indeed the grandest of syntheses.

As a result of Joyce's attraction to the Italian philosopher, Bruno occupies a bedrock position in criticism on the Irish author. The presence of his personage and philosophy in *Finnegans Wake* has been well documented, and Bruno's heresies may in fact underwrite the recurrent discourses surrounding consubstantiality and the Trinity in *Ulysses*. Primarily the criticism illustrates Joyce's use of Bruno's theory of the coincidence of contraries to place traditional antitheses in proximity to each other. Bruno is also the subject matter for two of the more memorable Joycean sound bites. In *A Portrait of the Artist as a Young Man*, Stephen Dedalus recalls a discussion with Father Ghezzi and enters in his diary: "He said Bruno was a terrible heretic. I said he was terribly burned" (249). Earlier in the novel when Heron called Lord Byron a heretic, Stephen's reply, "I don't care what he was" (81), shows his lack of regard for religious orthodoxy if aesthetic integrity is threatened with compromise. Moreover, the nineteen-year-old Joyce had already displayed his unflinching individuality and particular fidelity to Bruno; as he wrote, "No man, said the Nolan, can be a lover of the true or the good unless he abhors the multitude; and the artist, though he may employ the crowd, is very careful to isolate himself" ("Rabblement" 69). Robert D. Newman points out that "Joyce's attraction to Bruno began as admiration for the Nolan's uncompromising defense of his beliefs and increasingly developed into an employment of those beliefs in his own writing" (215). One of those manifestations is in "Clay," the short story written little over a year after his review of Bruno's philosophy.

If Bruno implores the readers of *Cause, Principle and Unity* to understand one idea, it is a call for the shared perception of the cyclical dynamics of nature: "Don't you see that what was seed becomes stalk, and what was stalk becomes corn, and what was corn becomes bread—that out of bread comes chyle, out of chyle blood, out of blood the seed, out of the seed the embryo, and then man, corpse, earth, stone, or something else in succession—on and on, involving all natural forms?" (102). In finding this dynamic process analogous to "stoking an engine," Joyce had Bruno's idea and diction in mind for Bloom's rumination in *Ulysses:* "food, chyle, blood, dung, earth, food" (144–45). The laws at work for Bloom and Bruno are the transference and conservation of energy as outlined by Newton's Third Law, and in *The Principles of Literary Criticism*, I. A. Richards argues that such scientific principles should be accepted as truth in literature. In light of his sense of thermodynamics, Bruno states that there "must then exist an unchanging thing which in itself is not stone nor earth nor corpse nor man nor embryo nor blood nor anything else in particular, but which after it was blood, became embryo, receiving the embryonic being; and after it was embryo, received the human being and became man" (103). The "unchanging thing" for Bruno is the "soul of the world," a substance-principle that can take animate or inanimate forms. Bruno's philosophy offers what most metaphysics do, an appeasement of the fear of death; through Bruno's rationale, the fear is quelled by the idea that humans have an essence that, after the death of the individual self, will eventually become human again.

The traditions that serve as the focus for Joyce's short story "Clay" promote belief systems mitigating the fear of death with a similar theory of recursion. "Clay" takes place on both the Catholic feast of All Saints' Day and the celebration of Samhain, the Celtic New Year. In name, the vigil of All Saint's Day (All Hallow's Eve) and, in ritual, Samhain spawned what we know as Halloween. Joyce originally entitled the story "Hallow Eve."[8] "Clay," the short story, and clay, the substance, both act as agents that unite the contrary pagan and Catholic holidays. The short story illuminates the holidays' simultaneity, and the substance indicates the state toward which all the participants on this and all other days tend. The traditions of both the Celts and the Catholics attempt to ease the angst accompanying existence with a system of regeneration based on rebirth or resurrection. Though Joyce uses elements of each tradition in "Clay," their divergence is circumscribed by Bruno's philosophy and the universal fate of decomposition into clay. In this process of synthesis, Joyce undermines both the conception of heaven and the canon for becoming a saint in Catholicism. In its repetition of elements of both Christian and pagan feasts, the story does not simply reproduce their cultural codes. The synthetic textual construction of "Clay" destabilizes the doctrine of canonization by subverting the divisions between the two competing traditions. At work in the story is the heresy of syncretism, which the next chapter discusses in detail. In his review of McIntyre's book on Bruno, Joyce claimed that his system "endeavors to simplify the complex" of metaphysics and has "a distinct value for the historian of religious ecstasies" (134). "Clay" is Joyce's syncretic simplification of the historical relation between two relevant religious feasts.

Oppositions abound in "Clay," but the effect of the story illustrates Bruno's idea of the coincidence of contraries through both setting and character. The central character, Maria, an aging, working-class Catholic woman, helps in the kitchen of "the *Dublin by Lamplight* laundry," run by Protestants to supply an institution to aid reformed prostitutes (83). Maria's piety and spinsterhood create the assumption that she, however, is a virgin. On another level of importance to the setting, she has the stereotypical characteristics of a witch: "Maria was a very, very small person indeed but she had a very long nose and a very long chin" (82). Though Maria is said to have at one time believed the Catholic stereotypical "bad opinion of protestants," she has reconciled herself to think that they are "very nice people, a little quiet and serious, but still very nice people to live with." Surrounded by reform-minded Protestants in an environment with proselytizing "tracts on the walls," Maria remains steadfast in her beliefs and plans to attend Mass on All Saints' Day, a holy day of obligation. The temporal parameters of the story, from the women having "their tea at six o'clock" to the following morning Mass, may be equated with the vigil before All Saints' Day (83–84). Prior to her communion with the saints, Maria however will indulge in the offerings of a purely pagan feast.

The setting of the story illustrates the temporal coincidence when the Celtic old year meets the new, the tenth month meets the eleventh, and all the evil souls are rampant, as the pious and canonized mutually pray for each other. The tension between Christian and pagan festivals lies at the heart of the story. In honor of this unique day in the Celtic and liturgical calendar, Joyce characterizes Maria in suggestive, nebulous terms that have elicited several allegorical readings of her significance.[9] Critics have tended to pick one of the festivals to explore and subsequently proceed to make the case for Maria as either the Blessed Virgin or a witch. Consequently, they neglect the significance of the fact that Maria personifies the simultaneity of the Catholic and pagan rituals. She is at once witchlike in appearance and saintly in demeanor. Maria's characteristics and the parallel in the story between the coincident traditions both allow for a coexistence of oppositions, in a date, in a person. Cóilín Owens has already delineated the Irish folklore and Mass of All the Saints that underlie "Clay." However, Owens fails to pursue the full implications of Joyce's "detailed and accurate" use of "popular folk customs and their roots in archaic tradition" (338). The story does not simply negate, as Owens supposes, the willingness to forsake earthly happiness by darkly invoking the Celtic and Catholic themes of self-sacrifice. Through the use of the overlapping Catholic and pagan celebrations, Joyce creates a paradox concerning the doctrine of canonization, not unlike that presented by Shaw and Donne, in which body and soul are equated.

When in 1904 Joyce began to write the story that would become "Clay," he had already published his first few stories in the *Irish Homestead*. Ashamed at publishing in this newspaper directed toward rural communities, what he referred to as the "pig's paper" in *Ulysses* (158), Joyce first published under the pseudonym Stephen Daedalus. Though the editor of the *Homestead,* H. F. Norman, had accepted the first three stories ("The Sisters," "Eveline," and "After the Race"), he asked Joyce to refrain from further submissions since readers had written letters of protest. An agrarian Irish audience that was perhaps already aware of the historical entanglement of the feasts might realize that Samhain had "a decisive influence in the establishment of the feast of All Saints on November 1st" (Hennig 152). Vestiges of myth and folklore endure more readily in the country, and in fact the word "pagan" originally meant "country dweller," in that Christianity grew first in cities. "Clay" had handled a subject that the Catholic populace would rather have left alone, the foundations of their beliefs. The rejection of "Hallow Eve" troubled Joyce, and for the next ten years the genteel sensibility of the printing world effectively censored *Dubliners.* Nevertheless, Joyce felt proud of his story (he exclaimed at one point, "ask the good gentlemen can they beat 'Hallow Eve'") (*Letters* 2: 77), and in a last ditch effort to have the story published on its own he told his brother to "[s]ell it to Mighty AUM." This reference to George Russell (A.E.) and his mysticism is a variant of Om, a word which Ellmann suggestively states signifies "creation, being, dissolution, and ultimate reality" (Joyce, *Letters* 2: 85).

In Bruno's mind, the first step toward a conception of the unity of being entails a breaking down of boundaries, and Samhain is the appropriate beginning of such an occurrence. Samhain, pronounced "sow'-in," meaning "end of summer," is the primary Celtic festival that ushers in winter and marks the start of the new year. James Frazer reports in *The Golden Bough* that "[w]itches then speed on their errands of mischief, some sweeping through the air on besoms, others galloping along the roads on tabby-cats, which for that evening are turned into coal-black steeds" (GBA 735). Indeed, Maria might be read as a witch given her freedom to roam about Dublin for the night. Of more importance, however, are the two relevant Celtic traditions performed in "Clay." On Samhain, bonfires and modes of divination celebrated the oncoming year. Divination games ascertained their players' destiny, and in "ancient Ireland, a new fire used to be kindled every year on Hallowe'en or the Eve of Samhain, and from this sacred flame all the fires in Ireland were kindled" (GBA 734). In modern times, the fires are hospitable gestures that welcome wandering souls to warm themselves at their old residences. Maria will return to Joe, whom she reared, warm herself by his fire and divine her own future to be clay.

The competing Catholic tradition for the evening is the Vigil of Our Lady and All the Saints, which begins at sundown on the night prior to November

1. The collectivity of the feast is appropriate in that Mary is the most exalted of saints. In explicating Maria's nature as a "veritable peace-maker," the story clearly alludes to the Sermon on the Mount, which is the Mass for All Saints' Day (Matt. 5:9).[10] When Maria assumes her "blessed" role as "peacemaker" in a sibling rivalry and puts "in a good word for Alphy," "Joe cried that God might strike him stone dead if ever he spoke a word to his brother again." However, Joe calms himself because "he would not lose his temper on account of the night it was" (87). The reference to restraint is part of Joyce's satire of superficial Catholic piety, calling attention to the arbitrary date of commemorating All the Saints.

As with many Christian holidays, the history of All Saints' Day reveals the Catholic Church's anxiety about the popularity of pagan rituals, in this case the ritual for the dead on Samhain. As part of its missionary work, the Church sought to subsume pagan rituals by superimposing an appropriate thematic and Christian observance, in this case a ceremony for departed holy souls. However, the persistence of Samhain traditions showed the mere simultaneity of All Saints' Day to be ineffectual in fully quelling the pagan observance, so the Church changed the perception of Samhain to one of pure evil and established All Souls' Day as an homage to the dead. The Church liked to think of the movement from the evening vigil to the morning Mass as a telic progression from chaos to control. The power of the pagan tradition kept resurging, and eventually the Church abandoned direct competition and suppressed the vigil portion of the celebration in 1955. Some critics of Joyce's story have misconstrued the genealogy of the feasts. For instance, Marvin Magalaner and Richard Kain claim: "the history of the church holiday actually establishes all the parallel background [Joyce] needs: The day set aside in honor of saints (like Mary) by Boniface IV has had its eve perverted by celebrants to the calling forth of witches" (129). To be sure, the usurpation of November 1 to serve as All Saints' Day shows the Church's common practice of molding, like clay, days of pagan rituals in order to serve its own purposes.

Central to "Clay" is Maria's homecoming and participation in Celtic traditions. Indeed, the plot outline of the story almost seems to have been formulated by Frazer's summary of the essence of Halloween. *The Golden Bough* could be a source text for the story. Throughout Europe, not just in Celtic lands, Halloween marked "the time of year when the souls of the departed were supposed to revisit their old homes in order to warm themselves by the fire and to comfort themselves with the good cheer provided for them in the kitchen or the parlour by their affectionate kinsfolk" (GBA 735). Part of the good cheer the hosts intend for Maria is the hope of a benevolent prophecy from the blindfold-and-saucer divination game. After the "two nextdoor girls had arranged some Hallow Eve games," they "insisted then on blindfolding Maria and leading her up to the table to see what she would get" (87–88). Traditionally, the game that they play consists of either four or five saucers distributed with water, a ring, salt or a coin, occasionally a prayer book, and in the less "genteel" versions, clay. The blindly chosen saucer divines a future of, respectively, migration or continued life, marriage, prosperity, entrance into a nunnery or seminary, and death. Though Joe Donnelly and his wife had intended a "genteel" version, someone, probably one of the next-door girls, had surreptitiously included clay for Maria's turn. As Maria "moved her hand about here and there in the air and descended on one of the saucers," she "felt a soft wet substance with her fingers and was surprised that nobody spoke or took off her bandage." By leaving the association to be made between the title-word, absent from the story, and the "soft wet substance," Joyce highlights the malleability of "clay" and hints at a unifying matter that synthesizes the metaphysics of the contrary Christian and Celtic heritages of Ireland.[11] Divination has revealed Maria's fate, a universal one, to her fellow revelers, yet she wants to believe "that it was wrong that time and so she had to do it over again." She ultimately picks "the prayer book." In agreeing that the first time "was no play" (88), the characters collectively repress the inevitability of death.

Through the amendatory act, the characters refuse to acknowledge the darker side of the game and, by extension, of life. François Laroque remarks that the characters' act of repression shows "that they deceive themselves and each other into forgetting" "the true meaning of the ancient rites." Therefore, "because of the collective amnesia of the Dubliners," "the reader has to reconstitute part of the missing data" (54). Replacing clay with the prayer book enacts the lacuna in the text, the strategic transformation of this holiday observance. Maria with her blindfold and her fellow revelers with their gentility cannot see this historical imposition. Through this subtle performance, Joyce hints at the arbitrary nature of the holiday and the Church's machinations. By emphasizing the syncretism of the pagan and Catholic rites, Joyce's return to origins invites a reexamination of the varying conceptions of death in the two traditions. In effect, "Clay" is a treatise on the presence of death in life and the inevitability of decay. In his review of Bruno's philosophy, Joyce found that it enabled a person not to "fear to die" since the "death of the body is for him the cessation of a mode of being" (134). The short story makes the sanctity of All Saint's Day seem strange, and disputes Catholic orthodoxy's sense of *the* ending. Instead, "Clay" offers the accessibility of "canonization" in the continuative process of life.

Joyce's later works also show a preoccupation with the biblical and deathly associations of clay. One of Joyce's later images of clay in *Ulysses,* "Born all in the dark wormy earth, cold specks of fire, evil, lights shining in the darkness" (198), inversely echoes a direct reference in the novel to Bruno's "soul of the world": "the obscure soul of the world, a darkness shining in brightness which brightness could not comprehend" (23). In associating clay with the "soul of the world," Joyce conflates two metaphysical systems of a cyclical nature, Bruno's and the Judeo-Christian one reflected by Genesis 2:7 and *The Dead Sea Scriptures:* "What is man, mere earth kneaded out of clay, destined to return unto the dust" (174). The association counters the fourth definition of "clay" in the *Oxford English Dictionary:* "the earthly or material part of man." Through Bruno's philosophy, Joyce could see the possibilities of not separating the clay of the body from its capacity to hold a vestige of the "soul of the world."

By repeatedly emphasizing a return to clay, Joyce undercuts the orthodox idea of heaven in that not only is clay the genesis and fate of the human body, but it is also connected to the soul. Moreover, Joyce points to the agrarian basis of Celtic culture and underscores the heretical idea that the body and the soul *only* return to clay. Substituting the prayer book for clay offers the condolence of a Christian afterlife; however, like most condolences, the replacement is a hollow contrivance. Through the replacement, Joyce subtly satirizes the arbitrary placement of All Saints' Day on the liturgical calendar. Maria's satisfaction in living a saintly life must be delayed, for death is requisite for canonization. On the other hand, complementing Bruno's philosophy with the qualities of clay suggests that all people are holy, molded from clay, and to clay they shall return. Therefore, the earthly, the "clay," should be canonized. The idea of universal synthesis is in some way a consoling projection itself, but perhaps not as superficial, for Joyce, as the one represented by the prayer book. Canonical transformations produce and are produced by the changing horizons of readers, and during the period from 1883 to 1924, a prominent agent of such a transformation was the heresy of syncretism. As the next chapter further illustrates, this form of synthesis found an intellectual frame in the philosophy of Bruno and other amenable schools of thought, while the array of pagan literature and myth supplied much of the material.

Chapter 5

Literary Paganism and the
Heresy of Syncretism

IN HIS LAST, unfinished, book, *Gaston de Latour* (1896), Walter Pater also illustrates the late Victorian recuperation of Giordano Bruno, and finds that his deification of the material world makes him a "true son of the Renaissance, in the light of those large, antique, pagan ideas" (82). As Gaston becomes influenced by the Renaissance scholar's philosophy in the chapter entitled "The Lower Pantheism," the narrative describes the germination of Bruno's heresies while he was in the Dominican order: the "young monk" puzzled "the good, sleepy heads of the average sons of Dominic with his neology, putting new wine in old bottles, teaching them their business." As we know, Bruno's new wine burst the bottle of his "brethren's sympathy," so he looked to "pagan writers" as "having a kind of natural, preparatory kinship with Scripture itself" (72).

The rediscovery of classical paganism characterizes much of Renaissance art, and Pater's own landmark *Studies in the History of the Renaissance* (1873) led, in part, to a similar return of paganism during the late Victorian and modernist periods. A profound fascination with new and buried products of science and art dominate each historical period, and Pater's aesthetic treatise became a staple of the "art for art's sake" movement and its desire to harmonize form and content. A common derivative of this approach saw a proliferation of literary works which collocated correspondent pagan and Christian rituals, images, and ideologies. This syncretic form of heresy often drew on the conclusions of cultural anthropology, and preoccupies the work of such artists as Pater, Hardy, Gauguin, Hudson, Lawrence, and Joyce. As this chapter illustrates, Pater's *The Renaissance* championed a reconciliation of pagan and Christian aesthetics, while fiction with critical cultural implications such as *Tess of the d'Urbervilles* often used such a heretical synthesis to trouble the repressive complacency of orthodoxy.

The philosophical pantheism behind the canonization of clay in Joyce's story about All Hallows' Eve reflects a turn toward the spirituality of "this world." In *Gaston,* Pater states that "'Nature' becomes for [Bruno] a sacred term" (74), and, though he helped "himself indifferently to all religions for rhetoric illustration, his preference was still for that of the soil, the old pagan religion" (80). One result of this mystical trend, perhaps best exemplified by Theosophy and the Hermetic Order of the Golden Dawn, saw a theoretical interest in pagan religions and an anthropomorphism which found spirituality in the vagaries of *human* endeavor. As literary experiments with paganism became more daring, the sexuality of various primitivisms that affirm "this world" came to the foreground, and their implicit critique of Christian asceticism led to charges of indecency in the work of Hardy, Joyce, and Lawrence. Paganism does not blaspheme, being outside the pale of Christianity, but it could be "obscene."

Take, for example, the scandalous beach scene in the "Nausicaa" episode of *Ulysses,* the serialization of which initiated the obscenity charges against Joyce's novel. Margaret Anderson had been publishing Joyce's work in her journal the *Little Review* since 1918, and she described the obscenity trial of 1921 as "a burning at the stake as far as I was concerned" (Crispi). In "Nausicaa," Joyce doubly frames the voyeuristic masturbation of Leopold Bloom and Gerty MacDowell with the tolling of steeple bells as Canon O'Hanlon confers the Blessed Sacrament in honor of the Virgin Mary, and with a bat frightened from the belfry "at the same time" flying "through the dusk, hither, thither, with a tiny lost cry" (298). A bat traditionally emblematizes both pagan and sexual agency, and these associations appear throughout the novel, notably in "Proteus" the parallel episode to "Nausicaa." In the earlier beach scene, Stephen Dedalus thinks: "He comes, pale vampire, through storm his eyes, his bat sails bloodying the sea, mouth to her mouth's kiss" (40). As the bat flies around in "Nausicaa," the passage, key to the censorship trial of the novel, begins when Gerty leans back to reveal her undergarments and Bloom masturbates, as literal fireworks dapple the sky overhead. The narrative voice later states that their orgasmic encounter "was their secret, only theirs, alone in the hiding twilight and there was none to know or tell save the little bat that flew so softly through the evening to and fro and little bats don't tell" (300–301). In his study of modernist obscenity and censorship, Adam Parkes notes many "blasphemous" elements in this episode including the unflattering simultaneity of the Mass, the associations of Gerty with the Virgin Mary, and the secret and "pornographic" elements structuring the scene like a confession. Acknowledging Foucault's idea that the confessional "turns desire into discourse and so regulates sex," Parkes argues that in the confessional the "priest's privileged access to women's sexual secrets replicates the structures of power exhibited in pornography." Parkes also points out that Bloom and Gerty's secrecy is violated by readers who are "implicated in the process of creating obscenity," and that "Joyce challenges us to reflect critically on the implications of our spectatorship, and to recognize its subversive possibilities" (83–86). One of these possibilities is pagan; the narrative heretically inserts the "little bat" in the confessional position reserved for priests who also "don't tell." Readers do tell, though, and the telling use of the pagan image reveals one of Joyce's many heresies. The bat's "lost cry" echoes beyond the chime of church bells as it sanctions Bloom and Gerty's sexual delight.

Joyce's novel, though, does not refrain from mocking the pagan revival common at the turn of the century, and this is a crucial qualification to Pater's and Hardy's use of paganism analyzed in the following sections. The pagan elements of *The Renaissance* and *Tess of the d'Urbervilles* subvert orthodox Christianity without any necessary intention to reinstall paganism as the privileged religion. In *Ulysses,* for instance, Stephen Dedalus thinks "To ourselves . . . new paganism . . . *omphalos*" (7), and dismissively lumps together these *fin-de-siècle* cultural movements. The "new paganism" is a reference to another use of pagan sexuality in the short-lived *Pagan Review* launched by William Sharp in 1891.[1] The solitary edition had seven "frankly pagan" titles that advanced "the new paganism," a movement which aimed at "thorough-going unpopularity" while appealing to the "younger generation." Sharp found that the "religion of our forefathers . . . is no longer in any vital and general sense a sovereign power in the realm." To revitalize the world, Sharp declared that the "duel between Man and Woman is to cease," and that literature should reflect the "various forces of the sexual emotion" (1–3).

During the 1890s, writers of "decadence" in particular wallowed in various forms of sexualized paganism, and welcomed the comparison to the late stages of ancient Greece and Rome. Oscar Wilde's ribald and erotic poem, "The Sphinx" (1894), epitomizes the themes and values of the Decadent decade. By addressing a hairless cat, perhaps of the sphinx breed, as the actual Sphinx of Greek and Egyptian legend, the poetic voice desires to revive the ancient myth and its accompanying sexual passion through a style that catalogs and gathers the god "scattered here and there." In blazoning the "sphinx," the resultant grotesque imagery conflates a panoply of deviant sexual acts and offers no discretion among the so-called wrongs. The poem reconstructs the sphinx's sundered body parts and implies that Egyptian myth is only fallow because "Only one god has ever died." However, with this introduction of Christian imagery, the poet turns away in guilt and self-loathing from the sphinx who wakes in him "each bestial sense" and makes him what he "would not be" (820–24).[2]

Pater also stresses the aesthetic value of a pagan sensuousness in his study of the Renaissance. Though he does not discuss Bruno until *Gaston*, the "thick stratum of pagan sentiment beneath" (76) Bruno's thought clearly makes the chapter an addendum of sorts to *The Renaissance*. As in his treatment of other Renaissance figures, Pater links Bruno's "flights of intellectual enthusiasm" with "those of physical love." Pater states that Bruno's "nature so opulently endowed can hardly have been lacking in purely physical or sensuous ardours," and he believes that the "theorem that God was in all things whatever, annihilating their differences" awoke in Bruno "a constant, inextinguishable appetite for every form of experience" (75–77). The "soul of the world" grows through acts of creation such as the products of love and the imagination. Jane Spirit believes that within "the context of *Gaston* it would seem then that the protagonist discovers in Bruno's system not only a theoretical justification for the integration of mind and matter, soul and body, but also an example of the fulfilment to be found in attaining such harmony." Here was a new way to bottle wine and make a celebratory toast. However, Spirit points out that Pater found Bruno's doctrine of the coincidence, or "indifference," of contraries troublesome to the "distinctions" between "art and life," "good and evil," and "pain and pleasure" (225). In a way, Pater identifies with Bruno in that each of their theories could be dangerously appropriated by a decadent approach to life even though each "was cautious not to suggest the ethic or practical equivalent to his theoretic positions." Therefore, Pater stresses the need to make the "distinction," as later modernists would do, "between what was right and wrong in the matter of art" (82–83). In *The Renaissance*, though, he emphasizes the initial need to reject any a priori authority regarding aesthetic taste.

The "Curious" Pagan Spirit of Pater's *The Renaissance*

Of the many famous dicta born with Pater's "Conclusion" to *The Renaissance*, perhaps the most subversive of his mandates for aesthetic criticism overtly calls for a consistent questioning of authority: "What we have to do is to be for ever curiously testing new opinions and courting new impressions, never acquiescing in a facile orthodoxy, of Comte, or of Hegel, or of our own" (189).[3] Pater's plea yokes together two terms to privilege the paganism that he finds subtly apparent in Christian iconography. To be "curious" in the face of "orthodoxy" is both what Pater values in his chosen Renaissance artists and what he strove for in his own life. Indeed, Pater's projection of autobiographical concerns onto his subjects emphasizes his desire for harmony between an artist's life and work. In his treatment of Pico della Mirandola, Leonardo da Vinci and Johann Winckelmann, Pater admires most in them the principle that the artist's work relates to his life, and asserts that the form of his artwork should also convey the array of sentiments associated with its historical and philosophical content. For Pater, this principle of *Andersstreben* explains both how the particular historical quality of the Renaissance, a pagan sensibility, appears in art and how correspondent aesthetic qualities become sublimated in the person. In his discussion of Giorgione, Pater explains his usage of *Andersstreben* in describing the relation between painting and music: "each art may be observed to pass into the condition of some other art, by what German critics term an *Anders-streben*—a partial alienation from its own limitations, through which the arts are able, not indeed to supply the place of each other, but reciprocally to lend each other new forces" (105). Pater's argument throughout *The Renaissance* implies that a similar productive dialectic undergirds the historical relation between Christianity and paganism, and his defense of "curiosity" and a "pagan spirit" distinguishes the work as a cohesive, unified treatise delineating in component parts the historical, aesthetic, and political relations between paganism and Christianity.

As a correlative of *Andersstreben,* the prominent metaphor and preeminent form of art in *The Renaissance* is music, an art form in which it is impossible "to distinguish matter from the form." Pater declares therefore: "*All art aspires towards the condition of music*" (106). Analogously for the religious concerns of *The Renaissance,* Pater tries to bring to the foreground the pagan "matter" repressed historically in the "forms" of Christian symbols and tradition. Pater finds that the unique dialogue between paganism and Christianity in Renaissance art is its masterstroke, in that they too "lend each other new forces." Curiosity is the driving force behind this genius. While criticism has generally seen *The Renaissance* as a disjointed collection of essays, the reciprocal function of curiosity and a pagan sensibility constitutes a dominant, consistent argument throughout Pater's work. In the third (1888) and fourth (1893) editions, Pater's inclusion of "The School of Giorgione" and the discussion of Amis and Amile within "Two Early French Stories," and the restoration of the "Conclusion," cultivate the coherence of a curious, pagan spirit. As part of this thesis, Pater argues that a curious, pagan spirit achieves a "serenity" and potentially harmonizes form and content through a desire for beauty and a search for historical and aesthetic continuities between paganism and Christianity.

The emphatic rhetoric of the first sentence of the essay on Pico della Mirandola equally applies to a predominant theme subtending Pater's work: "No account of the Renaissance can be complete without some notice of the attempt made by certain Italian scholars of the fifteenth century to reconcile Christianity with the religion of ancient Greece" (23). Pater later implies that history can synthesize Christianity and paganism, albeit at the expense of orthodoxy. As a result, Pater's "Conclusion" elicited a stern rebuke from the Bishop of Oxford, and "scandalous" and "notorious" came to be mentioned in the same breath as the "Conclusion." Pater's paganism informs both the late Victorian debates between established religion, comparative anthropology, and evolutionary thought, and T. S. Eliot's later attempt to debunk Pater's view of form and content. In defending the Christian tradition as the "true" content of art, T. S. Eliot continued the charges against Pater, who "knew almost nothing" about "the essence of the Christian faith" and only offers a "degradation of philosophy and religion" ("Pater" 388–91). To be sure, Pater champions "curiosity" as the relentless, unsettling characteristic of artists who challenge the thoughtless acceptance of "tradition." Pater suggests that the unmitigated love of beauty accompanying any "proper" aesthetics far outweighs the threat to orthodoxy concomitant with the resurfacing of potentially oppositional internal elements. A curious look at Pater's "Poems by William Morris," an October 1868 review of Morris's *The Earthly Paradise*, helps to clarify the fact that the orthodoxy "of our own" that Pater is questioning in his "Conclusion" is indeed Christianity.

In its previously published form, the "Conclusion" occupied a similar structural position in also concluding the unsigned Morris review. Of interest, then, are the tone and subject matter that led Pater initially to such controversial remarks that promote "the love of art for its own sake" and declaim the "conventional" as having "no real claim upon us" (189–90). What follows is the paragraph in the review that immediately precedes what would become the "Conclusion":

> One characteristic of the pagan spirit these new poems have which is on their
> surface—the continual suggestion, pensive or passionate, of the shortness of
> life; this is contrasted with the bloom of the world and gives new seduction to

it; the sense of death and the desire of beauty; the desire of beauty quickened by the sense of death. "*Arriéré!*" you say, "here in a tangible form we have the defect of all poetry like this. The modern world is in possession of truths; what but a passing smile can it have for a kind of poetry which, assuming artistic beauty of form to be an end in itself, passes by those truths and the living interests which are connected with them, to spend a thousand cares in telling once more these pagan fables as if it had but to choose between a more and a less beautiful shadow?" It is a strange transition from the earthly paradise to the sad-coloured world of abstract philosophy. But let us accept the challenge; let us see what modern philosophy, when it is sincere, really does say about human life and the truth we can attain in it, and the relation of this to the desire of beauty. (309)

Denis Donoghue believes that, when Pater transposed the review into the "Conclusion," "he excised the passage about the pagan spirit, presumably because it was too closely attached to his broodings on Morris's poems" (53). Donoghue could not be more wrong here. The "pagan spirit" also best describes Pater's heretical stance that subtends *The Renaissance*. At once, the "shortness of life" and "sense of death" emphasized in the passage elucidates the inspired *carpe diem* motif of the "Conclusion" and suggests that a "pagan spirit" can provide insight into the relation between beauty and truth. One senses that Pater is not satisfied with the Keatsian proposition of the Grecian Urn. For Pater's curiosity is especially aroused by those artists who do "spend a thousand cares in telling . . . pagan fables." Here Pater hints at a nuanced reasoning behind his recurrent use of the word "curiosity." Etymologically, "curiosity" derives from the Latin *curiosus*, "full of cares" or "careful." Among the many theories of development blossoming in the 1860s, the discipline of etymology (<Gk. *etumos*, "truth, what is") began to promote an intersection of history and language as the "study of truth." One of Pater's colleagues at Oxford, Max Müller, reinserted the importance of etymology in philological studies and put forth "the notion that the meaning of a word was equivalent to its whole etymological history" (Burrow 200). In its multi-tiered linguistic history, the word "curiosity" plays several roles in *The Renaissance*, often denoting alternately "inquisitiveness" or "an interesting object," but never excluding any of its associated meanings.

By the time Pater wrote the bulk of the essays that comprise *The Renaissance*, Matthew Arnold's *Culture and Anarchy* (1869) had exerted considerable influence in critical studies of culture. The first words of the famous first chapter on "Sweetness and Light" claim that the "disparagers of culture make its motive curiosity" (204). Arnold believes that this has happened because, in English usage, the word "curiosity" solely conveys pejorative connotations. However, as he had noted in "The Function of Criticism at the Present Time" (1865), other languages use the term "to mean, as a high and fine quality of man's nature, just the disinterested love of a free play of the mind on all subjects." In this positive sense, curiosity is the controlling motive of cultural criticism (141). By combining this view of culture with the belief that societies try to improve culture and perform "the will of God," Arnold believes that "culture" then is "*a study of perfection*" ("Sweetness" 205). Though Pater would refrain from thinking of "the will of God," the word "curiosity" for Pater continues to carry all of its varied historical significances. Thinking of the "truth" linguistically buried in "etymology" sheds light on the passage from the Morris review: "The modern world is in possession of truths; what but a passing smile can it have for a kind of poetry which, assuming artistic beauty of form to be an end in itself, passes by those truths and the living interests which are connected with them" (309). Again Pater evokes the idea that language carries history residually and keeps the past alive. In miniature, hearing all the voices of a word exemplifies his humanist belief that "nothing which has ever interested living men and women can wholly lose its vitality," including any "language they have spoken" (38). Pater uses "curiosity" as a keyword to reveal and underscore a similar historical development from paganism to Christianity, and he struggles to show the need for the recognition and persistence of the pagan spirit.

In "Dallying nicely with words," John Hollander argues that, in a cross section of writers from Shakespeare to Hopkins, "words are often like some agents in a larger fiction, not so much an epic or drama, but more a complex romance, of language" (123). In this light, Pater's use of the word "curiosity" becomes an example of what Hollander calls "an allegorising of the etymological process" (130). Hollander suggests that literature can play "on English word and Latin etymon" and become a "valorisation of the relation between past and present usage" (130). Uncovering the etymological layers of the word "curious" would take us from "an object arousing interest" to "a desire to know or learn" to a process "full of cares" or of "healing."[4] When Petronius alludes to Horace's *curiosa felicitas*, he is referring to this linguistic dimension of "curiosity" by implying an "elaborate and painstaking care in composition" (Arrowsmith 185). The last sense, "healing," shows the word's cognate relationship with "cure." (On another level, the connotations of "curiosity" associated with "pornography" or "strangeness" speak to the erotic subtexts Pater often cultivates vis-à-vis his subjects, especially Leonardo.) By extension, the thought processes involved in such a search for roots represent to Pater a convalescence that tries to syncretize Christian icons with analogous pagan symbols. Implicit in this approach is a sentiment that finds a malaise or loss of integration in the present. Hoping to revive the healing serenity of "*Heiterkeit,* that pagan blitheness" (180), Pater promotes, throughout *The Renaissance,* a willful and independent inquisitiveness as a means to restore this "cheerful" contentment in humanity.

In his repetitive, incantatory use of the word "curiosity," Pater draws attention to the word itself as an object of interest and as an illustration of how dormant and archaic meanings of any word or practice can be recovered. The word informs *The Renaissance* from the "curious strength" and "curious interest" of "Two Early French Stories" (7–11) to the "curiosity, the initiatory idea," of "Pico della Mirandola" (25) to the call in the "Conclusion" "to be for ever curiously testing new opinions" (189). Clearly, though, the most playful repetition of the word occurs in "Leonardo da Vinci." Pater describes the genius of Leonardo as "composed, in almost equal parts, of curiosity and the desire of beauty, to take things as they came" (86). Pater then unfolds the dynamic between these traits by repeating the terms with slight variation for the rest of the essay. Once, the terms fuse into "curious beauty" (90), and, in the following sentence, Pater nearly begs the question in explicating the synthesis of the terms: "Curiosity and the desire of beauty—these are the two elementary forces in Leonardo's genius; curiosity often in conflict with the desire of beauty, but generating, in union with it, a type of subtle and curious grace" (86). Here we have the three central meanings of "curiosity" playing off each other, and, in the process, creating a dialectical system. Pater suggests that the general desire to know engages a particular object arousing interest, and consequently generates a "curious grace" or healing power. If there were any doubt as to the importance of curiosity to Pater, the conclusion of the Leonardo essay, the purple patch for curiosity, speculates how Leonardo dies looking "forward now into the vague land, and experienced the last curiosity" (101).

Reading the layered meanings of curiosity in *The Renaissance* becomes a key that demonstrates the parallel endeavor of the work to use a historical process to reconcile the Christian present with its pagan past. To be constantly curious presents a direct threat to authority: not only does curiosity challenge authority, but the progressive, continuative nature of inquisitive searching precludes the establishment of any fixed forms or orthodox doctrine. In this vein, curiosity for Pater is akin to the role of heresy in Shaw's "Religion of the Future." As Richard Dellamora argues, for Pater, a "curious" "cultivation of self implies religious unbelief" (137). From the "Preface" to the "Conclusion," Pater emphasizes the durative process of searching far above the need for any final answers. One of the few qualities that Pater does want to achieve—the healing serenity of *Heiterkeit*—would not curtail curiosity in its attainment. Conversely, a serenity would be incorporated into curiosity and replace the angst-ridden concern for origins burgeoning in Pater's time.

While the role of curiosity plays a subtle role in linking the essays in *The Renaissance*, the prevalence of pagan issues more overtly harmonizes the collection. The echo of pagan practices and images in the essays builds on the call to reconcile past and present and gradually culminates in the challenge to Christian orthodoxy in the "Conclusion." Pater particularly takes interest in the appropriation of pagan gods and symbols by Christianity. In the two chapters highly concerned with cultivating a methodology for linking past and present, content and form, Pater stresses Pico's listing of correspondences between the Greek and Christian religions and Giorgione's "'imaginative reason,' that complex faculty for which every thought and feeling is twin-born with its sensible analogue or symbol" (109). In the *Doni* Madonna, for another example, "Michelangelo actually brings the pagan religion . . . into the presence of the Madonna" and gives her "much of the uncouth energy of the older and more primitive 'Mighty Mother'" (37). And, in Leonardo's *La Gioconda*, Pater sees in Mona Lisa all "the thoughts and experience of the world" including "the return of the Pagan world" (98). In these works and in the "strange likeness" between Leonardo's paintings of Saint John and Bacchus, Pater invokes "Heine's notion of decayed gods, who, to maintain themselves, after the fall of paganism, took employment in the new religion" (93). Pater, as a Platonist, is drawn to those art forms that slightly reveal this transmogrification by foregrounding a residue of an earlier connotation of the subject. Furthermore, the idea of former pagan gods lying fallow in Christianity leads Pater to make the bold claim in "Winckelmann" that "the broad foundation . . . of all religions as they exist for the greatest number, is a universal pagan sentiment, a paganism which existed before the Greek religion, and has lingered far onward into the Christian world, ineradicable" (160).

Consequently, criticism that speaks of paganism in *The Renaissance* generally focuses on "Winckelmann." Paul Jordan-Smith calls the essay Pater's "remarkable confession of faith," which "would bring back the spirit of paganism with its earthliness, its naturalness, and unite it to the gentleness and sympathy of Christian thought" (242). In his exhaustive study of the persistence of ancient Greek influence in Victorian Britain, Frank Turner interprets Pater's discernment of a "universal pagan sentiment" to indicate "humankind's acute awareness of its vulnerability in the natural world"; consequently, through "the myths, human beings sought to make themselves less estranged from nature and by religious ritual to exercise some vague control over it" (98). In discussing the Leonardo essay specifically, Dellamora contrasts John Ruskin's love of medieval Christian art with Pater's work, which "prefers 'pagan' to 'Christian' art precisely because it is 'pagan.'" Dellamora also argues that Pater's method "discloses processes basing and shaping Leonardo's art which afford guidance to contemporary artists in creating new forms." Therefore, he believes that "Pater's work does not merely mark the advent of modernism; it is itself modernist" (136). These modernist processes involve a non–a priori curiosity and a drive toward dialectical synthesis, both of which are central functions of the discourse of heresy in the transitional period from 1883 to 1924.

Early on in the preface, Pater argues that the actual value of trying to develop a universal formula for art arises concomitantly "in the suggestive and penetrating things said by the way" (xix). By valorizing the very process of aesthetic criticism, Pater seeks no other goal than the constancy of reinvestigation and the questioning of accepted norms. In his egalitarian and unrigid approach, Pater underscores the naive attempts of Pico della Mirandola to come to terms with historical process. Though Pater believes that Pico exemplifies the idea that "the Renaissance of the fifteenth century was, in many things, great rather by what it designed or aspired to do, than by what it actually achieved," Pater claims that it "remained for a later age to conceive the true method of effecting a scientific reconciliation of Christian sentiment with the imagery, the legends, the theories about the world, of pagan poetry and philosophy." During the Renaissance, Pater finds that the "only possible reconciliation was an imaginative one" (36), but suggests the modern possibility of synthesizing science and religion through a "proper" Hegelian historical sense. A proper historical summary or philosophy of the world also synthesizes "all modes of thought and life" (99). With an application of the "true" historical sense, built on the idea of process, Pater feels that he can fulfill this task.

In a striking passage from the first essay in *The Renaissance*, "Two Early French Stories," Pater sets forth the internal dynamics of his hermeneutics for thinking about the period. For any interpretation of the amalgam of Christian and pagan sentiments seen in Renaissance art, Pater suggests that the three methodological desiderata are an affinity for the sensuous, a willingness to be unorthodox, and an application of the historical sense. In this light, "Two Early French Stories" serves as an overture for the central themes of *The Renaissance*. By establishing a "continuity" between twelfth-century France and fifteenth-century Italy, Pater believes his approach will effect a "*healing* [of] that rupture between the middle age and the Renaissance which has so often been exaggerated" (2, emphasis added). Here, in the opening pages of the book, Pater foreshadows his use of the word "curiosity" and responds to Ruskin's recent praise of a sparse, sublime Gothic art antithetical to the decadent effusions of the Renaissance.

The Oxford Movement had helped to revive medievalism at Pater's institution, so his valorization of the successive period in history and its particular paganism confronted both established religion and aesthetics. However, in adopting a view of history as a constantly unfolding process, Pater clearly identifies with the developmental theories prevalent in his time. By supporting a methodology that casts suspicion on the immutability of the word of God, *The Renaissance* executes a critique of the idea of any *lex eterna*. In the following passage from "Two Early French Stories," Pater supports the particular challenge to the law of the church by lauding the heresy of antinomianism:

> One of the strongest characteristics of that outbreak of the reason and the imagination, of that assertion of the liberty of the heart, in the middle age, which I have termed a medieval Renaissance, was its antinomianism, its spirit of rebellion and revolt against the moral and religious ideas of the time. In their *search* after the pleasures of the senses and the imagination, in their *care* for beauty, in their worship of the body, people were impelled beyond the bounds of the Christian ideal; and their love became sometimes a strange idolatry, a strange rival religion. It was the return of that ancient Venus, not dead, but only hidden for a time in the caves of the Venusberg, of those old pagan gods still going to and fro on the earth, under all sorts of disguises. (18–19, emphases added)

As this passage reveals, Pater's preoccupations in *The Renaissance* are foreshadowed again by "Poems by William Morris." In addition to stressing the terminology, "a medieval Renaissance," he champions once more a "spirit of rebellion" in confronting the hegemonic religion of the time. Curiosity, though unsaid directly in the passage, remains the central heretical element. In the "search" that has a "care for beauty" (two senses of "curiosity") "people were impelled beyond the bounds of the Christian ideal." The opposition of Christianity and curiosity clearly echoes the call in the "Conclusion" to be "curiously testing" "orthodoxy." The French stories become an example for Pater of how to revive dormant pagan gods. While a desire to see historical elements in present appearances will discover the gods in their "disguises," Pater underscores the primary need for a vigorous antinomian ethics. Antinomians preach a doctrine that frees Christians, saved by grace, from the observance of any law. Etymologically, they are "against" the "law."

Prior to the call to "burn" with a "hard, gem-like flame," Pater's "Conclusion" highlights "the tendency of modern thought" to regard both the physical world and the human psyche as fundamentally mutable and fleeting. In each case, the "Conclusion" responds to the germination in the 1850s and 1860s of Higher Criticism and evolutionary thought, the seeds for what became the modernist crisis in Catholicism. Various scholars began applying notions of process and development to language, historical texts, and even, in bold moves, the Old Testament and the Gospels. Pater similarly opposes the static tenets needed by orthodoxy with the contemporary view of "physical life" as "a perpetual motion" of "elements, phosphorus and lime and delicate fibres," which "are present not in the human body alone." The interconnectedness of the material world humbles humanity, and viewing human beings as part of an evolving, internecine web of nature focuses attention on "this" world. In terms of the psyche, Pater notes that "the inward world of thought" illustrates that the "whirlpool is still more rapid." The experience of "this" world becomes a linguistic and impressionistic function that isolates the individual and leads to Pater's *carpe diem* conclusion to observe as many of these "unstable, flickering, inconsistent" impressions as possible. Pater's definition of "success in life" then directly opposes orthodox views of morality and destiny which require "the sacrifice of any part of this experience." For the Oxford don, asceticism and living with a goal of achieving heaven "have no real claim upon us" (186–89). While the implications of this perspective led to Pater's apotheosis during the "art for art's sake" movement, the influences informing his school of thought should not be separated from those that elicited the modernist crisis.

While the Catholic modernist threat to orthodoxy did not weigh as heavily on Protestantism, all Christian sects still were brought into the imbroglio perpetuated by a heretical interpretation of the Bible. For instance, the Bishop of Oxford, John Fielder Mackarness, followed the strategic response of Catholicism by defaming Pater as an internal dissenter whose philosophies should be quelled. On April 25, 1875, the bishop addressed the religious skepticism being promoted at Oxford: "To speak the simple truth, a considerable number of Graduates who hold office in the University, or

Fellowships in the Colleges, have ceased to be Christians in anything but name;—in some cases, even the name is repudiated, when arguments based upon its retention are pressed." Though he did not cite Pater by name, the bishop quoted three passages from the "Conclusion" to *The Renaissance* as examples of the emphasis that skeptics place on the ephemerality of life and the consequent need for reaping a manifold set of experiences.[5] Additionally, the bishop critiqued the rise of a scientific historical method: "The historical facts of Christianity fare no better than its precepts: deference to scientific criticism (whatever that may mean), forbids them to be taken for true." As a result of this form of education, the bishop believed that wayward youths would develop a "selfishness of character" and lose "all motive for serious action" (Seiler 95–96). In contrast, for Pater, Pico della Mirandola presents a serious attempt to synthesize all forms of thought out of a magnanimous, humanist gesture.

In the essay on Pico, Pater uses his compelling but failed attempt to syncretize paganism and Christianity as an illustration of the need for a proper historical criticism. Still, Pico's endeavor to list 900 theses arguing that all Western philosophy and religions share the same underlying truths lead Pater to consider the Renaissance humanist scholar his spiritual precursor, who also personified "curiosity" and believed "that nothing which has ever interested living men and women can wholly lose its vitality" (38). Like the Quaker librarian in Joyce's *Ulysses,* Pico had a "desire to hear all voices" (27). Above all, Pater finds Pico to be an attractive figure because he is a "picturesque union of contrasts" himself and a person who "wins one on, in spite of one's self, to turn again to the pages of his forgotten books" (37). A figure like Pico who was so desirous of all forms of knowledge inspires others to be so curious. Indeed, Pater certainly thinks of himself as continuing the approach of Pico, who was "one of the last who seriously and sincerely entertained the claim on men's faith of the pagan religions" (33).

In 1486, Pico planned on debating his 900 interdisciplinary theses at a conference to which he invited scholars from across Europe; however, Pope Innocent VIII declared thirteen of his theological theses to be heretical. When Pico avoided being burned at the stake by withdrawing the plans for his conference and acquiescing to work in a Dominican order, his life, according to Pater and his view of *Andersstreben,* became "so perfect a parallel to the attempt made in his writings to reconcile Christianity with the ideas of paganism." Still holding a "tenderness" for his earlier life, Pico wrote *Heptaplus, or Discourse on the Seven Days of Creation* (1490), a series of sonnets which strives to syncretize the works of Plato and Moses through an "unbroken system of correspondences" and, of particular interest to Pater, a rigorous and inspired analysis of the "double meanings of words" (34–35).

Despite admiring Pico's intentions, Pater hints that a "modern scholar" occupied by a similar problem would not treat religious traditions as hermetically sealed texts and divorce them from their cultural contexts. By placing the varied contexts at hand in light of the "gradual education of the human mind," Pater declares that the "basis of the reconciliation of the religions of the world would thus be the inexhaustible activity and creativeness of the human mind itself, in which all religions alike have their root, and in which all alike are reconciled." However, the historical sense required for this type of methodology would not develop until at least Hegel. During the Renaissance, Pater finds that scholars, despite exemplifying "a curiosity of the human mind" to compare religions, had to rely on the "quicksand of allegorical interpretation." Lacking historical tools and stuck within a geocentric view of the universe, fifteenth-century scholars tried to reconcile religions, "not as successive stages in a regular development of the religious sense, but as subsisting side by side." As a result of such a spatial methodology, the interpretations tended to "misrepresent" the material because, set "side by side, the mere surfaces could never unite in any harmony of design" (25–27). Pater, thus, pokes at Pico's overly nuanced attempt to force a harmonization where there was none.

On the other hand, Pater feels that the results of such an endeavor, successful or not, chiefly hold import in the loss of the "religious significance" and the rise of treating "the subject" as "purely artistic or poetical." Foreshadowing his call in the "Conclusion" for the love of art for its own sake, Pater claims that "the natural charm of pagan story" caused Renaissance artists, unlike their scholarly counterparts, to value the beauty of the Greek gods solely out of aesthetic appreciation (23). In contrast to the wrongheaded attempts of scholars of the period to collocate the pagan and Christian as distinct complements, the art of the Renaissance cultivates a "practical truce and reconciliation of the gods of Greece with the Christian religion" (27). Here Pater foregrounds the capacity of the Renaissance artists to capture what their contemporary scholars could not—the method by which the past subtly persists in the present.

Owing much unacknowledged debt to Pater, T. S. Eliot refines the idea of a living past in his landmark essay "Tradition and the Individual Talent" with the famous line that "the historical sense invokes a perception, not only of the pastness of the past, but of its presence." [6] In his perspective on the Victorians, Eliot stridently heeds his own advice that a poet should distance himself "from his predecessors, especially his immediate predecessors" (4). For, in his 1930 essay on Arnold and Pater, Eliot attacks them for replacing "Religion" with "Culture" and, in Pater's case, for emphasizing a subjective impressionism in aesthetic interpretation. Eliot shuns their mutual "curiosity" that might dig up historical material unflattering or antithetical to Christianity. Then, Eliot quickly devolves into a personal attack on Pater's mental faculties and ultimately tries to decanonize him. Since Pater was "incapable of sustained reasoning," Eliot believes that his work will not influence "a single first-rate mind of a later generation" (390–92). The attempt to disempower Pater's influence by and large succeeded, for, as Nathan Scott points out, Eliot's ad hominem attack on Pater's aestheticization of religion, though "utter nonsense," "proved over the span of a generation to be something like a benchmark for contemporary criticism" (64). "Arnold and Pater" appeared after Eliot had been baptized into the Church of England in 1927. Thereafter, Eliot's writings overtly promote Christianity, yet he steadfastly maintains his critical position on the dynamic between the past and present—content and form. As a result, Eliot endeavors to promulgate Christianity as *the* Western tradition, *the* old wine to be funneled into new bottles.

The very distinctions made in the process of defining "tradition" mark the difference between Pater and Eliot. In each of their forms of rhetoric, the diverging pasts that they privilege illustrate the recurrently contested realm of canon-formation. For Eliot, the new work of art must "conform" to the "existing monuments" that "form an ideal order among themselves." While he states that the individual artist must make the canon alter "ever so slightly," the inclusion of pagan discourses through syncretism, for Eliot, would not entail "conformity between the old and new" ("Tradition" 5). In contrast to Eliot's privileging of a self-consciously Christian presence, Pater, as we have seen, stresses the pagan sentiment, which is "a part of the eternal basis of all religions, modified indeed by changes of time and place, but indestructible, because its root is so deep in the earth of man's nature" (160). In a wonderfully evocative description, DeLaura proclaims that Pater's writings strive to move beyond the "inevitably inhibiting Victorian timidity and fear of paganism" in order "to provide a new spiritual basis for modern life which incorporates nothing less than a 'comprehensive' view of the totality of man's past" (*Hebrew* 181). Indeed, Eliot responds so vehemently to Pater because he needs to counter a previous aesthetic critic who first put forth similar ideas of form and content, but with an oppositional viewpoint on what composed the tradition. In Pater's vision, the canon needs to be expanded in a more inclusive gesture.

The gesture would heal what Pater sees as the rupture between the medieval period and the Renaissance and concomitantly reveal the shared origins of paganism and Christianity. In his discussion of "Winckelmann," which propels his thesis beyond the Renaissance, Pater points at the fluid inclusivity of history: "Pagan and Christian art are sometimes harshly opposed, and the Renaissance is represented as a fashion which set in at a definite period. That is the superficial view: the deeper view is that which preserves the identity of European culture. The two are really continuous; and there is a sense in which it may be said that the Renaissance was an uninterrupted effort of the middle age." For Pater, the temperament of the modern age would benefit from knowing this continuity and the example of Winckelmann whose "*Heiterkeit,* that pagan blitheness," reflects "a kind of ineffectual wholeness of nature, yet with a beauty and significance of its own." In the rhapsodic denouement of "Winckelmann," Pater calls for a rebirth of the Hellenic healing ideals of serenity, balance, and unity. As opposed to the art of Christian asceticism, the serenity of "art in the pagan manner" kindles sensuousness while treating the subject "with no sense of shame or loss" (176–77). According to Pater, the revival of pagan subjects in art awakens the world "with eyes refreshed, to those ancient, ideal forms" (181). For the heretical modernist, conformity of tradition had little claim as a mandate for art since traditional content itself is mutable. The historically documented appropriation of pagan myths and rituals testifies to that. In a countermove, Thomas Hardy deployed an archaic pagan ritual in *Tess of the d'Urbervilles* in an attempt to change everyday life.

HARDY'S UR-PRIESTESS
AND THE PHASES OF A NOVEL

In the preface to the Fifth Edition of *Tess of the d'Urbervilles,* Hardy responds to the critics of the novel by calling some of them "modern 'Hammers of Heretics'" who discourage free thought because they "may have causes to advance, privileges to guard, traditions to keep going" (6). In reviving an epithet applied to, among others, Tomás de Torquemada (1420–98), the first grand inquisitor of Spain, Hardy scornfully dismisses the intransigent and stifling nature of orthodoxy that secures its continuity. The many scathing reviews of *Tess* had objected to several of its ideological heresies, including the lack of providence in the novel, the claim for Tess's "purity," and the presence of pagan inclinations in England. For example, R. H. Hutton, writing for *The Spectator,* argued against the intention he suspected Hardy had in writing the novel, namely, "to illustrate his conviction that not only is there no Providence guiding men and women in the right way, but that, in many cases at least, there is something like a malign fate." In contrast to the review in *The Bookman* which stated that the novel's "first aim is neither to upset nor to establish a system either of theology or ethics" (Lerner and Holmstrom 69; 74), the general tenor of the reviews reveals that the novel did in fact upset religious sensibilities and the "keeping" of traditions by imposing heretical views.

The reviews of *Tess* reveal religious conflict, the fundamental characteristic of heresy. Two competing ways of thinking converge, and a thorough orthodoxy must decide either to crush the upstart ideas or to adopt the new tenets. Through the convergence of Christian and pagan cultural values, *Tess* slyly turns this conflict onto itself in order to challenge tradition and generate a new mode of thought in its readers. In the same preface noted above, Hardy describes what we might call the "heresies" of the novel as the "shifting of positions," and he states that such "shiftings often begin in sentiment, and such sentiment sometimes begins in a novel" (6). While Hardy's statement not only implies a narrative intention to change the way people think, of more interest is its description of a "ritual of succession" performed by the novel and designed to influence the reception of its readerly horizons. The textual history or "phases" of Hardy's novel and new modes of interpretations such as New Historicism further illustrate the explicit use of ritual in *Tess* to produce the "shifting of positions." The myths and rituals of succession surrounding the Golden Bough structure several plot elements in *Tess,* and the novel invokes this contemporaneous anthropological material not only to show how things change, but also to perform and elicit change. *Tess of the d'Urbervilles*—sometimes the character, sometimes the novel—functions as *the* Golden Bough in the eponymous ritual that James Frazer delineates in his tome.

In his general conclusion (added to subsequent editions) to *The Golden Bough* (1890–1915), Frazer, with equanimity, puts his "search after truth" into a historical perspective that forecasts an inauspicious future for humanity while remaining enthusiastic about the process of "life" (GBA 824). Though he feels the progress of knowledge is inextricably bound to advances in science, Frazer acknowledges a doomed humanity that will not "have strength to speed afresh our slackening planet in its orbit or rekindle the dying fire of the sun." With dripping sagacity, he then develops a metaphor for seeing the history of thought as a "web woven of three different threads—the black thread of magic, the red thread of religion, and the white thread of science." Transitional moments between epochs show overlapping threads, and the fabric changes color over time as systems of thought supplant each other gradually. Frazer suggests that even science can be superseded and the "dreams of magic may one day be the waking realities of science" (GBA 826).

The idea of the succession of systems of thought is more important to understanding the relation between *Tess* and *The Golden Bough* than the recognition of cyclical or reproductive processes. As Frazer states in the preface to the first edition of *The Golden Bough* (1890), "[t]wo or three generations of literature may do more to change thought than two or three thousand years of traditional life" (GB viii). With *Tess*, Hardy wanted to be part of the process of changing thought. After he had received three successive rejections of the half-finished novel in the fall of 1889, and within a few months of the appearance of Frazer's work, he wrote "Candour in English Fiction" (January 1890) out of frustration with the tyrannical morality controlling serial publication.[7] Mary Jacobus reports that when Hardy returned to *Tess* "in the post-1889 phase of composition," the "first scenes to be written" follow the episode of Tess's and Angel's wedding night confessions, and that forced and inauthentic narrative intrusions symptomatize Hardy writing "under precisely the adverse conditions described by 'Candour in English Fiction'" (87–88). Hardy found that the late Victorian cultural context of serial publication made writers conform to prudery or face ruin, so an author often "can scarcely help . . . arranging a *denouement* which he [or she] knows to be indescribably unreal and meretricious, but dear to the Grundyist and subscriber" ("Candour" 130). In an attempt to make Tess more "pure," Hardy's emendations, Jacobus argues, "produced anomalies [such as the forced denouement] which the conventional moralists were quick to seize on when the novel finally appeared" (79). For instance, the review in *The Nation* stated that the novel "was well adapted to confuse judgment" (Lerner and Holmstrom 134).

The institutional forces at work in the publishing industry had forced Hardy once again to acknowledge the need to be subtle in promulgating his heresies. On January 1, 1892, he explained his compromise and the trivial textual inconsistencies in a letter to Frederick Harrison by revealing that the first draft of *Tess* "said much more on religion as apart from theology," but he "thought it might do more harm than good, and omitted the arguments, merely retaining the conclusions" (*Letters* 251). While Hardy may have repressed some of his religious arguments, the aftermath of Tess and

Angel's disastrous wedding and the manuscript changes in the novel reveal that he chose instead to convey his point through a figuration analogous to the myth of the Golden Bough, and that he went back and textured the previously composed narrative with corresponding elements. J. T. Laird reports that Hardy revised *Tess* between November 25, 1889, and the autumn of 1890, when he submitted an edited version for serial publication in *Graphic* (3–20).[8] *Graphic* published the edited version of *Tess* in twenty-four weekly installments from July to December of 1891. With the serialization of the novel finally secure, Hardy, as *The Early Life* reports, "spent a good deal of time in August and the autumn correcting *Tess of the d'Urbervilles* for its volume form" (F. Hardy 313). Within days of the first serialized installment of the novel, Hardy had finished reading *The Golden Bough*. The entry for July 7, 1891 in Hardy's *Literary Notebooks* documents his pointed reading notes on Frazer's work (45).

The intricate degree to which Hardy engages with the subject matter of *The Golden Bough* mandates that we remember Frazer's original aims in tackling his magisterial comparative survey of "Aryan" fertility rites. Frazer wanted to explain the custom of worshipping a slain god in terms of both the bloody ritual of succession to the priesthood of Diana and the associated legend of the Golden Bough that Aeneas plucked before his descent into the underworld. To paraphrase the legend, Frazer states that the sacred grove of Diana grew on the north shore of the lake of Nemi in Aricia, near Rome, and a priest who had achieved the title "King of the Wood" guarded a certain tree of which only a fugitive slave was allowed to hew a branch. If the slave broke off a bough, *the* Golden Bough according to antiquity, he could engage the reigning priest in battle and, if victorious, succeed to the throne of the King of the Wood. Though he does not discuss the role of the Golden Bough in *Tess*, Bruce Johnson compares Hardy's retrieval of the past with Frazer's analytical method. For example, Johnson states that "[w]e have lost the meaning" of the "murder of the priest in the grove," but "it can be recovered though penetration of the strata that comprise its particular formation and by a comparative mythology that aids that penetration" (259). *Tess* puts those findings to use as Hardy deploys the ritual for choosing a successor as a tool to capture and influence historical change. The ritual has appeal due to its pragmatic, diffuse, and varied nature. Indeed, Frazer explains the importance of beginning with an investigation of the rites of Diana's priesthood by stating that its rule of succession is not exceptional to Roman lore and actually appears dispersed throughout European culture. The centrality of vegetation to his study arises not for its own sake, but from the fact that trees, in particular, play a significant role in the various succession rites.

Unique in its presentation of a divinity suspended between heaven and earth, the myth of the Norse god Balder directly leads to Frazer's conclusion that the Golden Bough is mistletoe growing on a venerated oak. Balder, the son of Odin, prophetically dreamt of his own death, so all elements of nature were compelled to swear an oath against harming him. As Baler was too young to take a vow, mistletoe became his Achilles' heel. A trickster figure, Loki, subsequently taunted Balder's blind brother, Hother, into hurling some mistletoe at Balder, immediately killing him. To interpret the myth further, Frazer explains the mystical power attached to both mistletoe and oak trees in Druid lore. Thought to have fallen from the sky as a gift from the gods, mistletoe could function both as a panacea and as protection against fire and evil spirits as long as it never touched the humbling ground. Since mistletoe is evergreen, it was thought to give life to its host, the oak, traditionally seen as having divine blessing and power due to its proclivity to being struck by lightning. Mistletoe, in Frazer's reconstruction of the myth-makers' mindset, then became seen as a product of lightning. Through speculative substitution, Frazer concludes that the dying Balder personifies an oak whose life-giving mistletoe has been severed. Similarly, Frazer argues that the King of the Wood represented the oak and could be slain only by one of its own boughs. (In the novel, the once-revered d'Urbervilles were "made Knights o' the Royal Oak" [30]). Seeing mistletoe as interchangeable with the oak, Frazer accounts for the name of Aeneas's talisman by noting that primitive peoples believed mistletoe was the "tree of pure gold" and "shone with a golden splendour" because it gave life to the oak and emanated the "sun's fire" (GB 2: 365–68). Frazer later added the more natural explanation that mistletoe eventually changes from green to a "golden" color after being cut.

Embedded deeply in the heathen landscape of the novel, as I will explain, the ritual of succession concerning the King of the Wood and his talismanic weapon is at once a theme and a performance within the novel. Perhaps the "phases" of the novel most overtly illustrate this dual role of the pagan ritual cast as a motif of succession. In the Explanatory Note to the First Edition, Hardy hints at a profound temporal order in describing the novel as "an attempt to give artistic form to a true sequence of things" (3). Each section, or "phase," of the novel conveys the sense of primordial order at work, and the narrative develops a corresponding set of scenes, crucial to the plot, that suggest the problematic continuity of an ineffable "essence" beneath changing outward appearances. After Tess's violation by Alec, the narrative describes her as "the same, but not the same" (125). The narrative complication of this issue during Tess's and Angel's mutual confessions on their wedding night actually repeats the same question. In Angel's mind, Tess's confession makes her "another" person than the "woman" he had "been loving" (325). In her defense, Tess exclaims that their sordid stories are "just the same" (318), that she is still her "very self," and that what Angel is angry at is in his "own mind," "not in" her (325–29).

During these significant, suggestive philosophical moments, the narrative points to a buried cliché that history repeats itself with a difference. In the midst of transitional, historical moments, the values of the novel appear obscurely as, for example, the allusion to the "vague ethical being" which Tess "could not classify definitely as the God of her childhood, and could not comprehend as any other" (121). Hardy overtly structures the plot of *Tess* in terms of succession, but he is not candid about how he uses a pagan ritual to effect change, or with what values he exactly invests paganism. Sometimes patriarchy in general bears the brunt of the narrative attack as it points to the "wise" idea from *Hamlet* to "exclaim against [patriarchy's] own succession" (238–39), or as in the statement that the d'Urbervilles are "extinct in the male line" (16). But a matriarchal worldview is at best an indirect value of the novel. Often of more importance is the narrative concern with the possibility that the "old order changeth" (493). As a result, the reviews of the novel often capture the threat to orthodoxy posed by the novel without fully discerning what constitutes its heresies. W. P. Trent, of *The Sewanee Review,* described *Tess* as a "novel with a purpose," and Mrs. Oliphant in *Blackwood's Magazine* "objected to being instructed by the novel." However, the reviews remain unclear about the nature of the instruction other than, as Clementina Black noted in *The Illustrated London News,* the novel "disturbs" the "conventional reader" by presenting an "open challenge" to the "traditional pattern of right and wrong" (R. G. Cox 232; 203; 186). In contrast to the prominent heresies surrounding the sacraments of baptism, confirmation, and marriage, the deeper, subtler structuring device used to "shift positions" bypasses the censorious eyes of orthodoxy. The humbling, geocentric associations implied by the narrative function of the pagan ritual appear simply as results.

As the novel comments explicitly on the attempt to syncretize paganism and Christianity, *Tess* anticipates a clerical debate over the modernist heresy. The modernists, in their most fundamental characteristic, tried to reclaim the apparent aspects of "becoming" that the world unfolds, and assimilate these ephemera with the static tenets of orthodoxy. In *Tess,* the parson, "a new-comer" to the parish, embodies the synthesis characteristic of modernism in his "ten years of endeavor to graft historical belief on actual skepticism." Struggling with this inner turmoil, the clergyman yields to his "nobler impulses" and tells Tess that, yes, both the baptism and burial she performs for her child "will be just the same" as if he had conducted them. Hardy satirically points out how a modernist sensibility in a clergyman can be seen as untenable by lay as well as clerical eyes: "How the Vicar reconciled his answer with the strict notions he supposed himself to hold on these subjects it is beyond a layman's power to tell, though not to excuse" (135–37). As Jesus had bestowed priestly powers on his disciples, the vicar ordains Tess, and on both linguistic and ideological levels, the novel constructs Tess as a priestess of her own sect. As the central heresy of the novel, a pagan sensibility arises from a narrative that intrinsically links Tess, language, the land, and "essence" through rituals associated with the Golden Bough.

During the scene early in the novel when Angel Clare encounters Tess for the first time, the failure to harmonize pagan and Christian belief systems becomes a controlling theme of the novel. While Tess performs in a May Day Cerealia, her demure charm rises to claim Angel from his clerical-minded brothers who want to continue reading *A Counterblast to Agnosticism*.[9] Nevertheless, Angel is drawn to the jubilant atmosphere of the dancing nubile women. Angel does dance with a few of the women but overlooks Tess until the moment he has to leave. From this opening moment of frustration between the future lovers, the novel constructs Angel as a nonbeliever who initially retains Christian morals despite his loss of faith. The pagan and "natural" elements of Tess draw Angel near, but he does not recognize an alternative set of values regarding egalitarian love and premarital sex until they have grown estranged.

Angel does eventually change his values, though, and his "enlightenment" on hearing the "sublimed" remarks of "the large-minded stranger" in Brazil testifies to the power the novel invests in words (464). In another striking example, Alec d'Urberville recants his recent evangelism after hearing (decorously unnarrated for the genteel reader) Tess's "negations" of Christianity drawn from Angel's "merciless," objective "species of thinking" (439). The narrative states: "Tess's words, as echoed from Angel Clare, had made a deep impression upon him, and continued to do so after he had left her" (443). By extension of this power in words to change thought, the novel uses a ritual involving choosing a successor—a lingering layer of the past—with the idea in mind that repetition with a difference may disturb and change minds. Although the ritual of the Golden Bough may be a vacuous superstition, it may also have efficacy. From the large-scale "phases" of the novel to specific instances of revision, the novel cultivates a theme of supplantation woven into its structure and style. By understanding the metaphorical language attached to the ritual of the Golden Bough, readers can see how the novel includes an example of Mark Schorer's "analogical matrix," which suggests "experiences of meaning and of feeling that may be involved in novels, and responsibilities for their style which novelists themselves may forget" (24). In large part, a rite analogous to the Golden Bough develops the theme and defines the style of *Tess* and its conceptual understanding of a "true sequence of things." As Schorer states, "style *is* conception," and metaphorical language can show "us what conceptions the imagination behind that work is able to entertain" (45). One central analogy in the novel substitutes discourse for ritual, and through the power of words, the narrative voice suggests that education is possible beyond but through the landscape of a pagan world: "It was probable that, in the lapse of ages, improved systems of moral and intellectual training would appreciably, perhaps considerably, elevate the involuntary, and even the unconscious, instincts of human nature" (236).

With the ambiguously auspicious beginning when John Durbeyfield learns of his "descent from Sir Pagan d'Urberville" (14), Hardy had first put forth the theme of a latent pagan past that surfaces now and then to structure the course of the novel. In these moments, *Tess* picks up the thread of *The Mayor of Casterbridge* and *The Woodlanders* in that Hardy continues to use primitive rituals to portray an atavistic combat that increasingly fails to regenerate agricultural fecundity. The existence of paganism in *Tess* has been established by many earlier critics.[10] For instance, Charlotte Bonica points out the common desire of Hardy's later characters to search for "a system of value capable of replacing the traditional orthodoxies that no longer satisfy them" (849). Such a view can still elicit condemnation, for she claims that paganism "is nevertheless based on the impossible premise that the natural world can function as a source of human value" (852). Though using natural selection as a basis for political economy has implications antithetical to the basis of civilization, social Darwinism has in fact become a crucial defense for capitalism and the anti-welfare state. For less politically charged issues, nature has functioned as the basis for seasonal feasts, codes of environmental ethics, and physical laws influencing customs, science, and legislation. On the other hand, Bruce Johnson argues that the novel valorizes Tess's view of paganism while critiquing Angel's view of her associations with nature. Johnson states: "Hardy seems to associate the ability to be in touch with primeval, pagan meanings with the ability to be in touch with the emotional, primitive sources of one's own being" (261). Angel's view of Tess is disturbing because it enshrines and essentializes her, but this perspective does not necessarily divest the novel of placing a high value on nature or of having other variant portrayals of nature. To argue her point, Bonica distorts Johnson's numerous illustrations of how Hardy, Tess, and the novel do derive value from nature. Her critique confuses the idea of nature having an inherent morality with the possibility of nature being a source of value. Though nature is relatively powerless in conflict with civilization, this certainly does not mean its mechanisms, laws, and role in life are wrong or can be dismissed. The novel uses a pagan ritual as a means to draw attention to "this world" while avoiding any mythical elements associated with pagan spirituality.

More recently, Catherine Gallagher argues, in an explicit demonstration of New Historicism, that the novel needs to be read in the context of a late nineteenth-century fascination with comparative mythology and fertility rites. Also noting the influence of Pater and Robertson Smith, Gallagher addresses Hardy's implicit dialogue with Frazer's *The Golden Bough* and its persistent argument that the origin of civilization is inseparable from rituals promoting fecundity. She illustrates how the "lost rituals" surrounding Artemis and Diana "stand aloof from the plot" because "formal disconnections" imply that "archaic sacrificial urges survive" in "the acts of reading and writing novels" (429–30).[11] Gallagher's detailed attention both to Angel's allusion to Tess as Artemis and to the sacrificial undertones of the rape scene occupies the body of her argument; consequently, she neglects discussing Artemis' Roman counterpart, Diana, and the ritual perpetuating her priesthood. Though Gallagher finds that allusions to sacrificial rituals cue "the reader to look beneath [the plot] for a level of explanation that is not in the story we are reading," she misses the function of the Golden Bough, one of the "ritual possibilities" conjured "without naming them" (430–31). The possibilities raised by the dialogic exchange between the novel and *The Golden Bough* go unnamed, but the important point is that there are possibilities for alternative modes of thought and for change. Still, Gallagher skillfully shows how a ritual of sacrificing a supposed virgin is performed by discourse in the novel. She is less thorough in explaining *why* it does so. Wanting to see the novel "at cross-purposes with itself," she sees the ritual in the novel "as nothing more than a particularly intense instant in a rather dismal reproductive cycle" (439). She points to Tess's somberness in thinking about history: "what's the use of learning that I am one of a long row only—finding out that there is set down in some old book somebody just like me, and to know that I shall only act her part" (180). Tess's "dismal" view, what Angel calls the "ache of modernism" (177), is related for Gallagher to "the mere 'sadness'—or pessimism—produced by the historically minded paganizers of the late nineteenth century" (438–39). Still, "dismal," "mere," and "pessimism" are evaluative judgments that at least some modernist "paganizers" might not have held. Additionally, someone historically minded would be less concerned with the emotional effect of discussing a pagan past or the cycles of nature than his or her "truth" claim.

As Laird and Gallagher have shown, *Tess* and *The Golden Bough* share a dialogic exchange in many intricate and structural ways. This exchange must have begun in the post-1889 composition history of the novel after Hardy became familiar with Frazer's work, and at the time when he was pondering Tess and Angel's postnuptial future. The immediate repercussions of Angel's rejection of Tess most dramatically reflect the influence of *The Golden Bough* in the episode concerning the mistletoe. From this moment on, the novel activates rites analogous to those of the King of the Wood delineated in Frazer's book in an attempt to effect a change in cultural and intellectual thought. *Tess* performs a pagan ritual not necessarily to retrieve a pagan sensibility but to weave all of the alternative threads into its contextual scientific and religious fabric. As the narrative voice states, "Such supplanting was to be" (206). The double grammar of this fatalistic statement connotes both a comment on destiny and a metaphysical principle.

If the Golden Bough *is* mistletoe, the discourse surrounding the parasitic evergreen in the novel not only performs analogous elements of the pertinent myths and rituals, but it also uses the performance to supplant the old ideological associations. The narrative employs the ritual of succession against itself in order to elicit a new way of thinking by shifting the values of its component parts, and Hardy's change in calling the sections of the novel "phase[s]," instead of the original "book[s]" (Laird 6), connotes growth and supplantment as if the narrative were a form of metamorphosis. The composition history of the novel accentuates this affinity. As J. Hillis Miller states in *Fiction and Repetition,* the novel "is a story about repetition" without "some single accounting cause"; and the "relation among the links in a chain of meanings in *Tess of the d'Urbervilles* is always repetition with a difference, and the difference is as important as the repetition" (115; 141; 128). The phases of a metamorphic narrative such as the ritual of the Golden Bough repeat themselves with a difference.

On the other hand, the discursive exchange between the novel and the Balder myth (along with the manuscript changes and Hardy's narrative compromises) suggests that Tess suffers an agonistic performance of the ritual designed to reflect back on the function of discourse in the novel and effect change in readerly horizons. In effect, Hardy inscribes Tess in a religious discourse like the sign-painter whose scriptural graffiti on the stile inculpates her; he then leaves, like the sign-painter once again, the inscription's "application to the hearts of the people who read 'em" (113). However, Hardy also leaves outlines in the narrative that accentuate the idea that religion consistently evolves, and that part of this effect is due to forward-minded thinkers unfit for their generation. To participate in this evolution, the novel uses the Balder myth for reasons similar to those behind Alec d'Urberville's hiring of the sign-painter: "to paint these reminders [so] that no means might be left untried which might move the hearts of a wicked generation" (426). Hardy had *The Golden Bough* ready at hand and would not leave a stone unturned that might "shift positions." Words in the novel "are meant to be," like the sign-painter's, "[c]rushing, killing" (113). Repeatedly, the narrative underscores the susceptibility of religion to historical change, "creeds being transient" (331). For example, Tess can discern the incongruity of Alec's conversion since "animalism" could "become fanaticism; Paganism Paulism" (420). Old Lady Day can become Lady Day, or the Annunciation, and expose the arbitrariness of certain holy feasts (392). The narrative voice also states that some readers may respond to the sign-painter's accusatory scrawl by crying out "'Alas, poor Theology!' at the hideous defacement—the last grotesque *phase* of a creed which had served mankind well in its time" (113, emphasis added). Readers relate to ritual discourse in the novel in a manner similar to Balder's symbiosis with the mistletoe, through a mutually constitutive element that undergoes successive changes over the course of history. For Balder, divinity and the oak are interchangeable—for Tess and her readers, being and language. This narratological heresy draws from Frazer's conflation of Balder, the mistletoe, and the oak to offer its own parallel associations between Tess, language, and being.

First, though, the old ritual must be enacted. For his honeymoon with Tess in a farmhouse formerly of the d'Urberville estate, Angel had painstakingly secured some mistletoe in secret. When "they shopped as partners in one concern" on "Christmas Eve, with its loads of holly and mistletoe" (294), the *one* concern for Angel is the procurement of the mistletoe. While the narrative does not explicitly state the reasons for his actions, the mistletoe represents for Angel his consummation with and possession of Tess, a woman he considers a pagan and a "daughter of the soil" (180). The phrase, "with its holly and mistletoe," is a late addition to the text, one that explains when and where Angel bought his surprise gift and its understated presence prior to the wedding (Hardy, *Archive* 278). More importantly, the insertion pointedly reveals Hardy's late engagement with *The Golden Bough* and his desire to employ its central myth. After the purchase of the talisman, Angel dreams of fighting the man who had insulted Tess at market, and he wrestles in his sleep with the portmanteau carrying the plant (294–96). He presumably had just packed the mistletoe in the portmanteau. In a displacement of his role in the myth, Angel dreams of struggling to become King of the Wood and the high priest of his Diana. After the wedding, he is "glad" to see the arrival of this luggage at the farmhouse, and the added inference is that his satisfaction derives from now being able to hang the mistletoe above their bed (313–15). In sliding "the massive oak bar" (another recursive addition to the manuscript) across the door to the farmhouse (315), Angel proceeds with his ritual performance that he probably feels would (if he were a believer) sanctify and ensure fertility on the night of his wedding to a perceived virgin.

After Tess's disastrous confession and Angel's inability to see beyond his double standard, Tess, with the reader, can piece together "the explanation of that mysterious parcel" in the luggage when she finally sees the "bough of mistletoe" above their bed. Angel had not explained the contents of the package to her, "saying that time would soon show her the purpose thereof" (331). Like Balder, she feels intimations of her own mortality in the parasite—"forgot existence"—and thinks of suicide (332). However, as the narrative voice remarks how "foolish and inopportune that mistletoe looked now" (331), the time is not ripe for the ritual sacrifice. The mistletoe has not yet faded and become golden. At work here is Gallagher's notion of ritual "standing aloof from plot" and creating "formal disconnections." Schorer adds further illumination in stating that in straining "toward symbolism" metaphorical language "can even be counterposed to dramatic structure" (44). The mistletoe appears "foolish" and "inopportune" because of the break in plot created by the performance of the ritual. Hardy's additions to the text accentuate the narrative discontinuity. The irony multiplies in realizing that the emendations added concerning a "changing of the guard" are designed to create a new storyline about stories. When Tess later confesses to Angel her thoughts of self-destruction under the mistletoe, she states her belief that by her own hand she cannot set Angel "free" and tells him that he is the one "who ought to strike the blow" (338). Tidying up business at the farmhouse later, Angel synecdochically kills his former image of Tess: "The mistletoe hung under the tester just as he had placed it. Having been there three or four weeks it was *turning colour,* and the leaves and berries were wrinkled. Angel took it down, and crushed it into the grate. Standing there he for the first time doubted whether his course in this conjecture had been a wise, much less a generous one. But had he not been cruelly blinded?" (372, emphasis added). Here the mistletoe has become the Golden Bough in its dying splendor, and Angel the blind murdering brother of Balder.

Angel has tried to become a priest of his Diana, and, in placing her in "the empty stone coffin of an abbot" during the sleepwalking episode (350), he has tried to make her an abbess, a gesture that feminizes a patriarchal religion (abbot <Aram. *abba*, "father"). To persuade Angel to return to the farmhouse, Tess whispers the suggestion in his ear, and he "unresistingly acquiesced," after which his dream "seemed to enter on a new *phase*, wherein he fancied she had risen as a spirit, and was leading him to heaven" (351, emphasis added). However, each of these supplanting options ignores what Tess considers herself to be. While she retains much of both her Christian and pagan heritages, Tess does not "believe in anything supernatural" (438). Rather, in beginning her first sojourn in the "uplands and lowlands of Egdon," Tess "felt akin to the landscape" (146–47). Anticipatory of Heidegger's notion of *Dasein,* the novel emphasizes the relative consciousness of Tess, whose concern is the present, for "through her existence all her fellow-creatures existed, to her" (221). Tess's religion is tied to the land—in Hardy's world, the Heath. As a dairymaid or "field-woman," she is "a portion of the field" (124). After Tess's loss of innocence when "she could come to church no more," she would venture into "the woods" where "she seemed least solitary" (120). In these mystical moments, the narrative stresses the idea that the world is what we make it. Though Tess's "whimsical fancy would intensify natural processes around her till they seemed a part of her own story," the didactic narrative voice declares that "they became a part of it" since "the world is only a psychological phenomenon, and what they seemed they were" (121). This phenomenological view rubs against the ontological bulk of the novel, but it is used here to suggest that the world, in part, is vulnerable to linguistic manipulation.

While Hardy certainly does essentialize Tess, the novel also implies a common synthesis for all of humanity. To this end, the narrative uses trees to mark the outline and import of Egdon Heath, the locale of the "rally" phase of the novel, where Tess is most happy and the idyllic "world was drawn to a larger pattern" (148). The larger narrative pattern of the novel draws connections between humanity and natural cycles through its use of myth, etymology, and an arboreal allegory. For instance, during their blissful idyll, Tess and Angel "passed the leafy time, when arborescence seems to be the one thing aimed at out-of-doors," and the narrative voice then compares Tess to a tree: "She was, for one thing, physically and mentally suited among these new surroundings. The sapling which had rooted down to a poisonous stratum on the spot of its sowing had been transplanted to a deeper soil" (183–84). At the end of "Phase the Second," Tess wonders if "any strange good thing" might come with her arrival in Egdon Heath, "her ancestral land." She feels the irrepressible hope of youth, and "some spirit within her rose automatically as the sap in the twigs" (141). However, throughout the novel, trees signify the life of the land, rather than the divinity of a heavenly spirit. The novel changes the valence of the divine role of trees in Frazer's study of vegetation rites.

Rooted in the ground, trees and Tess both reflect Hardy's call to pay more attention to the concerns of this world. The narrative foregrounds this ethos most literally when the abandoned Tess walks toward her seasonal appointment on a tenant farm and encounters the man who had insulted her at market. To escape him and her past, Tess plunges behind "the foliage of some holly bushes" and buries "her hunted soul" beneath "the dead leaves." Enacting the traditional role of some fallen mistletoe beside its holly, Tess acutely feels her humbled position and contrasts this with "a most inadequate thought for modern days": "All is vanity." As a form of hewn mistletoe analogous to that in the myth of the Golden Bough, she can recognize the successive advance of thought: "Solomon had thought as far as that more than two thousand years ago: she herself, though not in the van of thinkers, had got much further" (384). Since she feels that "[a]ll was, alas, worse than vanity—injustice, punishment, exaction, death," Tess identifies with her "kindred sufferers," the shot pheasants, and considers herself "outside humanity" (384–86). In this light, her "pantheistic" "essence" (247) is similar to Balder's relation to the mistletoe. In 1890, Frazer had found that the mistletoe made Balder "a being whose life is thus, in a sense, outside himself," and which "must be strange to many readers, and has, indeed, not yet been recognised in its full" (GB 2: 296).

Tess similarly estranged its readers through its new conception of natural relations. In euthanizing the dying pheasants falling from "thick boughs" to the ground, Tess, whose career at the d'Urberville estate entailed caring for fowls, first confronts those who "destroy life," singularly characterized as "tenant-farmers, the natural enemies of tree, bush, and brake" (385–89). The pheasants had tried to escape the dreary, hunted landscape where there "was not a tree within sight" (392). In these moments, Tess not only participates in a pagan form of renewal but actually functions as the Golden Bough itself. Tess's self-burial most dramatically symbolizes and transforms the Golden Bough's position between heaven and earth when she yearns to lose the ideological inheritance of her avatars by bringing them down to earth.

Tess's linguistic associations, however, have been rooted in the novel since the dance scene when she is first introduced. The May Day "Cerealia" dance, a revision of a "traditional rite," is an example of how "some old customs of their [the forests'] shades remain" "only in a metamorphosed or disguised form" such as this "guise of the club-revel, or 'club-walking'" (20). Like the reader, Angel first encounters Tess dressed in pagan garb, though his brothers are afraid to be seen with "a troop of country hoydens" (24). From this initial description of Tess, Hardy linguistically identifies her with forests and the land, for "hoyden" derives from the same Indo-European root, *kaito-, "forest, uncultivated land," that lies fallow in "heathen" and "heath." "Hoyden" is also an emendation (of "girls") to the manuscript, suggesting that Hardy further cultivated Tess's ties to the forest in the process of revision. In the same opening scene, Hardy also describes the dialect of Tess's people: "the characteristic intonation of that dialect, for this district, being the voicing approximately rendered by the syllable UR, probably as rich an utterance as any to be found in human speech" (23). In addition to being embedded in the title of the novel, the utterance is particularly rich for purposes here because, in the Druidic tree alphabet, the equivalent to our "u," "Ur," is represented by the low-growing evergreen shrub, heather.[12]

An arboreal allegory continues when Tess goes to "claim kin" (37) from the new d'Urbervilles who have bought her ancestral name. The newness is brought home to her by the disparity between the d'Urberville estate of "recent erection" and "The Chase—a truly venerable tract of forest land; one of the few remaining woodlands in England of undoubted primæval date, wherein Druidical mistletoe was still found on aged oaks." The "sylvan antiquity," however, "was outside the immediate boundaries of the estate." Though Simon Stoke-d'Urberville constructed "his family tree on the new basis," the narrative points out that "a family name came by nature" and that these d'Urbervilles were not any more "of the true tree" than anyone else (50–52). The last instance of the word "tree" is a change from "stock" in the manuscript. In November 1891 when Hardy turned to publish *Tess* in novel form, he further accentuated the arboreal allegory in the book by referring to the book itself as a tree. In the Explanatory Note to the First Edition, he thanks the editors for enabling him "to piece the trunk and limbs of the novel together, and print it complete" (3). The limbs now sprout mistletoe. As a whole, the novel develops several fundamental conceptions around the image and associations of trees. Even the "ache of modernism" that Angel attributes to Tess originates in her response to the sylvan surroundings. She states that the "trees have inquisitive eyes," and their foreboding nature causes her to feel the seriousness of life and a deep angst. The trees represent the encroaching, successive "numbers of to-morrows just all in a line" (177). In its description of the ache of modernism, the novel links trees with succession, and though the ritual of the Golden Bough drives the changing of values in the novel, the trees themselves persist. In Hardy's dendrological world, such variants as "evergreen oaks" dominate the landscape and the final image as they partially "disguised" Tess's gallows' pole (542).

"Druid," "tree," "true," and "endure" all come from the I.E. root *deru, but, while *Tess* points to a truth in trees that endures, the novel does so to establish a link between language and being, not to posit any absolute truths beyond this fundamental connection. As John Paul Riquelme has shown, the echoes of "ur" and "murmur" throughout the novel equally serve to deconstruct "conventional structures of adult understanding, including grammar and logic" (513). Though Riquelme does not address how the novel describes the environmental import of "the syllable UR," he shows how "Tess d'*Urber*ville murmurs" (512) to create an indeterminacy in the novel that is exemplified by the opposing centripetal and centrifugal vectors of the last two chapters. The centripetal force leads Angel and Tess to Stonehenge where as a "heathen" she feels "at home" (536); the centrifugal drive is exemplified by Angel and Liza-Lu leaving Tess's hanging and, in my mind, by the reader recoiling from the modern world that condemns her and the sanctity of the natural world.

Tess is a dismal story, and the reader wrenches in despair as Tess suffers rape, the imposition of Angel's double standard, and the refusal of her author to destine her to anything except hanging. While the understanding that the novel performs a pagan ritual may let Hardy partially off the hook ("self-sacrificing" Tess must be sacrificed), her fate also suggests the idea that the modern world cannot yet abide her. In the following passage, the narrative ascribes fundamental change to bodily sacrifice: "the break of continuity between her earlier and present existence, which she had hoped for, had not after all taken place. Bygones would never be complete bygones till she was a bygone herself" (421). In this logic of ritual sacrifice, we might understand the disturbing appearance of Liza-Lu at the end of the novel as a "spiritualized image of Tess" as she becomes Tess's successor (541). In moments such as these, the narrative functions like the Golden Bough. Tess must die with the novel, by the novel, so new, more tolerant narratives can be born. Tess continues the legacy of heretics such as Bruno who suffered martyrdom for the cause of a grand inclusive synthesis. Through an evolving discursive process, Hardy's novel constructs language and being as mutually constitutive and suggests that being persists through natural cycles and the horizons of readers. To answer Tess's question, the use of learning about rituals and the past is not to recognize oneself as mindlessly homogenized by history, but to understand and participate in the process of how things change.

Chapter 6

Fictions, Figurative Heresy, and the Roots of English

THE FASCINATION WITH etymology evinced by the work of Pater and Hardy exploded during the span from late Victoriana to High Modernism. While there was certainly a "curiosity" about the "truths" that "endure," philology also presented language as the vessel carrying the record of historical change. Monumental studies quickly followed on the heels of each other from Walter Skeat's *Etymological Dictionary* (1879–82) to Ernest Weekley's *The Romance of Words* (1912) to Otto Jesperson's *Language: Its Nature, Development and Origin* (1922) to the *OED* in its many fascicles from 1884 to 1928. With such rich glosses ready at hand, the modernist literary experiments with myth and religion often drew attention to the linguistic root or history of a word in order to compel close analysis and exploit the dependence of knowledge and being on language. Etymology explores the ruptures in signification that a word can display diachronically, though the discipline also evokes a centripetal drive for original wholeness and primordial synthesis. However, the search for integral words always ends, at best, in a speculative, reconstructed root. Such studies reveal the multiple and vexed origins that certain words have and, more importantly, how words themselves become the site at which issues of power are decided. For many of the literary modernists, the Word, by inference, became no longer either implicitly divine or immune from the processes of history. At the end of this chapter, a brief analysis investigates how two major modernist texts responded to these developments. T. S. Eliot's *The Waste Land* (1922) and E. M. Forster's *A Passage to India* (1924) both play comparative religion and the shared origins of Indo-European languages off each other for very different ends. While Forster's work continues the Edwardian legacy of synthesis, Eliot's work demonstrates the turn toward authoritarian traditional choices.

The early twentieth century also saw the birth of modern structural linguistics with Saussure's *Course on General Linguistics* (1916). While Saussure was teaching this course in Geneva, C. K. Ogden began his forays into semantics while establishing the notoriety of the Heretics Society. He ventured into a correspondence with Lady Welby and used her theory of "Significs" as a starting point for his own thoughts on language. Welby also sent off her famous letters regarding signification to Charles Peirce. Hans Vaihinger published his *Philosophy of "As If"* (1911) in which he argues with the buttress of Kant's *Critiques* that most forms of knowledge arise from the willing acceptance of "fictions" by humanity. Later in this chapter, the construction of an "aesthetic fiction" of the sublime (to use Vaihinger's phrase) can be seen at work in D. H. Lawrence's *The Rainbow* (1915). The early 1920s saw further semiotic developments in Wittgenstein's *Tractatus* (1921) and Ogden and I. A. Richards's collaboration on *The Meaning of Meaning* (1923). By 1924, Ogden had translated both Wittgenstein's and Vaihinger's work as he began to use Jeremy Bentham's "Theory of Fictions" as an apparatus for devising Basic English. These issues are discussed in greater detail in the afterword where *Finnegans Wake* and *Nineteen Eighty-Four* represent two opposing trajectories of the development of this flurry of linguistic thought.

Amid the postwar fervor for all things English, Richards became one of the first professors in Cambridge's newly launched School of English. The Great War also had dealt a death blow to faith in nonbelievers' minds, and, while also an active Cambridge Heretic, Richards began promoting the study of literature as "capable of saving us" since it is "a perfectly possible means of overcoming chaos" (*Science* 82–83). In Richards's mind, poetry provides the grandest example of the organization of complex and competing impulses, and it could therefore serve as a bulwark against the fragmentation rampant in modern society. The refinement of analytical skills in organization would then transfer into everyday life. F. R. Leavis became one of the first students in the School of English, and his textual mode of criticism evaluated literature for its moral character and promotion of humanity. His wife, Q. D. Leavis, would note later that reading literature can be described as the "desire to obtain assistance in the business of living, formerly the function of religion" (69). Such was the turn of the study of literature in the 1920s, and the Cambridge Clark Lectures and Heretics Society both participated in this amalgamation of humanitarian and textual approaches. For example, Charles Percy Sanger addressed the Society with his seminal piece of criticism, "The Structure of *Wuthering Heights*" (1926).

As the discipline of English literature germinated in the 1920s, the critical focus on the formal elements of a literary work eventually complied with the religious orthodoxies behind much of New Criticism, the praxis of which sought to harness the sway toward religious disavowal potentially elicited by reading. At the forefront, Cleanth Brooks declared that "poems never contain abstract statements" since their meaning "cannot be divorced from the [dramatic] context in which they are embedded." The aim of the poet, in his mind, is to dramatize intricately "the total situation" so that "it is no longer a question of our beliefs, but of our participation in the poetic experience" ("Irony" 801; 806). The effect of this view of criticism can be to derail the capacity of literature to change the way people think, since, as Brooks claimed in "The Problem of Belief and The Problem of Cognition" (1947), even in understanding the poetic experience the reader "is not asked to give up his own meanings or beliefs or to adopt permanently those of the poet" (*Urn* 226). As in his critique of the "heresy of paraphrase," Brooks believes that the poetic experience should not be translated into everyday words or situations.

Though Brooks made these statements in the 1940s, they owe much to Richards's work on what he interchangeably terms the "equilibrium" or "synthesis" within literature in his forays into literary criticism during the 1920s. For Richards, "poetry of inclusion" synthesizes a manifold variety of oppositions (e.g., self and society, subject and object), and tragedy best exemplifies the perfect culmination of this wholeness. Oscillating between the creation of pity and terror, classical tragedy effects a catharsis that confronts the spectator with the dissonances of "life." In Richards's view, the best tragedies are firmly rooted in secular affairs, and he claimed that the "least touch of theology which has a compensating Heaven to offer the tragic hero is fatal" (*Principles* 246).

While an Honorary Member of the Heretics Society, Richards established a methodology for analyzing poetry of "inclusion" and "synthesis" in the landmark *Principles of Literary Criticism* (1925). Brooks builds on Richards's argument that poetry generally is not conducive to verifying statements of belief, and he aligns Richards's work with T. S. Eliot's test for the validity of a poetic statement, one which makes all statements the result of dramatic situations, and therefore irrelevant to evaluation by independent belief systems ("Irony" 801). However, Brooks had appropriated Richards's methodology for his own purposes, to argue that a principle of poetic unity precludes all discussion of belief. In fact, in his *Principles*, Richards hopes "we can devise a more adaptable morality" (57), and the last chapter, "Poetry and Beliefs," constitutes a veiled deconstruction of religious beliefs. His heretical leanings are so subtle, though, that they are easily appropriated by an orthodox view.

In "Poetry and Beliefs," Richards distinguishes between scientific and emotive belief, and, since poetry generally consists of emotive statements, "only the very foolish would think of attempting to verify [them]" (272). The foolish are those who believe literature can create an absolute foundation for religious belief. On the other hand, Richards does believe that poetic statements, such as those of Leopold Bloom noted earlier, can be verified by scientific truths "such as the laws of thermodynamics" and therefore can be "brought into connection with what else we know" (285). He argues that "certain highly complex and very special combinations" of references in verse "can be either true or false" if they "correspond to the ways in which things actually hang together" (272). Scientific beliefs hold true in all contexts, whereas "revelation doctrines," to mention his chief example, are emotive, depend on dramatic situations, and "will readily attach themselves [as Ellmann notes] to almost any reference, distorting it to suit their purpose." Richards wants to distinguish between "beliefs which are grounded in fact" and those "which are due to other causes, and merely attach themselves to such references as will support them." Dramatic situations often create a series of relations which are conducive to religious beliefs, but a sincere modern intellectual cannot make religion cohere because of the "break-down of traditional accounts of the universe" (279–81). Brooks turns the fruits of Richards's methodology into the unilateral conclusion that poetry does not state independent propositions because they are part of a dramatic situation. In fact, Richards does imply that religious belief cannot attach itself to scientific truths expressed in verse, but those same truths can conversely debunk a religious view. This critique is buried in the last few subtle pages of *Principles of Literary Criticism*. Heresy underwrites the origins of New Criticism, the haven of orthodoxy.

In noting the traditional view that the arts convey a mystical sense of beauty, Richards explains how emotive relations in art create beliefs in such "Eternal Absolute Values" (286). These values remain solely emotive, though, and he cites two examples of analysis which beg the question in reviving them. In *The Necessity of Art* (1924), Percy Dearmer argues: "[h]uman speech bears constant witness to the universal conviction that Goodness is beautiful, that Beauty is good, that Truth is Beauty. We can hardly avoid the use of the word 'trinity,' and if we are theists at all we cannot but say that they are one because they are the manifestation of one God. If we are not theists, there is no explanation" (180). Richards then cites another example of a critic inserting "God," "the greatest of all emotive words," into the trinity of truth, beauty, and goodness. Though Richards refrains from the "easy," "wrong approach" which finds "such utterances 'meaningless,'" he equally cautions against mistaking "the incitement of an attitude for a statement of fact." He does believe in positing some interpretive propositions, though, and he closes his study with a jibe at Dearmer's claim that "[i]f we are not theists, there is no explanation"; Richards states, "after all there *is* another explanation, which would long ago have been quietly established to the world's great good had men been less ready to sacrifice the integrity of their thought and feeling for the sake of a local and limited advantage" (286–87). If we are not theists, Richards implies, the world would become a better place since the belief in God may result in political advantage at the expense of intellectual integrity.

Richards's critique of "belief" in literature not only reveals a decided heterodoxy below a seminal account of literary criticism, but also establishes a methodology for understanding the synthetic heresies embedded in its contemporaneous literary structures and forms. As a modernist critic, Richards exemplifies the common desire to come to terms with the incommensurability of orthodox Christianity and developments in scientific and historical analysis. As several critics have noted, his analysis of the combination of references in a literary work also parallels that of the Russian Formalists, and anticipates the reading strategies posited by Wolfgang Iser. Each critical school allows for the reader to become estranged by the unique combination of traditional discourses in a text. In *Principles* and even more so in *Practical Criticism* (1929), Richards empowers the reader with the authority to determine the authenticity and sincerity of events and ideas presented in a text. The equipose in a reader's mind generated by poetry of synthesis becomes a substitute religion. For Iser, the "repertoire" of the reader enables the recognition of gaps in a text which then defamiliarize conventional codes of reference and transform the reader's belief system. It is a small step to link these close reading strategies with the discourse history and ideology of a literary text's structural elements. The repertoire of a reader can include historical and political analysis, and, as etymology shows, even each word has a history too.

The informed reader is one who will not ignore the political implications of a text, and, as Jonathan Culler argues, criticism has been remiss in discussing one specific political dimension of literature, its presentation of religion. Culler argues that "an uncriticized religious discourse helps to legitimate a variety of repressive and reactionary movements," and that "the teaching and criticism of literature may work to legitimize religious discourse and strengthen its political power rather than to foster a critique of religion and religious authoritarianism" (71). The advent of New Criticism, veiling its orthodoxy, and the previous neglect of the innumerable modernist heresies discussed herein testify to Culler's point. In short, if we are honest and thorough in literary criticism, religiosity in literature must be debated. Modernism is a boon to such a study, for intellectuals from all schools hotly contested religious issues, and literary writers often composed synthetic heresies in a constructive manner through the complex formal combination of Christian and pagan elements. Texts such as Pater's *The Renaissance,* Joyce's "Clay," and Lawrence's *The Rainbow* put together synthetic heresies in a manner beyond the limitations of Richards's and Iser's response theories. Richards internalizes the readerly conflict within the literary form, and Iser's approach is built on the negativity of gaps. D. H. Lawrence's *The Rainbow* (1915), for instance, instead constructs a fiction of the sublime in its endeavor to transport the reader beyond the text by acting as if its heretical transfigurations would become manifest in reality.

Synthesis and the Sublime in *The Rainbow*

After the outrage that *Jude the Obscure* evoked, the inheritance of Hardy's heretical voice fell primarily to Lawrence, who, in a sense, rewrote the battle in Hardy's last novel between the flesh and the spirit in his own first novel *Sons and Lovers* (1913). However, a closer parallel to Jude's education appears in the coming of age of Ursula Brangwen in *The Rainbow.* This novel also follows *Tess of the d'Urbervilles* in its use of a structural pattern designed to elicit change in its readers. Soon after the outbreak of the First World War, Lawrence wrote "A Study of Thomas Hardy" (1914) "[o]ut of sheer rage" against the "colossal idiocy" of the war, and this philosophical piece of criticism informs the concurrent composition and publication history of *The Rainbow* (*Letters* 2:212). In particular, Lawrence's treatise points to the synthetic temperament he finds in Hardy's novels and deploys in the structure of his own contemporaneous novel. In the "Study," Lawrence argues that humanity must "reconcile the two" "Absolutes" of "Law" and "Nature" and of "Love" and "Knowledge" (123). History has witnessed the great expression of "Law" or "Love" but never in equal measure, and Lawrence believes "the supreme art" will be the "perfect utterance" which conveys the two elements justly as "Two-in-One" (125–28). His own simultaneous attempt at "the supreme art" met with a stern backlash of propriety.

Despite Lawrence's elision of certain objectionable phrases in the novel, *The Rainbow* was suppressed in November 1915 under the 1857 Obscene

Publications Act. Specific passages in the novel, in the words of the Hicklin standard of 1868, tended to "deprave and corrupt." As the prosecutor in the case argued, "[a]lthough there may not be an obscene word to be found in the book, it was a mass of obscenity of thought, idea, and action, wrapped up in language which in some quarters might be considered artistic and intellectual" (qtd. in Parkes 21). The affront to conventional taste lay in the frank depictions of sexuality of the novel, not its linguistic form. *The Rainbow* is a stellar example of Ellmann's point that Edwardian writers felt free to use the Christian lexicon heretically, for the formal pattern is indebted to the symbol of the covenant, the sacrament of marriage, and the doctrine of transfiguration. Lawrence's use of these religious metaphors, however, seeks to transcend conventional morality.

Though the putative obscenity of *The Rainbow* functioned like heresy in obeying the laws of decorous language, the open portrayal of sexuality drew the attention of the censors because, like *Jude,* it was *too* open. Furthermore, Lawrence believed that the lack of subtlety in his impiety principally caused the legal action; as he wrote to the publisher, Martin Secker: "The scene to which exception was *particularly* taken was the one where Anna dances naked, when she is with child" (*Letters* 3:459). While Adam Parkes speaks of the "blasphemous implications" of the ritualized allusion to David dancing before the Ark (23), Anna's performance of the sacred rite in a highly sexualized manner also entails an earnestness that suggests the scene is better understood as heresy. Lawrence's sincere efforts to liberate the body ran counter to wartime morality rallying around orthodox Christianity, but his literary sorties were first and foremost serious, and a credible new bedrock of scripture to him. A "becoming" view of the world and a revitalization of gender relations form part of what might be called the Lawrentian "school of thought."

The significance of heresy in fulfilling the hope associated with the imagery of pregnancy and the rainbow pointedly structures Lawrence's "allotropic" novel in which Tom, Anna, and Ursula Brangwen embody a primal, atavistic force evolving across generations. At two key moments in the novel, Anna and Ursula each have a mystical experience after becoming naked in their search for both solitude and consummation. Anna is pregnant with Ursula during the ritual dance of "lifting her hands and her body to the Unseen, to the unseen Creator who had chosen her." In a reversal of the gender roles in the biblical scene, Will is Michal to Anna's David, and witnessing his wife's dance makes him feel "he was being burned alive" "as if he were at the stake" (170–71).[1] Will needs to be "born at last unto himself," to "let go" of his control of Anna, and to create a stronger sense of his own self (176). When his "absolute self" becomes manifest and Ursula is born, Anna feels the tension between the "here" and the "beyond," recognizes that "[d]awn and sunset were the feet of the rainbow that spanned the day," and sees "the hope, the promise" in the biblical symbol of the covenant (181). Similarly, Ursula needs liberation from Skrebensky during the sublime beach scene of the denouement, in which "she gave her breast to the moon, her belly to the flashing, heaving water" (444). She has faced the might of nature, overcome her fear, and then wants a destination apart from her mechanical lover. After Ursula breaks from him, the narrative states: "She was as if tied to the stake. The flames were licking her and devouring her. But the flames were also good" (448). Ursula has performed the rites she learned in utero and links them with pregnancy. Again *The Rainbow* associates the imagery of burning a heretic with promise and hope for the future when Ursula first mistakenly thinks she is with Skrebensky's child before she finally sees "a band of faint iridescence colouring in faint colours a portion of the hill" and "the rainbow of the earth's new architecture" (458–59).

In these structural repetitions, *The Rainbow* suggests that the promise of a new covenant depends on sacrifice in the spirit of heretics burned at the stake. Similarly, at the end of *Jude the Obscure,* Jude identifies with Nicholas Ridley (c. 1500–55), who was declared a heretic and burnt at the stake in Oxford. Jude, too, feels that he is giving his "body to be burned" (296). While he had believed that he might serve "as a frightful example of what not to do" (256), Sue reminds him that his "worldly failure" is to his "credit" not "blame" since the "greatest among mankind are those who do themselves no worldly good" (284). In Lawrence's novel, the rainbow, pregnant with the symbolism of a new covenant and the symbolism of pregnancy, implies that in order to be born, a new architecture of life must perform and sexualize sacred rites and then endure the consequences of heresy. Lawrence rewrote the sacred script in order to account for and reveal, as he stated in "Morality and the Novel" (1925), the "changing rainbow of our living relationships" (532). The novel illustrates that chasing rainbows puts a literary career at stake, but Lawrence, Hardy, and the other various heretics in the period from 1883 to 1924 considered such an endeavor to be a morally obligatory and realizable pursuit.

Chasing rainbows for Lawrence entails a desire for a unified sense of being emblematized most pointedly in the novel through marriage. In the world of *The Rainbow,* an ideal marriage synthesizes two beings in a consummate and complementary set of gender and sexual relations. Mark Kinkead-Weekes argues that the novel asks readers "to think in terms of forces impelling men and women to seek the marriage of opposites," which for Lawrence "involves a kind of death of the self, and a kind of rebirth" (25–26). For example, Tom and Lydia achieve "entry into another circle of existence" and discover "complete confirmation" and a "new world" after he let himself "mingle with her, losing himself to find her, to find himself in her" (90). This "confirmation" is their transfiguration, a recurrent trope often followed by the vision of the rainbow and its promise. Tom and Lydia "now met to the span of the heavens," and Anna "was free to play in the space beneath, between" (91). This new covenant born of transfiguration recurs across the three generations of Brangwens as Anna later forges a household with Will "under the arch of the rainbow" (182) that creates a "door" through which Ursula can eventually see the "earth's new architecture." While this arch of the novel illustrates Lawrence's idea of an allotropic ego at work, the genealogy also extends and encapsulates the struggles of Jude who found that it "takes two or three generations to do what [he] tried to do in one" (256). Hardy and Lawrence represent the two successive generations in the span from 1883 to 1924 who likened the conflicts of their heroes and heroines to being burnt at the stake for challenging tradition and orthodoxy. Jude and Ursula are heretics, to borrow Shaw's definition, because they were ahead of their time.

In *The Rainbow*, the narrative derives its power from the sublime. The novel feels obliged to pursue its humanist vision, elevate its readers, and confront being in all its infinity and awe, and it hinges the possible achievement of its ideals on philosophical underpinnings delineating the fictional nature of the sublime itself. The narrative reflects a composite of theories on the sublime in its portrayal of the terror of uncertainty and self-oblivion drawn by Burke and Schopenhauer, in its creation of the psychological dynamic of the experience posed by Kant, and in its elaboration of figures of speech to create the aesthetic quality as noted by Longinus. Bruce Clarke finds that from "*Women in Love* onwards" Lawrence "commits himself to a sublime style," which Clarke defines as "attempts to render in prose aspects of individual being that the *cogito* cannot possess" (450). *The Rainbow*, in fact, initiated this style with a signature trope to convey the development and synthesis of a sort of ideal ego that Lawrence described in a famous letter of 1914: "There is another ego, according to whose action the individual is unrecognisable, and passes through, as it were, allotropic states . . . of the same single radically-unchanged element" (*Letters* 2:183). In this description of a continuity of being passing through metamorphoses in the three generations of Brangwens, Lawrence had discovered his sublime subject matter, which for the novel carries much of the Romantic sense of the term. In a dramatization of sublime experience, the Brangwens recurrently face the dissolution of their sense of self, but Lawrence invests his narrative voice with an imaginative drive that restores their being and wills a new order of things.

As a formal innovation corresponding to its subject matter, the trope of "as if" is used by the narrative in *The Rainbow* to make the mundane sublime. In these iterations which pepper the novel and introduce its grand rhetoric, *The Rainbow* dramatizes the ideas of Hans Vaihinger's *The Philosophy of "As If."* In this work, Vaihinger shows his discipleship of Kant and argues that humanity willingly constructs fictions and then accepts these falsehoods as true in order to survive and thrive. The linguistic form "as if" characterizes the latent, conditional acceptance of fictions, and Vaihinger demonstrates this wish fulfillment at work in math, physics, philosophy, and religion. Once knowledge of the world is seen as a fictitious construction, novelistic discourse such as the transfiguration of the covenant in *The Rainbow* finds legitimacy for its potential realization.

Vaihinger's rather accessible major work pointedly informs *The Rainbow* in its explanation of the linguistic form of fictions and "the law of ideational shifts." In much of the treatise, Vaihinger illustrates how scientific conceptions such as infinity are fictitious at the core and simply instruments for furthering other conceptions of the world. Though the concept of infinity is "not a picture of true reality," it serves as a "logical expedient" for secondary constructions or hypotheses that depend on predicating its existence. In contrast, religious and mythological fictions are purely inventive in giving shape to the world, and aesthetic fictions adapt these constructs for new poetic ends. While Vaihinger readily acknowledges his debt to Kant in arguing that "the conceptual world is only a creation of the imagination," he wants to stress the fact that scientific and aesthetic concepts "are useful and necessary, though theoretically they are false" (63). On this note, he distinguishes his work from pragmatism, which, for him, allows utility to prove truth. Instead, Vaihinger embraces fictitious concepts and particularly poetic fictions which are "not merely legitimate but *necessary* fictions" for the construction of "refined types of social intercourse" (83). For example, the Kantian dynamic of the sublime parallels "fictive judgments" which Vaihinger finds to be characterized by the linguistic form "as if." For Kant, the sublime is to be found not "in the things of nature, but only in our ideas," and it "shows a faculty of the mind surpassing every standard of sense" (88–89). While the sublime is experienced subjectively when reason fails or is defied as in facing the boundless magnitude of nature, the mind can have this experience precisely because it is aware of both its cognitive limitations and ability nevertheless to rationalize an account of the infinite. When Kant "speaks of an Idea," Vaihinger claims, "an 'as if' is somewhere hidden" (94–95). People experience the sublime as if infinity or boundlessness can be understood as a whole. In "as if" formulations, Vaihinger argues that the expressions first deny "objective validity" or insist upon "the impossibility of what is stated in the conditional clause," but then assert that "this judgment, although subjective, is permissible or even necessary" (95). In both the Kantian sublime and "as if" fictive judgments, a process of elevation occurs despite the lack of rational certainty.

In the law of ideational shifts, Vaihinger illustrates how ideas develop in stages of being fictions, hypotheses, and dogmas, and how these ideas can also degenerate across this spectrum. Fictions become hypotheses because of their similar instable core construction, but while fictions remain subjective formulations, hypotheses endeavor to receive verification in objective reality. Yet hypotheses do not have the rigidity of a dogma and therefore create a "tension which must be exceedingly disagreeable to the mind." The pure subjectivity of fictions makes this tension greater and furthers their tendency toward becoming hypotheses. The transition from hypothesis to dogma Vaihinger explains along the same lines; the psyche strives to avoid the disquieting feeling of instability implicit in a hypothesis, and makes it "more stable through repeated confirmation" (125). This also explains how a fiction can immediately become a dogma. He states that "the psyche" is "impatient to rid itself" of the tension concomitant with the inability to make ideas cohere (127). Doubt turns a dogma into a hypothesis and eventually a fiction, and Vaihinger believes this process of decay is apparent in religions from those of ancient Greece to Christianity. He believes all dogmas are illegitimately founded, and he even cautions against transforming fictions into hypotheses. Instead, he declares that we must not "substitute for reality what has been deduced from the fiction"; instead we should "recognize them as fictions and be content with this knowledge" (90). In the law of ideational shifts, there is a parallel for the process by which a heresy often will become accepted as orthodoxy. Previous orthodoxies will become crusty and doubt-ridden, and heresies take their place as the new doctrinal dogma. Lawrence's syntax of "as if" creates a figurative heresy that defamiliarizes the doctrine of transfiguration; the "as" draws in the comparison with familiar biblical references, but the conditional "if" sends them away as an impossible fiction. For instance, when Tom discovers "another centre of consciousness" through Lydia, he felt "as if a strong light were burning there, and he was blind within it, unable to know anything, except that this transfiguration burned between him and her, connecting them, like a secret power" (38).

Through the lens of Vaihinger's treatise, Lawrence could envision the world as an elaborate set of fictions whose successful actualization depends on rhetoric. In this vein, the argument of *The Rainbow* parallels Bloomsbury's use of Moore's *Principia Ethica* to convince others of what is "good." One of the major strengths of the rhetoric in *The Rainbow* lies in the insistency with which the narrative invokes its signature simile. "As if" appears on nearly every page, and the trope clusters around figurative moments when the narrative leaves off simple description and reaches for the sublime. The second paragraph of the novel sets forth this technique in its general description of the family: "There was a look in the eyes of the Brangwens as if they were expecting something unknown, about which they were eager" (9). Tom feels his surrogate lineage in Anna since it "was as if his hope had been in the girl" (120), and when Will discovers his "absolute being," he feels "as if now he existed in Eternity" (179). As in the Kantian movement of the sublime, Will's contentment follows much strife. Perhaps the most painful degree of his loss of self occurs just before he gave up "the master-of-the-house idea" when Anna makes him feel a fool regarding the miracle at Cana and his hold on the religious doctrine dissolves. The following narrative description of his psychological conflict epitomizes Vaihinger's philosophy: "The water had not turned into wine. But for all that he would live in his soul as if the water *had* turned into wine. For truth of fact, it had not. But for his soul, it had" (160). Here the "as if" trope blurs with the modernist doctrine of "vital immanence" in that it too compels a "special sentiment" striving to manifest "the reality of the divine." The make-believe games of Ursula's childhood intuit what she can express later in describing her beliefs as solely based on humanity and love. The prepubescent games were "a sort of fiction to them" (244), but she keeps a sense of this childlikeness in the philosophy of her coming of age: "Truth does not lie beyond humanity, but is one of the products of the human mind and feeling" (317). Truth is a construction for Ursula, and the sense of "fictions" underwriting the novel adumbrate post-structuralism.

Much of the criticism on Lawrence's novel has focused on issues relevant to other concerns of this study, for the Lawrentian legacy understandably carries forth his retrieval of primitivism, concomitant liberation of the sexual body, and battle against the resultant charges of obscenity. The early works, *Sons and Lovers* and *The Rainbow,* strove to make necessary breaks from tradition and orthodoxy in order to catalyze Lawrence's vision. As a result of this critical emphasis, Lawrence, as Garrett Stewart notes, "has had scant attention paid . . . to the words he used to gain his leverage on the literary imagination." Instead, Stewart asserts that Lawrence's style is "characteristically good, complex, and uniquely resonant," and intricately shows this craft at work in Lawrence's "transcendental vocabulary and grammar of 'to be'" (219; 218). Stewart's essay surveys most of Lawrence's major works and nuances their allotropic style of representing being, so it is not surprising that analysis of specific scenes escape its purview. The marriage of Will and Anna, in particular, demonstrates at once Lawrence's formal innovations regarding the grammar of being, the axiom of synthesis, the imagery of heresy, and the trope of transfiguration.

In the opening scene of "Wedding at the Marsh," the narrative anomalously breaks into the present tense to describe the temporality from the arrival of the carriages to the conveyance of the wedding party to the altar where Tom gives Anna away. The present tense is capturing the passing on of her hand as if it were the passing on of an allotrope. The verbal tense is quite conspicuous in documenting this wedding presence from how there "is a great bustle," to how there "begins to be more room," to how Anna "puts her hand very lightly on [Tom's] arm," to how "she is in ecstasies with herself for making such a lovely spectacle" (124–25). Anna, who "was in the present" (125), and Will become transfigured in this marriage of beings, and the narrative present tense strives to act as an apotheosis of this synthetic moment of being. Will is a changed man and feels "as if the surface of the world had been broken away entire" since "a man wasn't born before he was married." The preceding "as if" clause introduces a catalog of the everyday which then "peeled away into unreality" in the face of "one's own being . . . suddenly become present" (139). Amid this all, Tom must suffer the pains of the heretic. As they "stood before the altar," he sacrifices his claim to Anna in order to enable the transfiguration as if his stare "at the burning blue window" could see through his "pain" to the future when he "was finished." In the window which "burned alive in radiance," Tom feels "the clue" that one may "never get old, never die" (125–26), and this experience leads to his epithalamium which concludes with the synthesis that "an angel is the soul of man and woman in one" (129). In his "Study of Thomas Hardy," Lawrence states that, though no one has yet found "perfect consummation of marriage," "every generation can get a little nearer" (127). For Lawrence, "the supreme art" eyed this angelic synthesis in human terms as its goal that could be achieved by acting as if the reconciliation were a *fait accompli*. As the enactment of "Two-in-One," a "Consummate Marriage" for Lawrence enables the continuity of being, and the allotropic quality of being allows for subsequent generations to adapt to and transform the fictions of their time.

The wine of one generation might be vinegar to the next. Lawrence's use of the allotropic metaphor closely parallels Hardy's play with "phases" in *Tess*. While the ritual of succession to the King of the Wood points to "creeds being transient" in Hardy's novel, the trope of "as if" propels the creation of new religious fictions in *The Rainbow*. In each novel, these telic discourses orient toward the sublime. Since "religion" had been "another world" for Ursula and "she held that that which one cannot experience in daily life is not true for oneself," the novel constructs a sublime fiction out of her quotidian existence. After the first of two chapters entitled "The Widening Circle," Ursula has reached a stage in her life akin to one of Vaihinger's ideational shifts in which religion is no longer a dogma but a fiction. Religion "now fell away from reality, and became a tale, a myth, an illusion, which . . . one knew was not true—at least for this present-day life" (263). Once orthodox religion is just a fiction she becomes free to create her own.

Hence Ursula begins to experiment with both heterosexual and homosexual love to satisfy her curiosity for knowledge, and she wants to make her mark in what the novel calls "the man's world" and associates with education. In a striking passage describing her scholarly preferences, Ursula experiences intimations of the sublime. Since she found "the close study of English literature" to be the "[m]ost tedious" subject, she asks "[w]hy should one remember the things one read?" The answer to her seemingly disillusioned question immediately follows since "in odd streaks" she received "a poignant sense of acquisition and enrichment and enlarging" (310). Such elevation to the sublime moves within her in moments when she actually reads literature. The first case mentioned simply notes her reading of *As You Like It*, the Shakespeare play probably chosen for the resonance of the title with the wish fulfillment nature of the "as if" iterations. Ursula also "heard a passage of Latin" "with her blood" and "knew how the blood beat in a Roman's body," and she then forever "knew the Romans by contact." Ursula even "enjoyed the vagaries of English Grammar, because it gave her pleasure to detect the live movements of words and sentences" (310–11). In *The Rainbow*, the "as if" clause produces the "live movements" of the narrative as the trope which turns the transfiguration theme and transfigures the covenant. For instance, Ursula went with Skrebensky "out of the church, as if her feet were beams of light that walked on flowers for footsteps" (282). Ursula becomes self-luminous like Christ in his Transfiguration. The novel too seems to "enjoy" the vagaries of the conditional and subjunctive clauses, and the emphasis on the "live movements" and "the present-day" in the preceding passages self-referentially points back to the present tense of Will and Anna's wedding scene.

In the malleable world of the novel in which orthodox dogmas have become fictions, the "as if" clauses strive to elevate the present to the sublime. As Vaihinger states, "[a]esthetic fictions serve the purpose of awakening within us certain uplifting or otherwise important feelings," and are "a means for the attainment of higher ends" (82). The struggles of the Brangwen family across generations between the "here" and the "beyond" remain rather unresolved at the end of the novel, but the narrative, in all its transfiguring tropes, lays the foundation for Lawrence's new architecture of consummation that Ursula will find in the companion novel *Women in Love* (1920). To achieve this end *The Rainbow* narrates a series of generational phases in which each of the allotropic characters experiences the sublime by oscillating between the terror of the dissolution of self and the surge of forging a grander union of being. Desire is the cause of this tension, and romantic relationships become Lawrence's touchstone for the dialectic between the pain of denial and the pleasure of intimacy. In his violent sensuality with Anna, Will experiences "ultimate beauty, to know which was almost death in itself" (219). When Skrebensky kisses Ursula, "she quivered as if she were being destroyed, shattered" (414), even though she had earlier thought he would lead her to "a consummation, a being infinite" (409).

The Brangwens experience an inner turmoil, likened to the martyrdom of heretics, because of a narrative desire to subsume the doctrine of transfiguration in an apotheosis of human relations. There could be nothing more sublime. The narrative strives to transcend Christian asceticism by using the inherent process of sublimation in asceticism to achieve its vision of the sublime. Ursula, in fact, ventures out ever further into the "widening circles" after recurrent renunciations of pleasure. The psychology of desire which constitutes so much of the novel incorporates a sense of the processes of sublimation, and another contemporaneous text, Freud's "On Narcissism" (1914), may have informed Lawrence on the topic. Without sublimation there would be no sublime. The allotropic changes across generations and the narrative delay of Ursula's fulfillment across novels ultimately stellify Ursula with Birkin in *Women in Love*. Just before their consummation and subsequent flight to the Continent, Ursula sees Birkin "as if she were enchanted, and everything were metamorphosed" (304). The fictions of transfiguration and the sublime have achieved full synthesis, and "philosophy and fiction" for Lawrence have "come together again." Ursula and Birkin's "perfect relation" in which they are "free together" (308) becomes a new creation-myth of a constellation that raises them to the heavens as "two single equal stars balanced in conjunction" (143). Lawrence's sublime style elevates his characters to celestial bodies as "Two-in-One," and the mutual gravitational pull of their orbit emblematizes the tension of centrifugal and centripetal forces at work in Bakhtin's notion of heteroglossia. While this may make the Lawrentian sublime postmodern and founded on the abyss in Lyotard's sense of the aesthetic term, it nevertheless illustrates the subtle development of heretical syntheses so characteristic of modernist literary history.

THE CHOICE OF TRADITION AND THE SYNTHESIS OF BEING

In successive years, T. S. Eliot and E. M. Forster each went up to Cambridge to deliver the esteemed Clark Lectures. Eliot's "Varieties of Metaphysical Poetry" (1926) and Forster's "Aspects of the Novel" (1927) both demonstrate the turn of English studies toward analysis of formal structures while decidedly retaining a humanist sense of the arts as the staple of civilization. Both lectures enable us better to understand the major works that preceded them, *The Waste Land* (1922) and *A Passage to India* (1924). In each literary piece, linguistic roots linking Indo-European languages and culture demonstrate the tension between centripetal and centrifugal forces that function in a text. The analysis of these two texts sketches the legacy of heresy at the tail end of this literary history; the afterword examines the fate of heresy in later like-minded texts. In the last section of Eliot's poem "What the Thunder Said," the poetic voice endeavors to control the divisions of a pluralistic, fragmented modern society with a ritualistic display of authorized subject and object relations. The heresy of the poem is etymological in its root sense of "choice," a function at work in dogmatically determining what traditions constitute the world. As Chesterton had advised, however, Eliot thinks his choices are "right" and considers them orthodox. In Forster's novel, what had been a fearful thunderclap ushering primordial peoples into caves becomes the echo of a linguistic past uniting being, language, and the religious discourses associated with mosque, cave, temple, and church. Here Forster continues the Edwardian mode of synthesis in a variation of his desire to "only connect."

A hotly contested issue in the study of Eliot's work has been the question of the "two Eliots" and whether his literature prior to his 1927 entry into the Church of England can be reconciled with the overtly Christian nature of his later work. F. R. Leavis sought to establish a consistency in Eliot's oeuvre through the value of classicism Eliot always espoused, and on this note Kenneth Asher analyzes Eliot's posthumously published Clark Lectures from 1926 to argue for "a strongly continuous Eliot, with no major rupture" (18). Asher believes that in these last statements before Eliot's conversion, the lectures build on his previous essay, "The Metaphysical Poets" (1921), but reduce the stature of Donne's "sensibility" and indirectly elevate Dante's. For Asher, this moves "Eliot closer to the religious center of a tradition he had always embraced on political grounds" (22). In the early essay, Eliot puts forth his famous notion of the "dissociation of sensibility" that set in after the metaphysical poets and sundered the "recreation of thought into feeling." At the same time, he lauded "the poet's mind" as a synthetic site "amalgamating disparate experience" and distanced it from the "ordinary man's experience" which is "chaotic, irregular, fragmentary" (246–47). All this is familiar and so too perhaps is the notion that the relationship between form and content in *The Waste Land* embodies the literary values of this and Eliot's other early essays on the use of tradition, emotion, and mythical order. In its synthesis of fragments, the form of *The Waste Land* acts as a performance of the rituals it discusses, and the performance orders the anxiety of modern experience and strives to overcome chaos, to paraphrase Richards. Eliot appreciated Richards's theory of equilibrium in a synthetic reader's mind and wanted to insert morals into the equation, but what I want to stress here is that Eliot's choice of fragments, rituals, glosses, and linguistic roots for the poem is sectarian and orthodox and further establishes the continuity of Eliot's career.

In Eliot's "Notes on 'The Waste Land,'" he famously directs readers seeking elucidation of the poem to Jessie L. Weston's *From Ritual to Romance* (1920) and "The Perilous Chapel" chapter in particular. He does also acknowledge the general influence of Frazer's *The Golden Bough,* but Weston's slim and highly speculative work takes precedence for its application of Frazer's voluminous documentation of rituals restoring fertility and social order to the legend of the Holy Grail. Though Frazer had subdued references to Christ as another in the line of mythical slain gods like Balder for his abridged edition (1922), Weston's book championed the Grail as "a living force" founded "upon the ruins of an august and ancient ritual" that can disappear only to "rise to the surface again, and become once more a theme of vital inspiration" (187–88). She even suggests that the Templars were condemned as heretics for keeping the ritual alive in secret, and this reflects the proclivity in modernist literary history for seeing heresy become the orthodoxy of future generations.

When the amalgamating voice in Eliot's poem asks about "the roots that clutch," it inserts "Son of man" at the end of the questioning lines before telling its "chaotic" readers "You cannot say" since they know only "broken images" (19–22). Though Eliot points to Ezekiel for his use of the phrase "Son of man," where it means "member of the human race," the line-break and its lingering pause establish the common association with Christ as at least an initial answer to what clutches. The genius and wonder of the poem rests on such ambiguity and duplicity with its surface tension of diverse, fragmented languages and apparent syncretism of diffuse myths and religions, while at a structural and theoretical level, it spins Indo-European roots, Buddhism, and *The Upanishads* for orthodox Christian ends. As the original title of the poem suggests, Eliot "do the police in different voices." The "Jug Jug" (103) of the poem may connote brutal sex and the sound of a nightingale on one level, but below that repetition is "The Jug" of Bentham, his euphemism for the juggernaut power of organized religion.

In "What the Thunder Said," the Christian tradition comes to the fore in the first stanza with allusions to Christ's trial and crucifixion and continues in a benediction of the Indo-European root *da- enacting Eliot's idealized relationship between subject and object, order and myth, and the individual and tradition. In the fable from *The Upanishads* about the meaning of thunder, Eliot had found an antecedent for his literary values in the Hindu mantra "datta, dayadhvam, damyata" (give, sympathize, control). Embedded in such words of ours as "democracy," "demagogue," "Zeitgeist," and "time," the reconstructed root *da- ("to divide") underwrites the variant interpretations of God's will in the fable, but the interaction of these divisions creates a sense of control. For the poem offers its own interpretation of the mantra by inserting, after a colon, an English version of the meaning of its divided parts defined by references to Christianity and the Fisher King. As Bakhtin argues, "Indo-European linguistics" directs attention "away from language plurality to a single proto-language" and helps to determine the "content and power of the category of 'unitary language'" and "its creative, style-shaping role in the majority of poetic genres" (271). The centripetal drive in the Ursprache of *The Waste Land* parallels its choice of tradition, and those included in the canon must serve the restoration of the social order.

Eliot considered "What the Thunder Said" not only the best section of the poem, but also a justification of the whole work, and this fifth part occupies both the position of catharsis in classical tragedian structure and the role in ritual order of replenishing the postwar European wasteland. The *da- root also runs below the word "daimon," the lesser deity which originally signified "divider and provider," as the thunder brings fear but also the nourishment of rain. In the first two interpretations of God's imperative in the thunder, "give" entails an individual subject putting feeling into form, but to create order out of myth and establish control, the subject must "sympathize" with traditional thought and narrative. *The Waste Land* betrays its sympathies in its choice of traditions, for they are strategically chosen to prop up orthodox thought. To paraphrase the lines of verse following the *datta* and *dayadhvam,* the poem suggests that to break out of the prison of our egos we should be receptive to Christ since nothing can compare with his self-sacrifice. Despite the resonance of the Hindu fable, the allusions to Eastern traditions in the poem are rather scant. Buddha's fire sermon is reduced to "burning" (311), and the ascetic plea misses the balance of The Middle Way. The fruitless love of Antony for Cleopatra and Aeneas for Dido segues into modern analogs for failed gender and sexual relations, and with further illustration of debased sex and the turn to spiritual concerns the ascetic tenor of the poem becomes clear. In this vein, *The Waste Land* exemplifies the claim of Jane Harrison's 1921 address to the Heretics, as discussed earlier, that modern religion improves life through "the function of choice and the practice of asceticism," which "is necessary for eminence in art." In contrast to the "complete *nonconformism*" of Surrealism, the modernist experimentation with form in Eliot's poem demonstrates how heretical discourses can be appropriated by orthodoxy. While heresies may become orthodoxy as Shaw, Harrison, and Weston suggested, such a process enables orthodoxy to react, learn to don the clothes of the heretic, and write such books as "A Primer of Modern Heresy."

The landmark nature of *The Waste Land* makes it not surprising that two years later Forster might have rewritten the import of "What the Thunder Said" in the etymologically inflected chant "Esmiss Esmoor," which creates a new legend in *A Passage to India*. In fact, Forster's novel alludes to both the beginning and end of Eliot's modernist epic. The famous first line of the poem informs the phrasing of time, "April, herald of horrors, is at hand" (124), when the travelers are about to venture into the caves, and the translation of the poem's concluding "shantih," "the Peace that passeth Understanding," frames the disastrous trek with this restful "gesture" that manifests when "the whirring of action ceases" (280). In the middle of this circumscription lie the dark caves whose echoic effects epitomize the "muddle" theme of the novel. The chant echoes through the remaining narrative and into Forster's discussion of two "Aspects of the Novel," prophecy and rhythm, that he presented as part of his Clark Lectures. Trying to be in tune with English studies at Cambridge, the lectures on textual analysis are primarily humanist in concern. Forster argues that prophecy is "an accent in the novelist's voice," the theme of prophetic fiction is "something universal," and, since it "proposes to sing," the "strangeness of song" in prose is "bound to give us a shock" (181). In his textual discussion of rhythm, Forster simply defines it as "repetition plus variation" (240) which makes the novel cohere "because it is stitched internally" (236). Forster's stature as a novelist by and large grants the lectures the critical import they retain, and the debt is further evident in the resonance of the lectures with *A Passage to India*. The continuities suggest that he could not help basing his analyses on his own creative practice, for the chant of "Esmiss Esmoor" is stitched with the Indo-European root *es-, meaning "to be" or "be," and the rhythm of this "song" reverberates through the denouement of the novel. The narrative voice declares that the "song of the future must transcend creed" (298), and the syncretic drive of the novel strives to subsume any traditional orthodoxy.

On several levels, *A Passage to India* dramatizes the susceptibility to misinterpretation that rises in the clash between cultures and languages. In addition to the trumped-up allegations that put Aziz on trial, Mrs. Moore's belief that her encounter with Aziz in the mosque could be misunderstood and Ronny's disparaging perception of Aziz' missing collar-stud point to the workings of *heteroglossia* and the idea that sectarian and colonial relations create a "muddle." The novel suggests that the origin of calumny and failed communication lies in the insularity of linguistic cultures and in language itself. Despite the differences between India and British cultural expectations, Aziz, Mrs. Moore, and Fielding all try "to bridge the gulf between East and West" (26). In particular, Mrs. Moore grants divinity to India and desires to see the land and its people on an equal standing in the world community. She states, "India is part of the earth" (53), and "God is here" too (18), yet she struggles to verbalize her feeling that "God . . . is . . . Love" (53). The ellipses will be filled in later at Godbole's religious ceremony, but "by an unfortunate slip of the draughtsman" the words become "God si Love" (320).

Amid a place "full of misstatements" that confuse English and Indian relations (117), Aziz wants "to symbolize the whole into some truth of religion or love" (16), and one of his verses went "straight to internationality" (329). The English and the Indian peoples are "Aryan Brother[s]" (26), anthropologically linked, but Aziz has the larger vision that "[a]ll men are my brothers" (125). He dreams of "universal brotherhood" that "became untrue" "when put into prose," and Mrs. Moore believes India needs "something universal" to have "barriers" "broken down" (160). Godbole's choir sings of loving the "whole universe," and "tiny splinters of detail" in the song momentarily create "universal warmth" (321). Forster claimed in his lecture that the "face" of prophetic fiction "is toward unity" and elicits "the sensation of a song" (197). He was not concerned with the "particular view of the universe" in the work of prose, but rather "its implication that signifies and will filter into the turns of the novelist's phrase" and "minutia of style" (182). The *es- root definitively emblematizes this "minutia of style" as one of the "splinters of detail" that imply a universal theme in the rhythmic repetition of the root linking language and being.

Despite prophesying a binding humanity, the novel illustrates the forces that work against this synthetic vision by repeatedly playing with the nature of writing and the origins of language. The reconstructed *es- root is part of a motif in the novel that centers on the linguistic change concomitant with the diaspora of the primordial Aryan people, the proto-Indo-Europeans. However, Godbole offers supplications for "[c]ompleteness, not reconstruction," and he wants to impel beings "to that place where completeness can be found" (321). The novel suggests that a reconception of being is necessary to attain such synthesis, and it begins by revisiting the origins of being and language in the Marabar Caves, which are "older than all spirit" and "unsealed since the arrival of the gods" (136–38). Pilgrims, however, "find too much of it" (136), as Adela Quested and Mrs. Moore discover. After they hear the "terrifying echo," it "began in some indescribable way to undermine" Mrs. Moore's "hold on life" (162–65). The dissolution of self into a larger conception of being is unbearable, and she experiences the sublime. Filled with despair, she cannot continue her journey into the caves, and pointedly she cannot finish her letter. She loses possession of her "sincere words," becomes terrified with the vastness of the universe, and "knew that" Christianity's "divine words from 'Let there be Light' to 'It is finished' only amounted to 'boum'" (166). She not only critiques the "fictions" of language here, but "boum," French for "boom," evokes a theory of language positing that cave dwellers began speaking in echoic imitation of natural sounds—in this case, thunder.

When the crowd at Aziz' trial begins chanting "*Esmiss Esmoor,*" a similar interplay of language, being, and divinity comes forth (250).[2] As the crowd "Indianizes" Mrs. Moore's name, the sibilant invocation tries to bring her into being. After the chant inflects her name with the call of the I.E. root for "to be," there grew "signs of the beginning of a cult" devoted to this newfound divinity (285). Still, the narrative voice acknowledges that meditations on divine being such as "He is, was not, is not, was" may just be "games with words," for being depends upon language (317; 307). In *The Order of*

Things, Foucault illustrates how the copulative function of the verb "to be" "is the indispensable condition for all discourse." The verb enables the "representation of being in language; but it is equally the representative being of language" (93–94). Forster's characters feel that in India "everything hangs together" and trouble to find the "connecting thread" (345). The chant of "Esmiss Esmoor" with its woven "eses" connects the thread of being and language, and Godbole finds that the significance of the choir's song to Krishna can become "audible through much repetition" (348). When Aziz later notes the rhythmic change in the chant, "in the interstice," he "heard, almost certainly, the syllables of salvation that had sounded during his trial" (352). In his lecture on rhythm, Forster described it as a "living being" that takes "various forms" like the "little phrase" of music in Proust. The nature of rhythm is "not to be there all the time," but in "its lovely waxing and waning" it can mean "everything to the reader" and "fill us with surprise and freshness and hope" (237–39). For instance, Godbole finds hope in Aziz' internationalist verse which "might be rendered into Sanskrit, it is so enlightened" (329), and this cue to the ancient language is helpful in looking at its verbal forms of "to be." The stem of the present forms is an "s" or "as," and "s-mas" means "we are." The "s-mas" in "Esmiss" not only suggests a reason for the change in her form of address, but these "syllables of salvation" in the chant also imply that the recognition of collectivity is necessary for existence. Indeed, the image of the Marabar and the catastrophe of the trek make Fielding feel that "we exist not in ourselves, but in terms of each others' minds" (277–78).

When a word from a master discourse becomes appropriated by a subjugated counterpart, the word itself at this transitional moment informs the mechanisms of power potentially revealed by etymology. In the case of "Esmiss Esmoor," etymology points toward Bakhtin's notion of re-accentuation, which he states is "enormously significant in the history of literature" since every "age re-accentuates in its own way the works of its most immediate past" (420–21). The assibilation of Mrs. Moore's name is "an accent in the novelist's voice" that re-accentuates the antithetical divisiveness of the *da- root. Bakhtin explains that re-accentuation in the novel occurs with "a change in the background animating dialogue," and these new dialogic conditions not only resist parodic intentions, but also "may emit bright new rays" of meaning since the "*living* word" is "true to *itself*" (419–20). In all its *heteroglossia,* the hissing chant of the crowd at the trial challenges the legal system and invokes a new conception of being which subsumes India and England, undermines the eminence of any religion, and subverts any missionary justification for colonization. Amid this prophetic universalism that demands, as Forster claimed in his lecture, "the absence of the sense of humour" (197), the narrative points to one last synthesis, "the inclusion of merriment" to complete the spiritual "circle" of "salvation" (324). The disruptive nature of laughter makes it a fundamental centrifugal force in discourse, and Forster's nod to its importance not only lightens the spirit of the prophetic fiction, but also points to the centrifugal imagery ending the novel when Aziz and Fielding cannot be "friends" and "swerved apart" (362). Forster knew of limits to the desire to connect. The awareness of the novel of the instability of *logos* in the face of the syncretic drive of the narrative adumbrates postmodernism and the desire both to control and to liberate language discussed in the afterword, which follows.

The "Empires of the Mind" and the Control of Heresy

In Umberto Eco's medieval murder mystery, *The Name of the Rose* (1981), the cleric who destroys the last surviving copy of Book II of Aristotle's *Poetics* justifies his criminal acts by stating that in the treatise on comedy, "the function of laughter is revered, it is elevated to art, the doors of the world of the learned are opened to it, it becomes the object of philosophy, and of perfidious theology." While the Catholic Church could control "the heresy of the simple" by granting "the moment of feast, carnival, fair," intellectualizing and defending such Dionysian and centrifugal elements is the most dangerous heresy in the cleric's mind (474). Indeed, he sets fire to the labyrinthine library because he found that "behind the veil of mirth it concealed secret moral lessons" (437). The subversive effects of a "pagan laughter" and the references in the novel to the "great Lyotard," along with Eco's previous work on Joyce and semiotics, clearly make one of the effects of the novel the blurred distinction between orthodoxy and heresy when seen with a poststructuralist lens. In a pointed turn of phrase, William, the rationalist English Franciscan, explains that he had forsaken his post as an inquisitor because of "the problem of difference itself" (196). He could discern "little difference between his mystic (and orthodox) faith and the distorted faith of the heretics" (123). The principle of difference causes questions of heresy to become relative and arbitrary.

The seeds of poststructuralism were sown during the modernist period, and often High Modernist authors such as Joyce and Woolf have become the darlings of deconstructionists, with Derrida's work on the Irish writer leading the way. As we know, deconstruction grew out of a critique of the claims of structuralism, and at the same time as the radical modernist literary experiments with language, Saussure's work on semiotics, the Prague school of linguistics, and others sought to decode fundamental structures below language and literature. C. K. Ogden's development of Basic English during the 1920s shares this fascination with the centripetal desire to impose order on language. In a sense, Basic English is a cross between such structuralist endeavors, and the dogmatic manifestoes, proliferating at the time, which variously sought correctives to perceived social, aesthetic, and political problems. To examine briefly the currency and control of heresy in the period immediately beyond the scope of this study, two literary encounters with Ogden's work on Basic emblematize oppositional historical trajectories of the discourse of heresy. Joyce's continued cultivation of heresies in *Finnegans Wake* dissolve in Ogden's translation into Basic of an excerpt from Joyce's last work. In *Nineteen Eighty-Four*, George Orwell drew on his knowledge of Ogden's universal language to forecast the dangers to unorthodox thought posed by language control.

The translation of the excerpt from *Finnegans Wake*, in Ogden's words, put "the simplest and most complex languages of man" "side by side" ("Anna" 93), and this emblematic moment speaks to the stereotypical antithesis between the Edwardians and the modernists which Joyce so quintessentially troubles. He is neither the dogmatic modernist nor the apolitical aesthete, and not quite the politically committed Edwardian harmonizer of history. Ogden, too, was of that generation who matured before the First World War, but who were still young enough to try to adjust to advances in modern thought and the changing global political landscape. Before the war, he had helped to found the open-minded Heretics Society; afterward he turned toward what he called "Orthology" and began to profess what he claimed were the proper corrective measures for social interaction. In miniature, his career embodies the rise and fall of heresy during the modernist period. Ogden the Heretic became Ogden the Orthologist. In this light, the outcome of his lucubrations, Basic English, can be seen as another in the series of modernist manifestoes. Ogden repeatedly overemphasized the importance of Basic by claiming it was the last chance for world peace and global understanding since he thought, as we might think of another connotation of "translation," that his "universal language" could "put" the world, like the *Wake*, "into simpler terms." Translating the passage from the *Wake* into Basic English erodes its heresies, and Ogden's "orthology" emblematizes Chesterton's point that thinking a school of thought "right" changes the face of heterodoxy. It shines with self-righteous authority.

Ogden's purpose in developing Basic was akin to the humanist ideal of "synthesis" in that the modern world would be a less fragmented place if everyone could understand an auxiliary language. This fact is important to remember because the most common misconception of Basic is that it sought to replace English and other languages. While concerns about cultural imperialism arise nevertheless, in name, Basic only courted traffic in the human affairs its acronym suggests: British American Scientific International Commercial. For the international business traveler, Basic touted itself as being able to fit all of its 850 words on one page and thus capable of being learned in one day. Eventually, Basic received the financial support of the Irving Trust and the Rockefeller Foundation. It is no wonder that Churchill and Roosevelt found Basic attractive during the Second World War. Churchill in particular saw it as a new way to colonize and exert influence in those countries where Basic had already achieved footholds in the 1930s—India, China, Egypt, Russia, Mexico, and nearly thirty others. By the early thirties, H. G. Wells, I. A. Richards, Bernard Shaw, John Dewey, and Paul Robeson had already officially declared the urgent need for Basic.

For Ogden, the key to developing his language system lay in the ideas of Jeremy Bentham's Panopticism and Theory of Fictions. Ogden found Bentham's thoughts on linguistics to be a forerunner of Vaihinger's philosophy of "as if," which he translated from the German as he began to use Bentham's views on substantives and paraphrase to subtend the agenda and methodology of Basic. W. Terrence Gordon finds that in Bentham's work, Ogden "saw an appealing progression from the analysis of language to the laying of a foundation for a specific program of language reform" (45). What Ogden called the "Panoptic Eliminator" reduced words through the use of negation and opposition, and he designed his patented Panoptic Word Wheel in order to teach correct word order and enable envisaging the entire Basic vocabulary in one glance (see figures 6 and 7). He explained that the Word Wheel was "named the 'Panopticon' because all the necessary units are seen together" (*System* 305). Through substitution at the syntactic level, one could imagine where to insert the rest of the 850 words. By 1932 when he delivered the Bentham centenary lecture at University College London, Ogden had become the leading Bentham scholar of his time, and he attributed "the final synthesis" of panoptic elimination and the birth of Basic to his close reading of Bentham's works ("Universal" 5). Initially, in fact, Ogden called his auxiliary language "Panoptic English." Synthesis, for Ogden, had become a set of limiting choices, in the spirit of the modernist manifestoes, designed to make the world coherent.

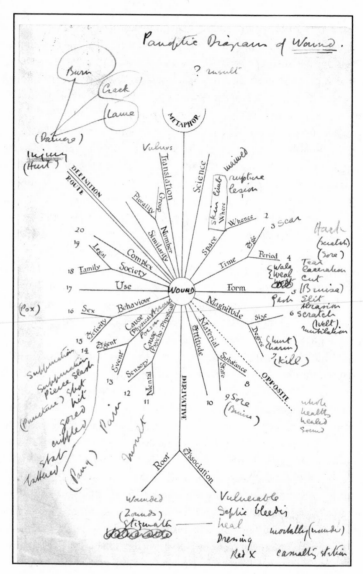

Figure 6. The Panoptic Eliminator. C. K. Ogden designed this diagram as an aid for developing the word list for Basic English, or Panoptic English as he initially called it. By putting an essential word in the center, one could eliminate words on the periphery from the Basic vocabulary, since their meanings could be conveyed through a combination of operators and the essential word. The annotations for the illustration are in Ogden's hand. (*Source:* C. K. Ogden fonds, McMaster University Library, MCMA 132.16)

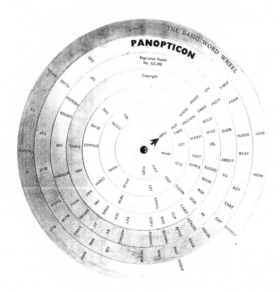

Figure 7. The Panopticon, or Basic Word Wheel. Ogden patented the Panopticon, which is seven cardboard circles whose rotation is designed to teach English syntax. (*Source:* C. K. Ogden fonds, McMaster University Library, MCMA 128.7)

THE ABCs OF ALP: BASIC ENGLISH AND *FINNEGANS WAKE*

A year after Aldous Huxley's *Brave New World* appeared in 1932, H. G. Wells responded with a positive vision of a totalitarian future as told through a "dream book" that narrates the short history of the world from 1929 to 2106. This utilitarian utopia, *The Shape of Things to Come* (1933), imagines an international "Modern State" founded on scientific principles and run with a "Puritan Tyranny." Wells envisions a new world order made possible after a period of apocalyptic war, plague, and barbarism. When the world becomes a *tabula rasa* again, unity and peace eventually blossom after people let global concerns override personal interest. Behavior modification, technology, and a socialized economy make life a model of efficiency and, in the vein of one of G. E. Moore's addresses to the Heretics Society, what Wells calls "common sense" determines political decisions. Since an objective "intellectual organization" of "scientific men" may be able to "prove that this, that, or the other course is the *right* one," Wells entertains the idea that a "dictatorship of "common-sense" should "some day rule the earth" (*Democracy* 202–3). In the novel, one example of the supposed refinements enabled by logic is the use of Basic English as the lingua franca of the world.

Wells' historical narrative looks back on the year 1929, and to illustrate the development of language it compares two ongoing linguistic experiments of that year, Joyce's work on the *Wake* and C. K. Ogden's creation of Basic. Wells supported Ogden's endeavor and dismissed Joyce's, and the narrative likewise reveals these biases in stating that "while Ogden sought scientific simplification, Joyce worked aesthetically for elaboration and rich suggestion, and vanished at last from the pursuit of his dwindling pack of readers in a tangled prose almost indistinguishable from the gibbering of a lunatic" (416). In his personal dealings with Joyce, Wells was more pleasant. In 1928, he wrote to Joyce explaining that he could not support openly the linguistic experiments of *Finnegans Wake:* "The frame of my mind is a world wherein a big unifying and concentrating process is possible. . . . For it, I want language (and statement) as simple and clear as possible. . . . Perhaps you are right. . . . But the world is wide and there is room for both of us to be wrong" (Joyce, *Letters* 1: 274–75). In contrast to Joyce's explosion of language, the polar extreme of Basic English functioned with only 850 words and led to Wells' imagined world in which "all understand another" through this "synthetic language," and everyone lives "in one undivided cultural field" (417).

In her discussion of the Basic English translation of "Anna Livia Plurabelle," Susan Shaw Sailer explains that, since Basic does not capture the vernacular or mythic functions of language, it can only "communicate information on a national [or international] scale" (865). Therefore, she concludes that "Ogden's translation errs in activating cultural values that Joyce probably did not intend to be operative," and is "a completely inadequate tool for translating *Finnegans Wake*" (865–66). Certainly this is true, but by looking more closely at the respective values operating in the texts, two prime examples of what synthesis meant in 1929 come to the fore. Sailer describes a "conceptual similarity" between Basic English and the *Wake* as a "notion of the universality of human nature that characterizes much modernist art and thought" (853). However, their attempts at creating a synthetic universal language to convey a common human experience drastically diverge in terms of the method by which all things putatively can be said. One is amalgamating, subversive, and liberating, the other isolating, directive, and colonizing. The late Victorian heresy of syncretism culminates in the substance and style of the *Wake*, while Ogden's word "choice" imposes artificial limitations in his synthesis of natural English. It would take Orwell's *Nineteen Eighty-Four* to forecast the dangers of reducing and controlling language as a means towards controlling thought. For that is what Basic English sought to do. Although fundamentally beneficent in his goal, Ogden believed he could improve thought processes by ridding language of what he called "word-magic" and "fictions," after Bentham and Vaihinger.

Unlike Wells, however, Ogden approached Joyce's work judiciously and saw the latter's linguistic experimentation as an illustrative contrast to his own language system. The feeling was mutual. By 1929, when Joyce solicited Ogden to write the introduction to *Tales Told of Shem and Shaun*, both men had begun struggling to garner support for their radical projects. In return for the introduction that Joyce found "useful" (*Letters* 1: 279), he brought recognition to Basic English by recording onto gramophone the last four pages of "Anna Livia Plurabelle" at Ogden's Orthological Institute in London. This encounter and the subsequent translation of these same pages into Basic English are the meetings of the heterodox synthetic mind and its standard-izing corrective counterpart.

To questions about the style of the *Wake*, Joyce would explain that he had to invent neologisms and use other languages because English had enough words, "but they aren't the right ones." In his novel, which extends the impli-cations of etymology, he wanted "a language which is above all languages, a language to which all will do service" (Ellmann, *Joyce* 397). For his synthesis of English, Ogden emphasized the Greek roots in his use of the term "Orthol-ogy" (*orthos*, "correct," and *logos*, "word"), and he described Basic English as "the International Language of 850 words in which everything may be said."[1] Each man would search for the *mot juste* to achieve his ends, and Ogden reports that during the recording session Joyce "expressed a desire to see how far the effects at which he was aiming with a vocabulary of say 850,000,000 words could be conveyed with the 850 words of Basic English" ("Anna" 92–93). Though the *Wake* has been translated into other languages, the linguistic explosion of Joyce's narrative suggests that it is against control, is its own peculiar, self-referential linguistic community, and is therefore theoretically untranslatable.

In his brief preface to the Basic English "Anna Livia," Ogden states that "the reader will see that it has generally been possible to keep almost the same rhythms." He further champions his translation by stating that though "the sense of the story has been changed a little," Joyce had stressed the impor-tance of achieving "these effects of rhythm [rather] than to give the nearest Basic Word every time" ("Anna" 93). Ogden would have it that Basic English is so extensive and supple that *it* was compromised by the translation, and the international language, if it wanted, could better capture the sense of the *Wake.* In privileging rhythm, however, a difficulty arises for Ogden's translation, for as John Bishop has shown in his tour de force explication of the chapter, the sense, the meaning, at least partly lies in the nongraphic sound and rhythm of blood circulating through HCE's ears. The most commonly recognized device of the *Wake,* the inundation of names of rivers, works to create the echoic effects of rushing waters or pulsating blood. Bishop then shows how this conception underwrites both the form and content of "Anna Livia," so the question arises whether the sense can change without disrupting the rhythm. The issue becomes further complicated when one notes that Joyce, according to Ogden, had a hand in the translation while sojourning in London during the summer of 1931.[2]

One salient aspect of the Basic translation is its arbitrariness. Sometimes it adheres to the syllabic pattern, sometimes it takes liberties with its own lexicon, and sometimes it retains the names of people and the names of rivers. For example, "Godavari, vert the showers" (*Wake* 213.20) becomes "*Godavari* keep off the rains," and the river in India is now clearly asked to hold back water. However, translating "vert," another river, into "keep off" as if it were "avert" works against the fluidity principle of the chapter. Etymologically, "vert" (Lat. *vertere,* "to turn") would actually suggest turning on the showers. Reproducing "Godavari" is an interesting choice because, for the rest of the chapter, Ogden tends to suppress the mention of divine concepts. Indeed, the translation here has even asked the "avaricious God," "varied gods," or "God of ours" embedded in the river name to stay out of the business of this world.

Rational thought does not want to account for the vagaries of the irrational, and Basic English either categorizes deities and blessedness as "the good" or lumps spiritual questions under the term "religion." Consequently, the same "Godavari" is asked only to provide "support," not bestow "grace," and the translation simply elides words evocative of divinity such as "Holy" (214.30), "Lord" (214.18), "gloria" (213.31), and "Seints of light" (214.31). Rather than "Ho, Lord" (215.28), Ogden's version exclaims "O, Laws," and Sailer notes that this instance "reveals as much about Ogden's secular vision as about Basic English" (866). Taking the pun "the load is with me" (214.19) as a cue, the load of lordly language becomes in the translation a "weight" ("the weight is with me"), which humbly brings the travails of human endeavor down to earth. The "kingdome gone" (213.31) is just "the land of the dead," and in Basic the washerwomen beseech the "Earth" to "give peace to their hearts and minds" rather than "Orara por Orbe and poor Las Animas" (214.6), a phrase closely akin to the Spanish for "to pray for the Earth & the Souls" (McHugh 214). There is no need to pray when in Basic "All have livings" and "All is well," and in this new expression the echoes of alleluia fade from "Allalivial, allalluvial" (213.32).[3] Certainly, the Basic translation is partly right in orienting "Anna Livia" around life and "this world." Much of what ALP and her "mamafesta" (104.4) stand for is life-affirming and anti-patriarchal. However, the loss of ambiguity created by clearly withdrawing the divine from the course of events erodes the tension and significance of the *Wake*.

William Empson, that heretical classifier of ambiguities in the late 1920s, could support Basic while still critiquing its representation of literature. He explained his position by explicating the conflict between authority and freedom in the moment when Wordsworth devotes himself to poetry in *The Prelude*. Empson's reasoning also particularly applies in the case of the Basic ALP; he states: "the effect is that this beautiful morning is like a sign of some good secret at the back of all experience. As so frequently in Wordsworth, in fact, there is an idea of religion not clearly in view. It seems to me that putting the lines into Basic makes this turn of thought much clearer, for the very reason that Basic is so short of words like 'magnificent.' The effect is like taking the cover off a machine" ("Basic" 170).[4] Similarly, the Basic "Anna Livia" removes much of the wondrous hydraulic apparatus from the chapter, and Joyce would possibly expect this in collaborating with Ogden, whom he considered "a mathematician," on the *Wake*, "which he insisted was mathematical" (Ellmann, *Joyce* 614).

One technique of the *Wake* that could be considered mathematical, Bruno's heretical coincidence of contraries, suffers from Basic's inability to replicate amalgamations. For rhythm, "Anna Livia," as Bishop notes, is "partitioned into intricate binary patterns" (350). While the Basic version often equivalently repeats words for sonorous effect, it fails in particular to account for the inclusive gesture of rivers running past and bringing forth historical and religious contradictions. The synthetic coincidence of contraries owes much to the effect of rivers, and, as Bishop pointedly explains, "rivalry" is "a formal principle of 'Anna Livia'" partly "because it derives from the Latin *rivalis* ('one using the same stream')" (350). Those rival city-builders of Latium, Romulus and Remus, sent adrift on the stream Tiber, would be nursed by Dea Tacita, "the silent goddess" also known as Acca Larentia. Before the fratricide happened and the murderer founded his eponymous Rome, Dea Tacita, or "Deataceas" (213.30), had reconciled their rivalry with a surrogate mother's love.

The Basic translation's omission of the allusion to Dea Tacita causes the loss of this emblematic coincidence of contraries important to the dream works of the *Wake*. As Bishop states, "all things manifest on the surface of the text act only as vectors pointing to far more turbulent rivalries and conflicts everywhere 'lying below' the evident surface of things" (351). The surface tension of "Deataceas" develops further when HCE, the archetypal male figure and another city-builder, appears syncretically as an "Etrurian Catholic Heathen" (215.20). Changing this cipher of HCE to "Etrurian Catholics of hated religion" dramatically exposes the biases of the translation. Whereas the *Wake* amalgamates the various types of religion that have lived along the Tiber, the Basic "Anna Livia" not only changes the rhythm and elides the tension embedded in the cipher, but it also imposes a value judgment on the religious relationships. In the *Wake*, the mysterious Etruscan religion, Roman Catholicism, and a general heathenism all survive simultaneously, and, as Ogden himself described Joyce's style, "this synthetic proliferate agglomeration" produces "the timeless condensation of the dream" (Preface x–xi).

For several years after the Basic English translation, Joyce continued with his *Work in Progress*, and reversed the direction of Ogden's reductive and clarifying project. According to his friends, Joyce would go "over a passage that was 'still not obscure enough'" or solicit "a word that would be more obscure than the word already there" (Bishop 3). He relished adding more names of rivers. Like so many of his personal dealings, the experience with Ogden found its way into the pages of "The Letter," according to Danis Rose, "probably in the mid-1930s" (441). In preparing this chapter of the *Wake*, Joyce inserted several qualifications about universal languages into a passage describing the primordial "letter" and the nature of being human and being in love: "if the lingo gasped between kicksheets, however *basically English*, were to be preached from the mouths of wickerchurchwardens and metaphysicians . . . where would their practice be or where the human race itself" (116.25–30, emphasis added). The passage suggests that no language can justly convey the fundamental aspects of being and love. The more complicated discourses, such as philosophy or theology, only distort the human emotions, perhaps best saved for pillow talk "gasped between kicksheets." And if the church warden or the metaphysician spoke in Basic English about *caritas* or Plato's *Symposium*, they would possibly lose their erudite mystique, but also do a disservice to love. Limiting vocabulary might be good for clarity, but the varieties of human experience often depend upon the change and wealth of language.

When the passage later refers to "hapaxle, legomenon" (116.33), *hapax legomenon*, the context suggests that though a word may only have been said once in history, this should not diminish its significance, for, among other things, it could represent love for someone. Furthermore, there may be no other word for it; it is untranslatable. In a sense, then, Joyce's response to Basic English supports the idea that he had in mind Bishop's observation that the rhythmic effect of the rivers conveys love. Through an analysis of HCE's feeling of being in the womb, which bonds and blurs genders, Bishop argues that "the 'interior' of his body is suffused by the 'intimite' 'lisp' of a sound unconsciously signifying 'love'" (368). The love becomes lost in translation once productive rivalries turn to hate, once people exclude rather than synthesize worldviews.

THE BETRAYAL OF HERESY IN *NINETEEN EIGHTY-FOUR*

In the godless world of Oceania in Orwell's *Nineteen Eighty-Four,* "heresy" still functions as the term used repeatedly to describe all subversive and antiestablishmentarian thought. Shorn of its religious connotations, heresy is Winston Smith's last hope and the elusive discourse in his desire to resist the extreme authoritarian state. The narrative teases him with the opportunity to read "*the book,*" Goldstein's "compendium of all the heresies" (15), only to have him trapped just as he understood what he already knew, the mechanisms by which the state, or war machine, controls heresy. The telescreens and the official language of Oceania, Newspeak, are perhaps the two most salient inventions of Orwell's dystopia, and they represent, respectively, the common practices of surveillance and propaganda. When "Newspeak had been adopted once and for all and Oldspeak forgotten," the appendix to the novel, "The Principles of Newspeak," states that it "was intended" that "a heretical thought . . . should be literally unthinkable, at least so far as thought is dependent on words" (246). The Inner Party chases after words as the Inquisition pursued heretics; only it has learned from historical mechanisms of discursive control and tries to "convert" the heretic rather than "destroy him." Since in "the old days the heretic walked to the stake still a heretic, proclaiming his heresy, exulting in it" (210), the Party uses all forms of torture and mind control to rehabilitate dissidents outside of the public spectacle.[5]

In Orwell's novel, the telescreens enable "Big Brother" to keep watch on the entire population of Oceania at nearly every moment. As the narrative states, "[t]here was of course no way of knowing whether you were

being watched at any given moment" (6). Oceania is a version of Bentham's
Panopticon on the grandest scale. In this light, both predominant methods
of control in *Nineteen Eighty-Four*, Newspeak and the telescreens, owe their
creation, in part, to Bentham's reformist mind. While delivering his centenary lecture on Bentham, Ogden declared that "Bentham is the true father
of Basic English," and he pointed to the page of 850 words on which, he said,
"Bentham's ideas for an international language have at last been worked
out" (42–44). While Foucault's famous account in *Discipline and Punish* has
illuminated the Panopticon's peculiar role in the historical turn from torture
to rehabilitation, John Bender's *Imagining the Penitentiary* (1987) is one of
the few studies to link Bentham's work on incarceration with his theory
of fictions. Bender argues that Bentham's "ideas help us to understand the
novel and the penitentiary as fundamentally similar social texts" because he
"wished to master reality by reshaping, and by rendering visible, the modes
of its fictional construction" (36). The proponents of Newspeak in *Nineteen
Eighty-Four* view reality, like Vaihinger, as a linguistic construction, and they
simultaneously exploit and dissemble that proposition. As a skewed variant
of "Panoptic English," Newspeak imprisons people within language while
simultaneously letting them think they are free.

The parallels between Basic English and Newspeak are manifold and
obvious. Both are "founded on the English language as we now know it," and
each sought to cut "the language down to the bone" by overhauling the "great
wastage" which lies "in the verbs and adjectives" (*Nineteen Eighty-Four* 247;
45). While Ogden did think Basic could make, as Syme explains in the novel,
the "meaning" of a word more "rigidly defined" as in Newspeak, Orwell's
hyperbolic critique extrapolates the implication that "the whole aim of Newspeak is to narrow the range of thought" (46).[6] In both language systems, the
process of elimination depends heavily on the interchangeability of parts of
speech and the regularity of inflections. Not only are synonyms redundant,
but the negative prefix "un-" makes antonyms also superfluous since "[a]ll
that was necessary, in any case where two words formed a natural pair of
opposites, was to decide which of them to suppress" (248). As a result, a "few
blanket words covered" "heretical meaning words," as in the Basic translation of ALP, "and, in covering them, abolished them" (*Nineteen Eighty-Four*
251).

As Newspeak included the C Vocabulary for specialized work in science and technology, Basic English hurt its claim that only 850 words were
required for an international language by developing word lists for use in,
among other disciplines, science, economics, and literature. In "The Prin-

ciples of Newspeak," Orwell may even be poking at the acronym behind Basic English: "Even in the early decades of the twentieth century, telescoped words and phrases [such as Nazi and Comintern] had been one of the characteristic features of political language" (252). The description of Newspeak claims that "in thus abbreviating a name one narrowed and subtly altered its meaning, by cutting out most of the associations that would otherwise cling to it" (252–53). The Anglo-American industrial and corporate interests disappear behind a language system simply touting itself as fundamental. Finally, both Basic and Newspeak grew in large part out of the desire to control heretical discourse. Newspeak sought the "repression of heretical words" (247), and, as I noted before, Ogden reflected that one of the great advantages in running the Heretics Society was the repeated forum in which "to study the defects of verbal exposition, and argument, under the most favourable conditions." His study of Bentham drew his attention to controlling the instability putatively more inherent in the verb, which was "a sort of linguistic eel—a slippery rhetorical luxury" ("Lecture" 42).

While defenders of Basic English shun the unflattering associations of a comparison with Newspeak,[7] it is clear that Ogden's invention was a source text for the planned language of Oceania. Too many similarities exist for critics to claim that, though Orwell had worked with Ogden on Basic English, the universal language does not inform Newspeak since Orwell never condemned it or openly attributed aspects of Basic to the creation of Newspeak. Indeed, Orwell appreciated the ability of Basic to deflate vague and highfalutin rhetoric, and he defended it against false beliefs that "advocates of an international language aim at suppressing the natural languages, a thing no one has ever seriously suggested" (*Works* 16: 82).[8] Orwell even facilitated the broadcast of Basic English ideas on the BBC in India. Nevertheless, Howard Fink documents Orwell's familiarity with Basic, outlines several dimensions in which Newspeak parodies it, and claims that "the public notoriety of Basic during the 1940s made it a natural vehicle for Orwell's satire" (156). Jean Jacques Courtine affirms that the "satire of *Basic English* is transparent in *Newspeak*" (72). Arguing that in the 1940s "contemporary educated readers with linguistic interests" would have discerned the parallels between the invented languages, Roger Fowler offers the following judicious perspective: "Orwell is not attacking Basic through Newspeak; Basic is used rather as an analogy, an aid to readers to imagine what kind of linguistic system Newspeak might be" (220–21). If Newspeak is founded in part on actual experiences, the dangers of language control become more real. In fact, Orwell explained that the future of *Nineteen Eighty-Four* "*could* happen" because "the direction in which the world is going at the present time" exposed it to the dangers of continuously preparing for a war driven by the fear of terror, and of "the acceptance of a totalitarian outlook by intellectuals of all colours" (*Works* 20:134). Perhaps Orwell grew wary of Basic English during the mid-1940s when Ogden handed over the copyright for his language to the Crown and eventually settled for £23,000, the same compensation Bentham had received from the Crown for the rights to the Panopticon. The state had appropriated the work of Ogden, whose multifarious heresies had been brought into the fold and then lost in bureaucracy. Orwell's dystopic novel illustrates the results of the appropriation of altruistic syncretic discourse by the state apparatus.

The control of heretical discourses in *Nineteen Eighty-Four* represents the culmination of the prevalent betrayal theme underwriting the novel. From little children informing on their parents to Winston's broken loyalty to Julia, people betray each other in the face of institutional control. The state conducts false flag operations, and O'Brien pretends to introduce Winston to the underworld supposedly gathering around Goldstein's "compendium of all the heresies," only to assert his absolute power during the process of "rehabilitation." Eventually, the torture, starvation, isolation, observation, "merciless questioning" (199), and fear of the unknown lead to Winston's ultimate betrayal, the insertion of another body, Julia his love, between himself and his greatest fear, the rat mask.[9] After Julia's and Winston's mutual betrayal, she explains that "after that, you don't feel the same toward the other person any longer" (240). Once Winston Churchill, whose name it has been noted lends itself to Orwell's protagonist, called for an Anglo-American coalition promoting Ogden's language, a similar taint of betrayal infected Basic English.

In July of 1943, Churchill dictated his interest in Basic English to the Secretary of the War Cabinet, Sir Edward Bridges: "I am very much interested in the question of Basic English. The widespread use of this would be a gain to us far more durable and fruitful than the annexation of great provinces. It would also fit in with my ideas of closer union with the United States by making it even more worth while to belong to the English-speaking club." As part of this "special relationship," Churchill further suggested that "the B.B.C. should teach Basic English every day as part of their propaganda, and generally make a big push to propagate this method of interchange of thought" (*War* 571). During 1944, Churchill drew six ministries into the promotion of Basic, and this governmental support not only brought Basic into the quagmire of bureaucracy, but also elicited the withdrawal of American funding. When Churchill lost the election of 1946, the new Labour government pigeonholed Basic and effectively sealed its official fate. However, in accepting an honorary degree at Harvard in September 1943, Churchill had forecast the global hegemony of English: "Let us go forward as with other matters and other measures in aim and effect [as Basic English] . . . Such plans offer far better prizes than taking away other people's provinces or lands or grinding them down in exploitation. The empires of the future are the empires of the mind" (*Victory* 238).[10]

   Nineteen Eighty-Four is the demonstration of the colonization of a mind. Newspeak facilitates the "doublethink" that can cause a *"lunatic dislocation in the mind"* (204), and Winston's rehabilitative "cure" destroys his belief that "[n]othing was your own except the few cubic centimeters inside your skull" (26). Ogden, who once had been the "Arch-Heretic" at Cambridge (MCMA 114.3), and whose Heretics Society had taught him about the verbal "fictions" in the mind, welcomed the official totalization of his language system. He wanted a "strong 'Anglo-American Directorate' formed by the two governments to take control of its future expansion" ("World" 25). Diffusing English language handbooks in the name of globalization could be a boon to a British and American coalition exporting military and industrial technology.

   A month after Churchill's speech at Harvard, Ogden introduced his invention to a now captive national audience in a strange article in *The Picture Post,* "Can Basic English Be a World Language?" Ogden's promotion of the language system, interlaid with bizarre photographs of him in various masks, must have been disturbing to any dissident thinker. As he often did to promote his language, Ogden wrote the article in Basic English, with one mistake designed to turn the article into a deciphering contest. Several of the photographs underscore a sense of duplicity in that they include shots of Ogden in "different masks" worn "to suit different requirements" (23). In one photograph, he wears a Fu Manchu mask which somehow demonstrates "certain Eastern language effects" (24), and the caption below the opening photo asks if the "strange figure in the Orthological Institute" is "Mr. Churchill discovering Basic English" (see figure 8). No, it is Ogden in an affectless, white mask which he described as "that which has doubts about the chances of one's death taking place in one's bed" (23). The masks flavor Ogden's introduction of Basic to the national stage with an unsettling eccentricity akin to the effects of Charrington's disguise and the rat mask in Orwell's novel. Indeed, Mary Adam's recollection of Ogden's fascination with masks has an eerie resonance with the novel: "He would often don a mask. He had many masks. A wonderful collection. And he would wear a mask

Figure 8. "Mr. Churchill Discovering Basic English." C. K. Ogden wears a mask in the offices of the Orthological Institute. (*Source:* C. K. Ogden fonds, McMaster University Library, MCMA 138.13).

when he talked to you—and often put a mask on you" (qtd. in Gordon 3). Another photograph in the article shows Ogden holding a Panoptic Word Wheel nearby a "Janus," a tool used for teaching tenses (see figure 9). The associations of the two-faced god, the masks, and the eclectic artifacts in Ogden's study evoke the images associated with Charrington, the masked member of the Thought Police who entraps Winston in his curiosity shop.

While these images can only be speculatively associated with the novel, Ogden's discussion of the potential effects of mass media on the populace bears remarkable similarities to the "Two Minutes Hate" in Oceania. In the article, Ogden states: "One great step forward [toward international peace] would be news every hour of the day and night, in a simple common language, from one or other of 24 stations working with a common purpose through Basic. Five minutes would be enough . . . to give everyone the feeling that he was part of a Great Society which was slowly pulling itself together" (24). In Oceania, everyone gathers before a telescreen on the "eleven hundred" hour in preparation for the propaganda of the "Two Minutes Hate" (12). Whereas

Figure 9. C. K. Ogden holding the Panopticon, or Basic Word Wheel. (**Source:** C. K. Ogden fonds, McMaster University Library, MCMA 138.13)

the "horrible thing about the Two Minutes Hate" was "that it was impossible to avoid joining in," almost immediately a "hideous ecstasy of fear and vindictiveness, a desire to kill, to torture, to smash faces with a sledge hammer, seemed to flow through the whole group of people like an electric current, turning one even against one's will into a grimacing, screaming lunatic" (16). In an exact parallel to Winston's job in the Ministry of Truth, Ogden supposes the fruits of his imagined news broadcast: "We have been comforting ourselves for five minutes with current notes from the International History Bank whose managers are the experts of the Limited Language Company responsible for the news . . .—a Basic account of those events which in their opinion were, at that time of day, of greatest general interest" (25).

Such opinions certainly can be influenced by advertising and political leanings, and Orwell's novel shows how a similar form of propaganda could be used to cultivate "hate." The novel, in effect, challenges Ogden's claim that the diffusion of Basic English "would at least do no damage" (25). At a minimum, *Nineteen Eighty-Four* underscores the dangerous potential of language manipulation, and the disturbing, exploited historical truism that war makes both television and public approval ratings soar. About three weeks after Churchill's "empires of the mind" speech, Orwell tendered his resignation at the BBC, where he had been commissioning radio talks on Basic during the Second World War. He explained that "by going back to my normal work of writing and journalism [he] could be more useful." During this time, he drafted the first outline of *Nineteen Eighty-Four*, which ends with the entry "The Two Minutes Hate" (*Works* 15:368).

Unlike the hedonism of *Brave New World*, the promise of *The Shape of Things to Come*, or the comic elements of Eugene Zamiatin's *We* (1924), the absolute power wielded by Big Brother and the bleak general despair in Oceania clearly construct Orwell's vision of the future as a didactic dystopia. Aside from coteries of individuals nestled into the upper echelons of the military industrial complex, no one, however, reads the novel as a positive-minded teaching text. War makes people flock to the security of oversimplified, rigid policies. Only by opposition does the novel pose a series of lessons on how to keep heresy alive amid an authoritative state bent on its control. By exposing the mechanisms by which state apparati quash and regulate heresy, the novel points to sites of contestation within the *modus operandi* of surveillance, propaganda, and the appropriation of subversive discourse. Each intrinsically depends on language, and Orwell's work invests the power of words not only with the state, but also individuals. The omnipotence of the state may make Winston love Big Brother, but Julia's note of "*I love you*" causes Winston to "desire to stay alive" (90–91). The state may package all subversive thought within Goldstein's "compendium of all the heresies," and thereby limit its independence, but its presence nevertheless delivers a pointed critique, however tedious, of the politics of the Party.

The control of discourse by the totalitarian state is unmitigated, but most readings of the novel tend to expose various unrealistic elements of its portrayal. Readers resist, and perhaps the greatest misrepresentation lies in 85 percent of the population, the "proles." Orwell's own distrust of the proletariat certainly informs the narrative portrayal of the mass of people as readily appeased with gambling, sport, drink, and the "Two Minutes Hate." They are the sleeping giant forever snoring, but the narrative also repeatedly states, "*If there is hope . . . it lies in the proles.*" Winston's hope, though, immediately becomes flagged by the italicized, intrusive reflection which "might almost have been a transcription from one of the Party textbooks": "*Until they become conscious they will never rebel, and until after they have rebelled they cannot become conscious*" (60–61). He has begun to "doublethink."

In *The Act of Reading*, Wolfgang Iser explains that the repertoire of a text "contains familiar materials, but that this material undergoes a change," and that when the norms "are depragmatized, they become a theme in themselves." As a repertoire of the novel, Basic English points to both the themes of betrayal and the use of language to colonize the mind. Through the exposure of social norms, a text, Iser argues, enables the reader "to perceive consciously a system in which he had hitherto been unconsciously caught up, and his awareness will be all the greater if the validity of these norms is negated." In this process of defamiliarization, "the reader is constrained to develop a specific attitude that will enable him to discover that which the negation has indicated but not formulated" (212–13). While Newspeak negates Basic English in part, the version of Newspeak in the novel is only "a provisional one" since it "was expected" to "have finally superseded Old-speak . . . by about the year 2050" (246). Similarly, in 1928, Ogden believed that Basic English would "initiate a programme of scientific Debabelization which it may take a hundred years to carry through" ("Universal" 6). The futuristic and dystopic nature of Orwell's novel accentuates Iser's point that the "process of negation . . . situates the reader halfway between a 'no longer' and a 'not yet'" (213). Winston can still struggle to have heretical thoughts during the gradual inculcation of Newspeak. The process of negation in *Nineteen Eighty-Four* indicates that the education of the "proles" is key to staving off the world of Big Brother. The "proles" remain outside the agenda of the colonization of the mind, and the characterization of such a large percentage of the populace running rampant with relative impunity and ignorance draws attention to itself as an absurdity and a site of contestation. Or, in Iser's words, the lack of an educated proletariat "prestructures" the reader's "mental image" of Oceania as a "defined deficiency" and a "hollow form" (213). The "proles" are the large blank slate to be taught the skills of interpretation, for rebellion may feed consciousness, but education is its staple.

In the framework of the novel, heretical discourse is an impossibility for the "proles" because they do not have the language skills or historical sense necessary for interpretation. Even members of the Inner Party will supposedly not have these skills since the final absorption of Newspeak would preclude the use of other words. Interpretation disappears in such a linguistic community because Newspeak cannot be paraphrased by its own lexicon. It is the rendering plant of paraphrase. "The Principles of Newspeak" states that it was "possible to utter heresies of a very crude sort, a species of blasphemy," but such statements "could not have been sustained by reasoned argument, because the necessary words were not available" (254–55). Newspeak and Basic English both turn paraphrase cannibalistically onto itself. John Bender argues that Bentham's "signal contribution to narrative theory" was "the expository device of 'paraphrasis'" which he "invented to dispel 'the pestilential breath of fiction'" (214). For Basic English, Ogden directly applies this "paraphrasis of exposition" in one of the key reductive principles of its vocabulary—the "[e]limination of all words which can be defined in 10 other words" ("Universal" 5). For both Ogden and Bentham, the use of paraphrase can expose the "illusion of significance that attaches to fictional entities," and which inheres in "human language" (Bender 214). Bentham insisted, in Bender's analysis, that "substantives used in apparently significant sentences gain their meaning, even when they have no real reference, by the context of the whole sentence in which they appear and, critically, that the translation of such sentences into other sentences determines their significance" (214). For Basic English, Ogden directed this sentence-level analysis onto individual words.

In his later years, William Empson referred to the "doublethink" of *Nineteen Eighty-Four* as an example of how doctrinal statements often mask untenable propositions, disturbing premises, and irreconcilable contradictions. As his methodology shows, paraphrase is a valuable interpretive tool to illuminate the ambiguities often underlying authoritarian answers. During the Second World War, Empson also worked on Basic at the BBC, and he shared his concerns with Ogden that Basic lost its efficacy in necessarily including official quotations: "The problem about news, especially for the BBC, which has a policy of being cautious about news, is that half the time you are quoting a communiqué or some text which is the only authority for the story, and that source is itself couched in vague or puzzling terms" (*Letters* 140). Paraphrase can deconstruct such statements, and that is the reason Basic attracted Orwell and Empson. Its importance for heretical thought continues, for it can expose the workings of propaganda and the "doublethink" of an ideology that sees a "continuous war" become the given state of affairs and engender the definition "WAR IS PEACE" (7).[11]

Cleanth Brooks' denunciation of Empson's mode of critical analysis as the heresy of paraphrase exemplifies Foucault's point that "the importance that has been given for so long to the small techniques of discipline, to those apparently insignificant tricks that it has invented, and even to those 'sciences' that give it a respectable face" arises from the development of the "minute disciplines, the panopticisms of every day" as "the political counterpart of the juridical norms according to which power was redistributed" (*Discipline* 223). In Foucault's view, the panoptic principle is central to the origins of the disciplinary society. New Criticism is an example of a panoptic "minute discipline" which affirmed Bentham's and I. A. Richards' emphases on the whole literary context to determine meaning, while refuting the ability to speak of its significance in other words. As a result, New Criticism can reinforce the power of orthodoxy. Denying the validity of paraphrase deprives literature not only of the capacity for social critique, but also its ideal function of making better citizens.

As various elements of Orwell's world become more "real," the import of the novel increases concomitantly with the responsibility to teach and practice dissent, diversity, and other forms of heretical thought. To wage a continuous war, increased surveillance invades personal privacy in the name of homeland security, and national media control the dissemination of foreign press and the reports of political protests, always inflecting the end of the news blurb with dismissive trivialities or minor counter-demonstrations. Foreign policy creates a pariah out of a former ally, and constructs pure "evil" which then shifts its axis depending on the global climate. On the other hand, the rejuvenation of religious fundamentalism is a development Orwell did not foresee; "even religious worship would have been permitted if the proles had shown any sign of needing or wanting it" (62). Noting "how far education has abandoned its historic tasks, of combating superstition, encouraging skeptical debate about competing religions and their claims of their myths, and fighting religious dogmatism and its political consequences," Jonathan Culler suggests that teachers of literature might compare "Christianity with other mythologies when we teach works imbued with religion, [make] the sadism and sexism of religious discourse an explicit object of discussion," and "work to keep alive the critical, demythologizing force of contemporary theory" (78–81). In 1945, an aging Bernard Shaw additionally warned that "heretical teaching must be made irresistibly attractive by fine art," or nations will fall "at the feet of Pavlov and Hitler" (Postscript 292). This pedagogy could include modes of interpretation from the linguistic to the political and share the mechanisms of heretical discourse which veil critique, subvert the censor, expose ideology, and spawn difference. To cultivate the hope that lies in the "proles," literary scholars are ethically bound to discuss the education Jude Fawley sought and found, the education culminating in Stephen Dedalus' *non-serviam*, the education the Heretics Society fostered. While "new wine in old bottles" now may be a "dead metaphor" as Orwell jotted down in his notes for *Nineteen Eighty-Four,* heresy will survive (*Works* 15:367). Perhaps it will go under a different name such as progressive politics, radical theology, or deep ecology, but none has yet equaled the weight wielded by "heresy" in the era of Hardy, Harrison, Shaw, and Joyce.

Appendix

Meetings of the Heretics Society, Cambridge, 1909–24

a.) published addresses
b.) public lectures
c.) lecture added to original schedule
d.) strictly confined to full members of the Heretics Society
e.) published in revised form
f.) uncertain date
g.) uncertain title of address

Titles and forms of address are in original cases and spellings.

MICHAELMAS 1909

	Nov. 21	C. N. S. Woolf, "Blake the Mystic"
	Nov. 28	A. E. Löwy, "Evolution of Religion"
a. b.)	Dec. 8	Miss Jane Harrison, "Heresy and Humanity" (inaugural lecture)
a. b.)	Dec. 8	Dr. John McTaggart, "Dare to be wise" (inaugural lecture)

LENT 1910

	Jan. 30	G. W. Paget, "William Godwin"
b.)	Feb. 4	Prof. E. G. Browne, "The Adaptation of Heresy to its Environment"
	Feb. 6	S. H. Batty-Smith, "The Plays of Oscar Wilde"
b.)	Feb. 12	Dr. F. C. S. Schiller, "Pragmatism, Humanism, and the Religious Problem"
	Feb. 13	Mr. E. I. James, "The True Mysticism" (earlier titled "The Place of Mysticism in philosophy")
	Feb. 27	N. B. Michell, "Love"
b.)	Mar. 10	Mr. R. R. Rusk, "What is Religion?"
		Mr. L. H. G. Greenwood, "Agnosticism and Conduct" (joint meeting with the Emmanuel Religious Discussion Society)

EASTER 1910

b.)	May 12	Miss F. M. Stawell, "Hebrew Scepticism"
	June 12	N. B. Michell, "The Secular Education Movement"

MICHAELMAS 1910

a.)	Oct. 23	C. M. Picciotto, "Via Mystica"
b.)	Oct. 26	Dr. A. C. Haddon, "The Moral Ideas of Savages"
	Oct. 30	Mr. E. B. V. Burns, "von Hartmann's Critique of Religion"
	Nov. 6	F. F. L. Birrell, "On Idiotism"
b.)	Nov. 7	Mr. Aylmer Maude, "The Future of Religion"
b.)	Nov. 13	C. Bradlaugh Bonner, "Mithraism and Christianity"
	Nov. 20	G. E. Jackson, "Social Aspects of Disillusion"
a. b.)	Nov. 23	Mr. Harrold Johnson, "The Problem of an effective Lay Moral Education, with special reference to France and Japan"
d.)	Nov. 30	Miss E. M. Smith, "Self-Delusion and its Value"
	Dec. 4	Mr. Arthur Machen, "Symbolism" (previously scheduled for Nov. 27)

LENT 1911

	Jan. 22	A. Watkins, "Individuality and Convention"
a. b.)	Jan. 23	Mr. Edward Clodd, "Obscurantism in Modern Science" (joint meeting with the Emmanuel R.D.S.)
	Jan. 29	W. B. Copeland, "E. A. Poe"
	Feb. 5	P. Sargant Florence, "The value of Historical Method in Aesthetics"
b.)	Feb. 8	Mr. A. C. Benson, "Walter Pater"
	Feb. 12	Miss K. C. Costelloe, "The Relation of Pragmatism to Truth and Ethics"
	Feb. 19	C. K. Ogden, "The Progress of Significs"
b.)	Feb. 20	Rev. R. J. Campbell, "The Possibility of a Liberal Interpretation of Christianity" (earlier titled "Is a Liberal Interpretation of Christianity possible?")
b.)	Feb. 25	J. A. Hobson, "Sentiments regarding Heresy"
	Feb. 26	D. S. Fraser, "Hinduism"
	Mar. 5	A. J. Dorward, "Aristotle's Poetics" (replaces Mom Chow Skon "Orientalia" which had been originally scheduled for Feb. 5 under the title "Siamese Superstitions" and then apparently canceled)
	Mar. 12	A. L. Bacharach, "Thomas Hardy, the Poet of Heresy"

EASTER 1911

	Apr. 23	C. B. Bonner, "Servetus and Calvin"
	Apr. 30	C. K. Ogden, "The Inexplicable Indescribability of Post-mortem Psychoses"
b.)	May 1	Earl Russell, "Religion and Science"
	May 7	R. A. Fisher, "Whilom Eugenics"

	May 14	D. H. Pinsent, "Solipsism"
a. b.)	May 21	Dr. W. H. R. Rivers, "The Primitive Conception of Death"
a. b.)	May 29	Mr. G. Bernard Shaw, "The Religion of the Future"

MICHAELMAS 1911

	Oct. 15	A. Watkins, "Functions of Modern Drama"
	Oct. 22	Mr. S. H. Swinny, "Positivism"
a. b.)	Oct. 25	Mr. F. M. Cornford, "Religion and the University"
	Oct. 29	R. D. Macrae (canceled)
	Nov. 5	R. Smith, "The Philosophy of Bergson" (replaces lecture by C. B. Bonner)
a.)	Nov. 12	Mr. H. G. Wood, "The Christ-Myth (a criticism)" (originally scheduled for Nov. 19)
a. b.)	Nov. 17	Mr. G. K. Chesterton, "The Future of Religion" also called "Some Dogmas of Mr. Bernard Shaw" (reply to Shaw's address)
	Nov. 19	Mr. W. R. M. Lamb, "Principles of Plastic Art" (originally scheduled for Nov. 12)
	Nov. 26	A. E. Heath, "Hypothesis in Science" (earlier titled "Science and Hypothesis")
a. b.)	Dec. 3	Mr. J. M. Robertson, M.P., "The Historicity of Jesus" (originally scheduled for Nov. 25)

LENT 1912

	Jan. 21	H. F. Heard, "G. K. Chesterton"
	Jan. 28	G. F. Shove, "The Conception of the General Will in Modern Political Theory"
b.)	Jan. 29	Mr. Joseph McCabe, "Materialism"
	Feb. 4	Miss E. M. Smith, "Animism"
	Feb. 11	C. F. Angus, "Christian Discipleship"
b.)	Feb. 12	Mrs. A. W. Verrall, "Telepathy"
	Feb. 18	E. J. F. Alford, "Liberty"
	Feb. 25	T. E. Hulme, "Anti-Romanticism and Original Sin"
b.)	Feb. 26	Dr. C. S. Myers, "The New Realism"
a. b.)	Mar. 11	Bertrand Russell, "The Philosophy of Bergson"

EASTER 1912

	Apr. 21	T. Renton, "Egyptian Religion"
	Apr. 28	J. E. Wilks, "Conversion"
b.)	Apr. 29	Mr. E. Bullough, "Religion and Art"
	May 5	L. C. Robertson, "The Vedantic Philosophy"
	May 12	H. F. Jolowicz, "The Paradox of Ancient Religion"
	May 19	Dr. J. W. Oman, "Religion and Reality"
	May 26	Miss M. Gabain, "Pascal: The Consistent Christian"
	June 2	Mr. H. Wildon Carr, "Life and Logic" (a defence of Bergson)

b.)   June 5   Mr. Frank Harris, "Shakespeare as Friend and Lover"

MICHAELMAS 1912

	Oct. 20	P. Sargant Florence, "The Possibility of an Inductive Political Science"
b.)	Oct. 21	Prof. Patrick Geddes, "Mythology and Life—an Interpretation of Olympus as Rediscoverable"
	Oct. 27	Harold Munro, "Contemporary English Poetry"
	Nov. 3	V. Bugeja, "Scientific Intellectualism and Religious Belief"
	Nov. 10	Rev. P. N. Waggett, "Scientific Method in Religion"
b.)	Nov. 11	Dr. G. T. Wrench, "Nietzsche"
	Nov. 17	Dr. Ivor Ll. Tuckett, "The Evidence of the Supernatural"
	Nov. 24	E. B. Shanks, "The Technique of English Verse"
a. b.)	Nov. 25	Jane Harrison, "Unanimism: A Study of Conversion and Some Contemporary French Poets"
	Dec. 1	L. Macrae, "The Nature of Religious Knowledge"
	Dec. 8	W. L. Scott, "Against Mr. Moore"

LENT 1913

	Jan. 19	P. Sargant Florence, "Political Science"
	Jan. 26	H. F. Jolowicz, "The Greek Attitude towards Art"
b.)	Jan. 27	By a Member of the Facts Society, "The Truth about Telepathy"
	Jan. 28	Gathering to celebrate the 100th meeting of the Heretics
	Feb. 2	A. J. Dorward, "Evidence and Belief"
	Feb. 9	F. Bekassy, "Medieval Heretics"
b.)	Feb. 11	Dr. W. H. D. Rouse, "Some Principles of Education"
	Feb. 16	M. Georges Roth, "Unanimist Poetry"
e.)	Feb. 23	Rupert Brooke, "The Drama: Present and Future" (originally scheduled for Mar. 2)
b.)	Feb. 24	Mr. Haldane MacFall, "The Splendid Wayfaring: An Attack on Art-Criticism" (titled "Against the Art Critics" in contemporaneous issue of *Cambridge Magazine*)
	Mar. 2	Miss O. H. Persitz, "Anarchism: Past & Present" (originally scheduled for Feb. 23)

EASTER 1913

	Apr. 13	J. F. Harris, "Samuel Butler, the author of 'Erewhon'"
	Apr. 20	A. D. Richie, "Vitalism"
	Apr. 27	Mr. Kamaluddin, "Some Principles of Islam"
b.)	May 4	Dr. G. F. Rogers, "Hypnotism"
	May 11	Miss S. Fairhurst, "The Sorrows of a Psychologist"
	May 18	R. A. Fisher, "Nietzsche or Huxley?"
	May 25	V. Bugeja, "The Social Psychology of the Jesuits"

	June 1	Mr. H. Golding, "Kierkegaard, a forerunner of Ibsen and Nietzsche"
b.)	June 2	Mr. F. C. Conybeare, "Dreams"
	June 8	Mr. S. A. Cook, "Psychology and future Theology"

MICHAELMAS 1913

	Oct. 19	Mr. H. G. Wood, "Religion and the Unknown"
	Oct. 26	W. L. Scott, (1) "Bertrand Russell as a Neo-Platonist"; (2) "Dramatic Criticism Condemned"
a. b.)	Oct. 27	Mr. G. M. Trevelyan, "De Haeretico Comburendo"
b.)	Nov. 2	Mr. C. Reddie, "Sex in Education and Education in Sex"
a. b.)	Nov. 10	Mr. Holbrook Jackson, "The Artist as Heretic"
	Nov. 16	Mr. Halliday Sparling, "The Logic of the Bandar Log"
	Nov. 23	F. W. Stokoe, "Jules Laforgue"
b.)	Nov. 24	Mr. G. Sturge Moore, "Taste"
	Nov. 30	Mr. Hugh Elliott, "Scientific Materialism"
c. e. f. g.)	Dec. 1	Georg Brandes, "Nietzsche"

LENT 1914

	Jan. 18	F. Bekassy, "Hungarian Poetry since 1906"
	Feb. 1	Mr. R. D. Prowse, "Some Aspects of Modern Drama"
b.)	Feb. 6	Mr. G. Lowes Dickinson, "The Religion of Time and the Religion of Eternity"
	Feb. 8	Dr. R. Piccoli, "Croce's Aesthetic"
d.)	Feb. 15	Dr. G. E. Moore, "The Philosophy of Commonsense"
b.)	Feb. 16	Debate with the "X" Club, Oxford, "That in the opinion of this House the Churches are doing more harm than good"
b.)	Feb. 22	Mr. J. H. Badley, "Co-Education"
	Mar. 1	Mr. John Alford, "Walt Whitman" (canceled)
a. c. d.)	Mar. 1	Bertrand Russell, "Mysticism and Logic"
d.)	Mar. 8	Mr. A. Thorold, "The Philosophy of Anatole France"

EASTER 1914

	Apr. 26	G. Von Kaufmann, "The Monism of Wilhelm Ostwald" (originally scheduled for Jan. 25)
	May 3	W. J. Gould, "History of Individualism"
b.)	May 10	Miss Cicely Hamilton, "The Conventions of the Theatre"
	May 17	H. D. Henderson, "Morality and its Motives"
	May 24	A. J. Dorward, "Conventionality and Boredom"
	May 31	P. Vos, "The Reasonableness of the Jewish Religion"
c.)	June 3	Signore F. T. Marinetti, "Futurism"
b.)	June 5	Professor Gilbert Murray, "The Conception of Another World"
	June 7	Mrs. Graham, "Can we see God?"

MICHAELMAS 1914

	Oct. 18	Mr. E. J. Dent, "The Meaning of Music"
	Oct. 25	Mr. E. Bullough, "Nietzsche and the War"
	Nov. 1	Dr. N. Wiener, "Scepticism"
	Nov. 8	P. Sargant Florence, "The Key to Sociology"
c.)	Nov. 15	Prof. G. Santayana, "An Interpretation of Transcendentalism"
	Nov. 22	B. W. Downs, "Brieux" (originally scheduled for Nov. 15)
	Nov. 29	Dr. R. Piccoli, "The Philosophy of Michelstaedter" (originally scheduled for Nov. 22)
a.)	Dec. 5 or 6	Miss C. (Constance) Stoney, "Early Double Monasteries"

LENT 1915

	Jan. 17	Private Business
	Jan. 24	L. H. G. Greenwood, "Can the Promotion of Heresy be defended?"
	Jan. 31	Miss F. M. Stawell, "The Religion of Goethe"
	Feb. 7	Rev. E. W. Lummis, "In Praise of Faith"
	Feb. 14	M. Van Iseghem, "Romain Rolland"
c.)	Feb. 21	Mr. E. E. Kellett, "Mediaevalism in Milton"
c.)	Feb. 28	W. H. Bruford, "Friedrich Hebbel"
	Mar. 7	Mr. Harold Monro, "The God-Myth in Modern Poetry"
	Mar. 14	Mr. S. Thayer, "Aesthetica"

EASTER 1915

Apr. 25	Private Business
May 2	Mr. C. Delisle Burns, "The Debt of Modern Philosophy to Literature"
May 9	Mr. E. Bullough, "The Talking Horses of Elberfeld"
May 16	Miss I. R. Turner, "On Certain Theosophical Fallacies"
May 23	Mr. Shinji Ishii, "Freedom of Thought in Japan"
May 30	Mr. A. S. McDowall, "Are we Realists?"
June 6	Vernon Lee, "War, Group-Emotion and Art"

MICHAELMAS 1915

	Oct. 17	Jane Harrison, "Russia and the Russian Verb: A Contribution to the Psychology of the Russian People" (members' meeting)
a. d.)	Oct. 24	Miss E. Power, "Cult of the Virgin in the Middle Ages"
	Oct. 31	Charles Sayle, "Sir Thomas Browne"
	Nov. 7	Miss D. Jordan-Lloyd, "Facts and Fancies"
	Nov. 14	Desmond Macarthy, "Heroic Poetry"
	Nov. 21	S. K. Ratcliffe, "Billy Sunday and the Business of Conversion"
	Nov. 28	James Woods, "Cubism"
	Dec. 4	J. C. Squire, "Utopias"

LENT 1916

c.)   Jan. 16   Mr. W. S. Scott, "A Problem of Ethics"
        Jan. 23   G. E. Moore, "Intrinsic Value and its relations to Beauty and
                    Patches of Yellow surrounded by Red Rings"
b.)   Jan. 30   G. H. Hardy, "The Value of Knowledge"
        Feb. 6   G. G. Coulton, "Toleration"
        Feb. 13   L. Alston, "Marcus Aurelius"
        Feb. 20   P. G. Howlett, "Carlyle's Debt to Goethe"
        Feb. 27   W. E. Armstrong, "Happiness"
        Mar. 5   Miss L. A. Lomas, "Psycho-analysis and Poetry"
        Mar. 12   E. J. Dent, "The Musical interpretation of Shakespeare on the
                    Modern Stage"

EASTER 1916

        Apr. 30   F. S. Marvin, "The Reality of Progress"
        May 14   G. de Swietochowski, "Poland and her Religious Problems"
        May 21   Mrs. Bradlaugh Bonner, "Belief, Make-belief, and Unbelief"
        May 28   V. Peniakoff, "The Aesthetics of Mr. Clive Bell" (originally
                    scheduled for May 7)
        June 4   Julius West, "The Russian Intelligentsia"
        June 11   Dr. Raffaello Piccoli, "The Religion of Mazzini"

MICHAELMAS 1916

        Oct. 22   Dr. Raffaello Piccoli, "The Ethics of Intellect"
        Oct. 29   W. H. Bruford, "Anatole France"
        Nov. 5   Mrs. Constance Graham, "Soul-doctoring, a Profession for the Laity"
        Nov. 12   Mrs. Rebecca West (postponed)
        Nov. 19   Miss D. W. Black, "Some Conceptions of Comedy"
        Nov. 26   Sunday meeting transferred to open meeting q.v.
b.)   Nov. 28   Professor W. Bateson, "Evolutionary Theory and Modern Doubts"
                    (with Lantern Illustrations)
        Dec. 3   Mrs. M. A. Hamilton, "Henry James"

LENT 1917

        Jan. 21   Ernest J. Chaloner, "Art and Anarchy"
        Jan. 28   Miss Rebecca West, "Emotion and Education" (originally
                    scheduled for Nov. 12, 1916)
        Feb. 11   A. D. Waley, "Chinese Poetry"
        Feb. 18   Mr. Thomas, "Buddhism and Western Heterodoxy"
        Feb. 25   M. Jean Nicod, "Love of Life and the Instinct of Sacrifice"
                    (originally scheduled for Feb. 4)

Mar. 4   Mr. E. E. Turner, "The Futility of Utility"
Mar. 11   E. R. Brown, "Still Life"

EASTER 1917

Apr. 22   Mr. E. Vulliamy, "Is Reality an Object of Art?"
Apr. 29   Mr. Adrian Stephen, "In Defence of Understanding"
May 6   Mr. W. W. Rouse Ball, "Cagliostro"
May 13   Miss D. D. Ivers, "Origen and his Age"
May 20   B. W. Downs, "Four Novelists of the Grand Siècle"
May 27   Miss Gabain, "Eurhythmics"
June 3   Mr. John Copley, "Revolutionary Fetters on Art"

MICHAELMAS 1917

Oct. 21   Mr. A. E. Heath, "The New Realism"
Oct. 28   Dr. G. F. Rogers, "Hypnotism"
Nov. 4   Mr. E. E. Kellett, "The Nicene Creed"
Nov. 11   C. C. Chatterji, "Individual and Society"
Nov. 18   Mrs. A. E. Meyer, "Eugenics and Education"
Nov. 25   L. S. Stebbing, "The Utility of Metaphysics"
Dec. 2   S. K. Ratcliffe, "The Lower Middle Classes. A Problem"

LENT 1918

Jan. 20   Sworry[1]
Jan. 27   Miss E. A. Drew, "What was Shakespeare's idea of Comedy?"
Feb. 3   Mr. R. Demos, "The Nature of Organisation"
Feb. 10   Miss D. Wrinch, "The Inter-Relation of Science and Philosophy"
Feb. 17   Dr. G. E. Moore, "The Value of Religion"
Feb. 24   Mr. P. Tudor-Hart, "Unity in Art"
Mar. 3   Miss D. W. Black, "The Abbé Pluche and other Christian Apologists"
Mar. 10   Mr. Roper, "Education"

EASTER 1918

          Apr. 28   Sworry
a.)   May 5   Dr. Santayana, "Philosophic Opinion in America"
          May 12   Mr. John Drinkwater, "The Poet and Tradition"
          May 19   Mr. Shinji Ishii, "The Influence of Buddhism in Japan and the Psychology of Harakiri"
          May 26   Mr. Graham Wallas, "Rational Purpose"
          June 2   Miss E. B. C. Jones, "Walter de la Mare"

Michaelmas 1918

	Oct. 20	Mr. R. Demos, "Intolerance"
	Oct. 27	Captain Osbert Sitwell, "Intimidation in Art and Literature"
	Nov. 3	M. Mitrinevitch, "The realisation of reality"
	Nov. 17	F. C. Bartlett, "In Praise of Intolerance"
	Nov. 24	Meeting as announced
a.)	Dec. 1	Miss D. W. Black, "How to be Happy—Some 18th Century Recipes"

Lent 1919

Jan. 19 Mr. L. B. Walton, "The Imitative Faculty in Art"
Jan. 26 J. B. Conliffe, "Aspects of New Zealand University Life"
Feb. 2 Mr. E. Bullough, "My Experiences at Wilhelmshaven"
Feb. 9 Sava Popovitch, "Synthetic Art"
Feb. 16 W. A. Orton, "Artzibashef and the Russian Pessimism"
Feb. 23 J. Reineke van Stuwe, "Recent Currents in Dutch and Flemish Literature"
Mar. 2 Miss Strachey, "The Case against Modern Poetry"
Mar. 9 Mr. A. G. Pape, "A Plea for a New Motive in Education"

Easter 1919

May 4 Mr. B. W. Downs, "Is Drama a dead form of Art?"
May 11 Mr. J. C. Squire, "The Limitations of Heresy"
May 18 L. Smodlaka, "Scandinavian and Jugo-Slav ideals compared and contrasted"
May 25 Mr. E. Bullough, "The Film as a New Art"

Michaelmas 1919

Sabbatical Term

Lent 1920

Jan. 18 Mr. Robert Young, "State Religion in Japan"
Jan. 25 Mr. Ivor Richards, "Emotion and Art"
Feb. 1 Miss E. B. C. Jones, "The Art of Walter de la Mare"
Feb. 8 E. A. Walker, "Marcel Proust"
Feb. 15 Mrs. Vulliamy, "Dress"
Feb. 22 Dr. H. Crichton Miller, "The Making of a Heretic"
Feb. 29 Miss E. E. Power, "The Nun in Literature"
Mar. 7 Walter de la Mare, "Life in Fiction"
Mar. 14 Mrs. M. A. Hamilton, "Henry James"

SUMMER 1920

e.)   Apr. 25   I. A. Richards and C. K. Ogden, "The New Symbolist Movement"
        May 2   Miss E. E. Power, "A plea for the Middle Ages" (earlier titled "In
                    Defence of Mediaevalism")
        May 9   B. Dobree, "Laughter in its relation to Comedy"
        May 16   Miss E. Pedley, "The Sublime"

From June 1920 to January 1921, the records are incomplete.

a.)   Lytton Strachey, "Art and Indecency"

LENT 1921

        Jan. 23   Dr. G. E. Moore, "Some Problems of Ethics"
        Jan. 30   W. Whateley Smith, "Psychical Research"
e.)   Feb. 27   Jane Harrison, "The Religion of To-Day"

SUMMER 1921

        Apr. 24   Dr. W. H. R. Rivers, "The Origin of Caste"
        May 1   A. V. Burbury, "A Study in Reserve"
        May 15   Capt. L. De G. Sieveking, "The Unforeseen Effects of Flying on the
                    Mind"
        June 5   Mr. Harold Monro, "Can any Religion meet the Conditions of
                    Modern European Civilization?"

MICHAELMAS 1921

        Oct. 16   Dr. Marriette Soman, "Modern French Literature"
        Oct. 23   Prof. B. Muscio, "Behaviourism"
        Oct. 30   Mr. C. H. Hsu, "Readings in Chinese Poetry"
        Nov. 6   Miss Edith Sitwell, "Modern Criticism"
d. e.) Nov. 13   Mr. Arthur Waley, "Zen Buddhism"
        Nov. 17   Mr. G. G. Coulton, "Super Heresy" (by invitation)
        Nov. 20   Mr. H. Morris, "The Tragedy of Education"
d. e.) Nov. 27   Mr. Clive Bell, "Jazz Art"

LENT 1922

        Jan. 22   Mr. B. K. (Kingsley) Martin, "The Psychology of the Press"
        Jan. 29   Dr. H. Hartridge, "Sleep"
        Feb. 5   Mr. L. L. Whyte, "Adventures of Atoms"
        Feb. 12   Mr. A. Clutton Brock, "Some Difficulties of Literary Expression"
        Feb. 19   Mr. W. J. Turner, "Musical Heresies"

	Feb. 26	Mr. A. E. Heath, "Why are Mathematicians obsessed by the Mind?"
d. e.)	Mar. 5	Mr. and Mrs. Bertrand Russell, "Industrialism and Religion": (1) Bertrand Russell, "Traditional Religion"; (2) Dora Russell, "The Industrial Creed"
	Mar. 12	Prof. J. T. Wilson, "A Rational Universe"

SUMMER 1922

	Apr. 30	L. S. Penrose, "The Chess Problem; a neglected form of Art"
	May 7	A. B. Mathews, "Anthropology; its practical and theoretical applications"
	May 14	Miss E. E. Power, "India, China and Europe; a traveller's impressions"
	May 21	Mr. S. K. Ratcliffe, "The Intellectual Reaction in America"
	May 28	Mr. Julian Huxley
	June 4	M. H. A. Newman, "Can Physics be saved from the Mathematicians?"
	June 11	Mr. Eugene Goossens, "Contemporary Music". Economic Section
	May 18	M. H. Dobb, "The Decline of Capitalism"

LENT 1923

e.)	Feb. 4	J. B. S. Haldane, "Daedalus"
	Feb. 18	Walter de la Mare, "Islands and Robinson Crusoe"
	Feb. 25	Percy Turner, "Modern Art"
	March 6	Roger Fry, "Composition"

C. K. Ogden withdraws from managing the Society, and the records become scattered.

SUMMER 1924

| e.) | May 18 | Virginia Woolf, "Character in Fiction" |

Notes

Introduction

1. In *The Longest Journey* (1907), E. M. Forster clearly continues Arnold's and Hardy's critique of the modern "want of correspondence" between form and content. Surveying the cataracts near the road from Salisbury to Cadover, the narrative voice declares: "instead of looking towards the cathedral, as all the city should, they look outwards at a pagan entrenchment, as the city should not. They neglect the poise of the earth, and the sentiments she has decreed. They are the modern spirit" (288). For Forster, the form of modern dwellings here does not cohere with their intended purpose. Etymologically pagans are "country-dwellers." Forster plays on words to foreground the straying of "civilians" from the "civis" and the cathedral which had distinguished them from heathens.

2. In *After Strange Gods,* Eliot defines "tradition" as a set of "habitual actions" "of the same people living in the same place" (11), associates tradition with orthodoxy, and declares that "the right tradition for us must also be a Christian tradition" (22).

3. Kranidis argues that a prominent method used to achieve these ends was to synthesize "the conventional tradition-bound figure of womanhood with the enlightened New Woman" (xiv). Through this subversive technique, writers such as Mona Caird and Olive Schreiner could "successfully insert [their alternatives and criticisms] into mainstream discourses and maintain [their] political purpose . . . without compromising [their] message" (ix).

4. Perhaps the most evocative literary example of the literary and historical amnesia that accompanied the onset and aftermath of the First World War is Chris Baldry's mental erasure of the twentieth century in Rebecca West's *The Return of the Soldier* (1918). By suppressing the fifteen years from 1901 to 1916, Chris returns to a time in his life filled with poetics, romanticism, and a Victorian sensibility.

5. The aesthetic attempt at "completion," for instance, appears at the end of Woolf's *To the Lighthouse* (1927) as Mr. Ramsay finally arrives at the lighthouse. Lily Briscoe has her "vision" simultaneously and can complete her "blurred" painting, "an attempt at something," by drawing "a line there, in the centre" (208–9).

Chapter 1

1. In his discussion of the reception of Nietzsche's attacks on Christianity, René Girard wonders whether in academic circles there is "something inopportune or embar-

rassing about the theme" and whether it is "strategically advisable" to discuss critiques of religion (816). In his study of church attendance in England from 1870–1930, Jeffrey Cox notes the "religious indifference of the twentieth century" which finds that "the subject of religion often provokes boredom" and "is not supposed to be important" (3).

2. For example, Jacques Derrida, Gianni Vattimo, and Slavoj Žižek have brought religion back to the foreground of criticism. See Derrida, *Acts of Religion* (New York: Routledge, 2002); Derrida and Vattimo, eds., *Religion* (Stanford, Ca.: Stanford University Press 1998); and Žižek, *On Belief* (New York: Routledge, 2001). Several other studies have applied the work of Levinas and Bakhtin to extended treatments of religion, society, and literature. See Jeffrey Kosky, *Levinas and the Philosophy of Religion* (Bloomington: Indiana University Press, 2001); and Susan M. Felch and Paul J. Contino, eds., *Bakhtin and Religion* (Evanston, Ill.: Northwestern University Press, 2001).

3. References to Keynes' collected writings are cited parenthetically within the text by volume and page number.

4. Paul Levy describes the Apostles and Bloomsbury as giving "the impression that they could not be harmed, that they were not vulnerable," and he attributes this demeanor to the fact that "they were sure of their rightness" (245).

5. For example, the Bishop of Durham, Joseph Barber Lightfoot (1828–89), wrote several influential studies of St. Paul's Epistles, and his *Ignatius* (1885) decided the authenticity of St. Ignatius' epistles. Additionally, Lightfoot participated with Brooke Westcott (1825–1901) and Fenton Hort (1828–92) in the celebrated revision of the Greek New Testament (1881). The culmination of Westcott's thought appears in *The Gospel of Life* (1892).

6. For a more full discussion of college chapel and compulsory attendance at Cambridge, see Christopher Brooke, *A History of the University of Cambridge*, vol. 4 (Cambridge University Press, 1993), 106–21; and V. H. H. Green, *Religion at Oxford and Cambridge* (London: SCM Press, 1964), 297–333.

7. In 1913, J. E. M. McTaggart, a Heretic, put forth the successful motion at Trinity not to enforce compulsory chapel.

8. In 1929, the Master of Magdalene succeeded in reinstituting two attendances per week for all members of the Church of England. This statute lasted until the Second World War.

9. In the May 14 1909 edition of *The Church Times*, the Church of England newspaper with the largest circulation reported the state of affairs at Cambridge. The anonymous columnist tried to dismiss Chawner as an eccentric to be neither tolerated nor worried about: "Much distress has been caused at a large and important College by the publication of a pamphlet by the Master, in which he details his views on religion. Their somewhat elementary nature shows that he cannot have devoted much time—or at any rate much study—to the question, and his action has caused needless pain to both teachers and learners in the College, who are not prepared to see the whole supernatural element of Christianity thrown overboard without a protest. These inconsiderable utterances are much to be deplored" (*The Church Times* 14 May 1909: 651). Ogden clipped the review and pasted it in his copy of "Prove All Things."

10. Apparently Francis Cornford is one of the three who did not want their correspondence to be published. In his brief account of the Chawner affair, Don Cupitt includes an excerpt from a letter Cornford sent to Chawner on May 17, 1909, in response to "Prove All Things." He probably did not want his militant agnosticism to be exposed, for he called for "solidarity among the non-clericals here, and some organised protest" against denying the use of Swinburne's name for a University prize. He also stated that the "Theological School is a disgrace" (TCA 9).

11. At the October 3 informal meeting of the Heretics, Mr. Hodge of Trinity joined after forsaking the F. T. A. Lavington was there and did not.

12. The full list is: The Master of Emmanuel, Prof. E. G. Browne, F. M. Cornford, Dr. F. Darwin, G. Lowes Dickinson, G. H. Hardy, Miss J. E. Harrison, W. E. Johnson, J. M. Keynes, Dr. J. E. McTaggart, V. H. Mottram, D. S. Robertson, Prof. A. C. Seward, J. T. Sheppard, H. W. V. Temperley, G. M. Trevelyan, V. S. Vernon Jones, Dr. A. W. Verrall, and H. J. Wolstenholme.

13. A. E. Ward of Newnham was the first female committee member in 1910.

14. In one passage, McTaggart almost seems to parody William James' work in his overuse of the words "variety," "religious," and "experience" (5). The influence of James' book on English philosophy at the turn of the century cannot be overstated.

CHAPTER 2

1. The membership book is titled, in Ogden's hand, "Ye Worshipful Society of ye Heretics" (MCMA 114 Env.3).

2. Remembering the Christian presence in the Heretics, G. F. Fox reports: one of the "most vociferous members was a Roman Catholic from Montenegro. C. F. Angus was a Christian and gave us what was practically a sermon. He was listened to with profound attention, and there was no heckling in the discussion. Whereas another Christian speaker who addressed us in a patronising tone was given a nasty heckling later" (88).

3. For instance, W. J. Turner addressed the group on "Musical Heresies" in 1922, and Dr. H. Crichton-Miller wrote to Ogden in 1920 explaining that his contribution, "The Making of a Heretic," could also be called "Psycho-analysis and heretical tendencies" or "Heresy and the Subconscious" (MCMA 113.36).

4. Ogden's friend Mary Adams reports that he would ask people to wear masks because, he said, "[t]his enables me to talk in terms of ideas and not in terms of personalities. I blot you out. I only listen to what you say and the ideas you have" (CA 44).

5. The controversy created a deep bitterness in Chawner toward Raven since the Master had been responsible for Raven's appointment in the face of opposition from the Christian members of the governing body. Later, Raven would find he was too young and out of line in challenging Chawner (Raven 178–80).

6. The correspondence between Ogden and Welby is mostly housed at York University, Toronto. On May 16, 1911, she wrote to Ogden: "I agree that orthodoxy is just as bad as heresy,—and vice versa!"; "I don't wonder that you feel as you do about the 'divine.' I should welcome a term for the starry and the sunny and the rush of Spring beauty, which was free from outgrown references"; "As for Faith you must be consistent and socially canonise the deserter, the betrayer, the traitor"; and "I feel a little as if Heresy was becoming the opposite of a faith, that is becoming a *dogma*" (MCMA 112).

7. References to Russell's collected papers are cited parenthetically within the text by volume and page number.

8. Writing for *The Gownsman,* a reviewer of Benson's address questioned the "surprising omission" of "Pater's curious attitude toward the Church" (*Gownsman* Vol. 2 {February 11, 1911}: 363).

9. Virginia Woolf, *To the Lighthouse* (New York: Harcourt, 1989), 34.

10. Several of the budget sheets of the Heretics are housed in McMaster's collection (MCMA 113.38).

11. *The Great Heresies* (1938), Belloc's contribution to reactionary Catholic apologetics, takes pride in polarizing orthodox Catholic doctrine and tradition with a handful of

heresies. Above all, he wants to mark the differences by defining what exactly makes a heresy a heresy so that he can line up the "ranks" "as for a battle" (161). The war to be waged will decide "the whole future of our race" (161).

12. Forster's diary is housed in the Kings' College Archives at Cambridge University. Portions have not yet been opened to the public.

CHAPTER 3

1. During the 1909–10 academic year, 3,699 male undergraduates were enrolled at Cambridge. At the height of the First World War, only 575 enrolled for the Easter Term, 1916 (Brooke 331).

2. Dora Black would return to Cambridge in March 1922, after marrying Bertrand Russell. Together they addressed the Heretics on "Industrialism and Religion."

3. Each of the volumes in the Today and Tomorrow Series has a Latin or Greek title followed by an alternative title usually involving the word "future." Among personages formerly involved in the Heretics, the series includes Bertrand Russell's *Icarus, or the Future of Science*, Dora Russell's *Hypatia, of Woman and Knowledge*, J. B. S. Haldane's *Daedalus, or Science and the Future*, and Vernon Lee's *Proteus, or the Future of Intelligence*.

4. In *Jacob's Room*, Virginia Woolf must certainly have had in mind the address of her fellow member of Bloomsbury when an outraged Jacob Flanders reacts against bowdlerization and prudery and cites Shakespeare and Aristophanes for the argument in his essay "Ethics of Indecency" (69–78).

5. For instance, in H. D.'s *Notes on Thought and Vision* (1919), she claims: "Two or three people, with healthy bodies and the right sort of receiving brains, could turn the whole tide of human thought, could direct lightning flashes of electric power to slash across and destroy the world of dead, murky thought" (27).

6. In the December 1, 1923, edition of *Nation and Athenaeum*, Woolf first introduced Mrs. Brown in the short response, "Mr. Bennett and Mrs. Brown," to Arnold Bennett's critique of *Jacob's Room*. The address to the Heretics was the first substantial development of Woolf's illustrative contrast between Edwardians and Georgians, which T. S. Eliot would publish after major revisions as "Character in Fiction" in the July 1924 edition of *Criterion*. In October of that year, the Hogarth Press published this same essay as *Mr Bennett and Mrs Brown* in pamphlet form.

7. Virginia Woolf, "Character in Fiction," *The Essays of Virginia Woolf*, ed. Andrew McNeillie, vol. 3 (London: Hogarth, 1988), 503. This appendix to the collection of Woolf's essays is a transcript of her revised typescript address to the Heretics. Since "Character in Fiction" is also the title of the published version McNeillie collects in his volume, I will hereafter cite the address to the Heretics as CF1 and the published version as CF2 parenthetically within the text.

8. Samuel Hynes perhaps initiated the inaccuracy in reporting that Woolf delivered the lecture "to the girls of Girton College in May 1924" ("Contention" 31). Woolf's own version of the gender of her audience appears in a letter to Ethel Sands: "I've been lecturing at Cambridge on your beloved Arnold Bennett, and not a single young man or woman in the place has a good word to say for him!" (*Letters* 3: 112).

9. For example, Hirst declares that "Love" is the concept that "seems to explain it all" (315). Later, in order to repress the fact that Rachel was near death, Terence experiences a mystical view of the natural world: "Surely the world of strife and fret and anxiety was not the real world, but this was the real world, the world that lay beneath the superficial world, so that, whatever happened, one was secure" (343).

10. In the published version of "Character in Fiction," Woolf changed the example of

Jude to *The Mayor of Casterbridge*. This is a symptomatic shift. In the 1920s, criticism led by Eliot tended to bestow praise on Hardy's earlier novel (if he received praise at all) for its character development. Criticism could thus steer away from the scandal of *Jude*.

11. For example, in her discussion of Harrison's influence on Woolf's *Between the Acts*, Sandra Shattuck highlights the brilliant estrangement elicited by Miss La Trobe's dramatic use of broken mirrors as an instance of Harrison's ideas surrounding collective ritual performance.

12. R. M. O'Donnell underscores the importance of heresy to Keynes since "his earliest years," and considers this appreciation "a by-product of his interest in truth and reason and his attitude to preordained rules and duties." O'Donnell also clusters a set of allusions to heresy in Keynes' writings (367n5). Heresy defines the Bloomsbury economist's thought to such a degree that Robert L. Heilbroner entitles the relevant chapter "The Heresies of John Maynard Keynes" in his famous history of economic thinkers, *The Worldly Philosophers* (1953).

13. John Maynard Keynes, "The Economic Consequences of Mr Churchill," *The Collected Writings of John Maynard Keynes*, vol. 19 (Cambridge University Press, 1981), 441.

14. Keynes' endeavor illustrates the importance of both persuasion and synthesis to his approach to economics. The General Theory is one grand synthesis that inverts orthodox claims to generality and makes *it* the special case (O'Donnell 176). As Keynes himself argued, the limitations of orthodox economics make it "a particular theory applicable only to certain conditions; and this is my justification for calling my own theory a *general theory*, of which the orthodox theory is a limiting case" (14: 106).

15. The Rockefeller Foundation appears to have had a long-standing interest in language reform. In Shaw's *Pygmalion* (1913), Alfred Doolittle returns at the end of the play fearing that he will be caught in "middle class morality" now that he has been awarded a lifetime stipend by one "Ezra D. Wannafeller" (73–74). Doolittle had been part of Henry Higgins' offhand application for funding for the foundation of "Moral Reform Societies" and the invention of a "universal language" (74).

16. In an anonymous lampoon, "Those in Authority," published in *Granta* in May 1929, the author roasts Empson's untidy lifestyle and has particular fun with his recruitment of speakers for the Heretics. While attempting to interview "Bill," the author shuffles across the beer-stained carpet only to hear him say "Look here, it's lucky someone turned up. What can you read a paper on for next Sunday?" The author concludes by noting that "the interesting creature is on view every Sunday evening . . . where he may be seen preening himself beside his catch, and glowering at the assembled Heretics" (15–16). In this view, the President of the Heretics was always on the lookout for prey. On the hunted rather than hunting hand, we have Empson idealizing the conviction of heretics in *Milton's God*: "when I was a little boy I was very afraid I might not have the courage which I knew life to demand of me . . . if some bully said he would burn me alive unless I pretended to believe he had created me, I hope I would have enough honour to tell him that the evidence did not seem to me decisive" (89).

17. In *Milton's God*, Empson argues against the traditional view that Milton had inadvertently characterized God as a tyrant through the inconsistencies in the epic. Instead, Empson finds that the richness of the poem derives from Milton's honest investigation of the nature of God's ways. Sometimes God is wicked and sadistic, and punishment unfair, and this interpretation troubled the critical waters that mandated that Milton made mistakes since God's ways are necessarily good. Empson's book met a strong critical backlash, perhaps best summarized by Hugh Kenner as "surely the maddest critical book of the century" (213n).

18. In part, Empson developed his idea of equilibrium from I. A. Richards who uses the term interchangeably with "synthesis" and "wholeness."

19. Paul Fry notes the similar use of the seventh type of ambiguity in Empson's analysis of the function of the doctrine of the Trinity in *Paradise Lost* and that of Atonement in "The Sacrifice" (156–69). They both are dependent on divisions within the writer's mind. In a similar vein, Christopher Norris summarizes Empson's analogous approach: "in Milton's case this means trying to understand *both* how a doctrine like the Christian Atonement could implant itself so firmly in the Western cultural tradition, *and* how various thinkers within that tradition struggled to avoid its worst, most sadistic implications by telling the story over again while refusing—at whatever 'unconscious' level—to endorse the official creed" ("Introduction" 13–14).

20. The twentieth century witnessed an explosion of various schools of thought flying under the banner of "humanism." From Irving Babbitt's New Humanism to the Humanist Manifesto to the liberal humanism of E. M. Forster and the Cambridge Humanists, various groups of people appropriated the term. The resultant vagueness of the label often hid the ideology of the affiliations, and gives credence to G. E. Moore's complaint that, in comparison to "heresy," the name "humanism" was not "strong enough" (WCL 406).

21. Jonathan Culler explains that Empson became ostracized and labeled an "eccentric" because he wished "not only to open skeptical debate about Christian principles that are articulated in literature but to challenge the complicity with religion which neglects authors' oppositions to theological orthodoxies" (75). Stressing the importance of a political critique of religious discourse in literature, Culler adds that Empson was simply "trying to combat the unreflective acceptance of Christianity that makes attacks on it seem odd and tedious behavior" (76).

22. As Cleanth Brooks himself acknowledges, his previous discussion of Robert Herrick's "Corinna's Going-a-Maying" "is perhaps susceptible of this interpretation—or misinterpretation" (181). Though a "pagan appeal" persists throughout the presentation of the ritual in the poem, this is qualified by "the Christian view" and, "if we read it carefully," the "primacy of the Christian mores" (182). The qualification by the Christian view precludes the need to make statements about the poem, but Brooks believes that the critic can still use interpretive paraphrase to confirm that the poem states "that the May-day rites are not a real religion but a 'harmless follie'" (181–82). If it promotes Christian values and thwarts the appeal of pagan "follie," Brooks tolerates the heresy of paraphrase.

23. Many years after the dissolution of the Heretics Society, Kathleen Raine wrote to Julian Trevelyan after having heard one of Alistair Cooke's weekly broadcasts in which "he had talked to the new generation of rabble students." She remembered him describing "to them 'our' Cambridge: the talk, the hard work, the Heretics, the fullness of our days, innocence; and overheard one of the new guys saying to another—'do you know—that square—I really believed he *liked* it!' I almost wept" (TCL JOT 13/16).

CHAPTER 4

1. Noteworthy among their public spectacles was a mock trial of 1914 "solving" *The Mystery of Edwin Drood* in which Chesterton as the judge and Shaw as the foreman of the jury found John Jasper guilty of the murder.

2. The pamphlets of both Shaw's and Chesterton's addresses are reports transcribed by the Heretics for private publication. They include notes of applause, laughter, and gesture, and at the end they attach several excerpts from reviews of the events as reported by various national newspapers and journals.

3. Shaw's view of "The Heretic" is akin to the Italian miller whose cosmology Carlo Ginzburg describes in *The Cheese and the Worms* (1976).

4. For personal recollections of actresses who have played Joan, see Holly Hill's fas-

cinating collection, *Playing Joan* (New York: Theatre Communications Group, 1987). The revisionist, feminist narrative of Mark Rappaport's film *From the Journals of Jean Seberg* (1995) traces the career of the actress who debuted nationally as Joan in Otto Preminger's film adaptation of Shaw's play, *Saint Joan* (1957). Rappaport's film implies that there is a curse in playing Joan, and Seberg suggests that Preminger actually allowed her to be burnt during filming. An accident on the set while she is "burnt" at the stake did let the flames reach her.

5. On several occasions, Shaw's play points to the arbitrariness and failure of Joan's voices. The voices chose dubiously to speak to Joan "in French" (126). Joan states that she hears the voices "in the bells" (110). More importantly, she admits that "the voices come first," and she finds "the reasons after" (111). Finally, she even declares that her "voices have deceived" her because they "promised" that she "should not be burnt" (139–40).

6. Bruno's influence has also been noted in Spenser, Sydney, Bacon, Donne, and Coleridge.

7. In 1930, the Catholic Church canonized Cardinal Robert Bellarmino, the cleric in charge of Bruno's trial and punishment.

8. Joyce sequentially changed the title of the story from "Hallow Eve" to "The Clay" to "Clay," and these changes suggest a turn away from specificity, a movement that accords with Joyce's search for a larger order beyond Catholic orthodoxy.

9. Some critics point out that she bakes "barmbracks," the traditional Celtic food for Samhain, and that she returns to her old haunts, Joe's house. Other critics note how Maria is beyond reproach. The matron of the laundry finds her "a veritable peace-maker," and Joe frequently used to say, "Mamma is mamma but Maria is my proper mother" (110–11). From such comments and her apparent virginity, some criticism has cast her as the mother of God. Donald Torchiara summarizes the genesis of such variant readings: "Maria by name and appearance seems to be the expected confluence of Christian and pagan that makes up the modern Halloween" (151).

10. In an interesting further gloss of "Clay," Roman Catholic catechism polarizes the Standard of Christ, "blessed are the peacemakers," with the Standard of the World, "Am I my brother's keeper?" (Kelley 67). Maria regrets that the brothers she raised have become estranged: "Alphy and Joe were not speaking" (113).

11. Joyce may have entitled the story "Clay" to echo a moment in "A Little Cloud." Apart from the title of "Clay," the only mention of the word in *Dubliners* occurs in "A Little Cloud." While rocking his child, Little Chandler tries to read the second stanza of Byron's "On the Death of a Young Lady": "*Within this narrow cell reclines her clay, / That clay where once . . .*" (92). The fragment anticipates Maria's story, whose title knowingly follows another set of ellipses, the last line of "Counterparts": "I'll say a Hail Mary . . ." (109). Both of these fragments find completion in "Clay" and testify to the interwoven, molded nature of the stories in *Dubliners*.

CHAPTER 5

1. Edited by Sharp under the pseudonym W. H. Brooks, *The Pagan Review* was designed to be a quarterly journal. However, its serial nature never materialized after Sharp could not continue the tour de force of writing the entire contents (dramatic, narrative, and poetic) under varying pen names.

2. It is important to remember that, in the end, the poet cries "False Sphinx!" and asks to be left with his "crucifix." Here in miniature is Ellis Hanson's notion of the decadent turn to Catholicism. In *Decadence and Catholicism* (1997), Hanson synthesizes Christian, aesthetic, and erotic discourses in the work of Huysmans, Pater, and Wilde to show the

ways in which nineteenth-century Catholicism is "decadent," and the decadent movement Catholic.

3. Quotations are drawn from the fourth edition of *The Renaissance* (1893), the last, revised edition published in Pater's lifetime.

4. In the *OED*, the first definition of "curious" used as a subjective quality of persons is: "Bestowing care or pains." Demonstrating the relation of "curious" to "cure," John Ayto states that the "Latin adjective *curiosus* originally meant 'careful,' a sense preserved through Old French *curios* into English *curious* but defunct since the 18th century. The secondary sense 'inquisitive' developed in Latin, but it was not until the word reached Old French that the meaning 'interesting' emerged" (150).

5. Wolfgang Iser finds that the "skepticism of Pater's first essay [on Coleridge] remained fundamental to all his writings," and describes it, in the vein of "curiosity," as a "skepticism in the old classical sense of 'spying out, investigating, searching, examining'" (*Pater* 16–17).

6. In his essay on the subtextual Paterian echoes in Eliot's criticism, David DeLaura finds that, in "Sandro Botticelli," Pater "had given several hints which suggest a source for the criterion of the 'objective correlative'" ("Pater" 428).

7. Hardy published "Candour in English Fiction" in the January 1890 edition of *The New Review,* and Frazer dates the preface of the first edition of *The Golden Bough* March 8, 1890.

8. For a rich discussion of the composition history of *Tess,* see Juliet Grindle and Simon Gatrell's introduction and notes to the Clarendon edition of the novel, along with Gatrell's *Hardy the Creator* (Oxford: Clarendon, 1988).

9. Hardy's choice of both Tess's involvement in a "Cerealia" and the Clare brothers' reading of *A Counterblast to Agnosticism* occurs during the process of revision and points to his accretion of details furthering the opposition between paganism and Christianity in the novel.

10. Rosemary Eakins discusses several of the pagan and Christian allusions in the novel and concludes that this "traditional material becomes the very fabric of the book, woven into almost every aspect of the tragic story" (107). For the source of some of this material, she suggests, which others have confirmed, that Hardy possibly read Frazer's *The Golden Bough.*

11. In a brief survey, Gallagher draws parallels between the sexual and sacrificial rites performed by Artemis and the King of the Wood and "the main events of Tess Durbeyfield's destiny—sex in the primeval forest, murder by stabbing of the priest-husband, and the execution of the goddess herself" (429).

12. For further discussion of the Celtic tree alphabet, see Roderick O'Flaherty, *Ogygia,* 1685, trans. James Hely (Dublin: M'Kenzie, 1793); Robert Graves, *The White Goddess* (New York: Farrar, Strauss and Giroux, 1966); and Fergus Kelly, "The Old Irish Tree List," *Celtica* 11 (1976): 107–24.

CHAPTER 6

1. In the early drafts of *The Rainbow,* Lawrence compares Will's feelings to being "racked" rather than "burnt at the stake." The change further testifies to Lawrence's identification of the novel with heresy.

2. In the first draft of *A Passage to India,* the novel simply chants "Mrs. Moore." Forster's decision to inflect her name with the Indo-European root for "to be" reflects not only the stitched nature of the novel, but also the interwoven nature of language and being that is the most fundament universal synthesis.

AFTER WORDS

1. In November 1927, *transition* continued its serial publication of Joyce's *Work in Progress* (*Finnegans Wake*) with an early version of "Anna Livia Plurabelle," Book I, chapter 8 of the *Wake*. During 1928, Joyce revised "Anna Livia," and Crosby Gaige published it in booklet form. Two years later, Faber and Faber became the first English publisher to print "Anna Livia," also as a booklet. Ogden's translation into Basic English works from this edition.

2. In assisting with the Italian and French translations of the chapter, Joyce also stressed his concern with reproducing a similar rhythm, harmony, and consonance. Bishop dismisses any perception in these cases of Joyce's "apparent recklessness" in ignoring literal meaning, and emphasizes that he "knew quite well what he was doing" (457n23).

3. Additionally, in this instance, the translation loses the repetitive rhythm of Joyce's phrasing.

4. In the *Wake*, Joyce similarly critiques the inability of a limited lexicon to convey the richness of words such as "majesty": "I am told by our interpreter . . . that there are fully six hundred and six ragwords in your malherbal Magis landeguage . . . but yav hace not one pronounceable teerm that blows in all vallums of tartallaght to signify majestate" (478.8–13).

5. In 1931, Bernard Shaw pointedly suggested that the "Inquisition is not dead" since modern dictatorships will create a "secret tribunal dealing with sedition, with political heresy, exactly like the Inquisition" (qtd. in Holroyd 75).

6. Syme may be named after the counterinsurgent heresy hunter in Chesterton's *The Man Who Was Thursday*.

7. For instance, W. Terrence Gordon has often denied the connection between Basic English and Newspeak. Also see W. F. Bolton, *The Language of Nineteen Eighty-Four* (Knoxville: University of Tennessee Press, 1984).

8. In fact, Ogden had suggested that Basic could make English a study for antiquarians.

9. Orwell's own creation of a scandalous "blacklist" while he was writing the novel may have accentuated the theme of betrayal.

10. It is no wonder that the Axis accused England of using the promotion of Basic English "as a propaganda stunt designed to secure domination of the world" (Gordon 52).

11. In its final form, the Basic English word list includes both "war" and "peace," but in 1929 Ogden had defended his initial reasoning to exclude "peace." In an editorial for *Psyche*, he responded to the criticism of Basic by a writer for the Baltimore *Sun*. The unnamed critic had lambasted the omission of important words in the Basic lexicon, and highlighted the choice of "war" over "peace." Ogden retorted: "The significance of choosing 'war' as the more fundamental word is that when 'not at war' we have 'peace'; while peace is more naturally described in terms of war 'coming to an end' than vice versa" (Editorial 4). As in the given state of affairs in *Nineteen Eighty-Four*, war, in this mindset, is the fundamental and natural character of global politics.

APPENDIX

1. The term "sworry" is Ogden's humor. The Society held a soirée instead of a regular meeting.

WORKS CITED

Adamson, Robert and John Malcolm Mitchell. "Giordano Bruno." *Encyclopaedia Britannica.* 11th ed. 1910.

Arlen, Shelley. "'For Love of an Idea': Jane Ellen Harrison, heretic and humanist." *Women's History Review* 5.2 (1996): 165–90.

Arnold, Matthew. "The Function of Criticism at the Present Time." 1865. *Matthew Arnold: Selected Prose.* Ed. P. J. Keating. New York and London: Penguin, 1987. 130–57.

———. "Sweetness and Light." 1869. *Matthew Arnold: Selected Prose.* Ed. P. J. Keating. New York and London: Penguin, 1987. 204–27.

Arrowsmith, William. "Notes to *The Satyricon.*" Petronius. *The Satyricon.* Trans. William Arrowsmith. New York: Meridian, 1987. 166–92.

Asher, Kenneth. "Poetry and Politics in T. S. Eliot's Clark Lectures." *Yeats Eliot Review* 15.1 (Fall 1997): 18–23.

Ayto, John. *Dictionary of Word Origins.* New York: Little, Brown and Company, 1990.

Bakhtin, Mikhail. *The Dialogic Imagination.* Trans. Caryl Emerson and Michael Holquist. Austin: University of Texas Press, 1981.

Banfield, Ann. *The Phantom Table: Woolf, Fry, Russell and the Epistemology of Modernism.* Cambridge: Cambridge University Press, 2000.

Bell, Clive. *Art.* 1913. New York: Capricorn Books, 1958.

———. "Plus de Jazz." *Since Cezanne.* 1922. New York: Harcourt, 1928. 213–30.

Bell, Quentin. *Bloomsbury.* London: Weidenfeld and Nicolson, 1968.

———. *Virginia Woolf: A Biography.* New York: Harcourt, 1972.

Belloc, Hilaire. *The Great Heresies.* 1938. Rockford, IL: TAN Books and Publishers, 1991.

Bender, John. *Imagining the Penitentiary.* Chicago: University of Chicago Press, 1987.

Bennett, Arnold. Introduction. Adelyne More [C. K. Ogden]. *Fecundity versus Civilisation.* London: George Allen & Unwin, 1917. 3–6.

Bishop, John. *Joyce's Book of the Dark, Finnegans Wake.* Madison: University of Wisconsin Press, 1986.

Bonica, Charlotte. "Nature and Paganism in Hardy's *Tess of the d'Urbervilles.*" *ELH* 49.4 (Winter 1982): 849–62.

Braithwaite, R. B. "Keynes as a Philosopher." *Essays on John Maynard Keynes.* Ed. Milo Keynes. Cambridge University Press, 1975. 237–46.

Breton, André. "Manifesto of Surrealism." 1924. *Manifestoes of Surrealism.* Trans. Richard Seaver and Helen R. Lane. Ann Arbor: University of Michigan Press, 1969. 1–47.

Brooke, Christopher. *A History of the University of Cambridge*. Vol. IV. 1870–1990. Cambridge University Press, 1993.

Brooks, Cleanth. "Empson's Criticism." *Critical Essays on William Empson*. Ed. John Constable. Hants, England: Scolar Press, 1993. 123–35.

——. "Irony as a Principle of Structure." 1951. *The Critical Tradition: Classic Texts and Contemporary Trends*. Ed. David H. Richter. New York: Bedford, 1989. 799–807.

——. *The Well Wrought Urn*. New York: Reynal and Hitchcock, 1947.

Bruno, Giordano. *Cause, Principle, and Unity*. Translated with an introduction by Jack Lindsay. New York: International Publishers, 1962.

Buckler, William. Introduction. *Jude the Obscure*. By Thomas Hardy. New York: Dell, 1959. 5–11.

Burrow, J. W. "The Uses of Philology in Victorian England." *Ideas and Institutions of Victorian Britain*. Ed. Robert Robson. New York: Barnes and Noble, 1967. 180–204.

Butler, Samuel. *The Way of All Flesh*. 1903. New York: Modern Library, 1998.

Carlen, Claudia, ed. *The Papal Encyclicals*. Vol. III: 1903–1939. Raleigh, NC: McGrath, 1981.

Carr, H. Wildon. "On Russell's Reasons for Supposing That Bergson's Philosophy Is Not True." 1913. *The Collected Papers of Bertrand Russell*. Vol. 6. Ed. John G. Slater. London and New York: Routledge, 1992. 455–60.

Chawner, William. *Prove All Things*. Cambridge: Privately Printed, 1909.

——. *A Supplement to a Paper entitled Prove All Things*. Cambridge: Privately Printed, 1909.

——. *Truthfulness in Religion*. Cambridge: Bowes and Bowes, 1911.

Chesterton, G. K. *The Future of Religion*. Cambridge: Heretics, 1911.

——. *George Bernard Shaw*. 1909. New York: Hill and Wang, 1962.

——. *Heretics*. 1905. London: The Bodley Head, 1960.

——. *The Man Who Was Thursday*. 1908. New York: Modern Library, 2001.

Churchill, Winston. *Onwards to Victory*. Boston: Little, Brown and Company, 1944.

——. *The Second World War*. Vol. 5. *Closing the Ring*. 1951. Boston: Houghton Mifflin, 1985.

Clarke, Bruce. "Birkin in Love: Corrupt Sublimity in D. H. Lawrence's Representation of Soul." *Thought* 59.235 (December 1984): 449–61.

Coleridge, John Duke, Lord. *The Law of Blasphemous Libel: The Summing-Up in the Case of Regina v. Foote and Others*. London: Stevens, 1883.

Cornford, Francis. *Microcosmographia Academica*. 1908. Cambridge: Bowes and Bowes, 1949.

——. *Religion in the University*. Cambridge: Fabb & Tyler, 1911.

Constable, John. Introduction. *Critical Essays on William Empson*. Hants, England: Scolar Press, 1993. 1–14.

Courtine, Jean-Jacques. "A Brave New Language: Orwell's Invention of Newspeak in *1984*." *SubStance* 15.2 (1986): 69–74.

Cox, Jeffrey. *The English Churches in a Secular Society, Lambeth, 1870–1930*. New York: Oxford University Press, 1982.

Cox, R. G., ed. *Thomas Hardy: The Critical Heritage*. New York: Barnes and Noble, 1970.

Crispi, Luca et al. Curator notes. "James Joyce and *Ulysses*." Dublin: National Library of Ireland, June 2004–March 2006.

Crompton, Louis. "A Hagiography of Creative Evolution." *George Bernard Shaw's Saint Joan*. Ed. Harold Bloom. New York: Chelsea House, 1987. 31–51.

Culler, Jonathan. "Political Criticism: Confronting Religion." *Framing the Sign: Criticism and Its Institutions*. Norman: University of Oklahoma Press, 1988. 69–82.

Cunich, Peter et al. *A History of Magdalene College, Cambridge.* Cambridge: Cambridge University Press, 1994.

Cupitt, Don. "The Chawner Affair." *Emmanuel College Magazine* 53 (1970–71): 5–11.

———. "The Chawner Pamphlet." *Emmanuel College Magazine* 54 (1972): 17–30.

Dale, Alzina Stone. *The Outline of Sanity: A Biography of G. K. Chesterton.* Grand Rapids, MI: Eerdmans Publishing, 1982.

Daugherty, Beth Rigel. "The Whole Contention between Mr. Bennett and Mrs. Woolf, Revisited." *Virginia Woolf: Centennial Essays.* Ed. Elaine K. Ginsberg and Laura Moss Gottlieb. Troy, NY: Whitston Publishing, 1983. 269–94.

Deacon, Richard. *The Cambridge Apostles.* New York: Farrar, Straus and Giroux, 1985.

The Dead Sea Scriptures. Revised and Enlarged Edition. Garden City, NY: Anchor Books, 1964.

Dearmer, Percy. *The Necessity of Art.* London: Student Christian Movement, 1924.

DeLaura, David J. *Hebrew and Hellene in Victorian England.* Austin: University of Texas Press, 1969.

———. "Pater and Eliot: The Origin of the 'Objective Correlative.'" *Modern Language Quarterly* 26.3 (September 1965): 426–31.

Dellamora, Richard. "Pater's Modernism: The Leonardo Essay." *University of Toronto Quarterly* 47.2 (Winter 1977/78): 135–50.

Dickens, Charles. *Dombey and Son.* 1848. Harmondsworth, England: Penguin, 1975.

Donoghue, Denis. *Walter Pater: Lover of Strange Souls.* New York: Alfred A. Knopf, 1995.

Eagleton, Terry. *Literary Theory: An Introduction.* Minneapolis: University of Minnesota Press, 1983.

Eakins, Rosemary L. "Tess: The Pagan and Christian Traditions." *The Novels of Thomas Hardy.* Ed Anne Smith. New York: Barnes and Noble, 1979. 107–25.

Eco, Umberto. *The Name of the Rose.* Trans. William Weaver. New York: Harcourt, 1983. Trans. of *Il nome della rosa.* Milano: Bompiani, 1981.

Eliot, T. S. *After Strange Gods: A Primer of Modern Heresy .* New York: Harcourt, 1934.

———. "Arnold and Pater." 1930. *Selected Essays of T. S. Eliot.* 1932. New York: Harcourt, 1964. 382–93.

———. "The Metaphysical Poets." 1921. *Selected Essays of T. S. Eliot.* 1932. New York: Harcourt, 1964. 241–50.

———. "Tradition and the Individual Talent." 1919. *Selected Essays of T. S. Eliot.* New York: Harcourt, 1964. 3–11.

———. *The Waste Land.* 1922. *The Complete Poems and Plays, 1909-1950.* New York: Harcourt, 1962.

Ellmann, Richard. *James Joyce.* New York: Oxford University Press, 1982.

———. "Two Faces of Edward." *Edwardians and Late Victorians.* Ed. Richard Ellmann. New York and London: Columbia University Press, 1960. 188–210.

Empson, William. "Basic English in Literature." *C. K. Ogden: A Collective Memoir.* Ed. P. Sargant Florence and J. R. L. Anderson. London: Elek Pemberton, 1977. 169–73.

———. *The Complete Poems of William Empson.* Ed. John Haffenden. London: Penguin, 2000.

———. *Milton's God.* 1961. London: Chatto & Windus, 1965.

———. *Selected Letters of William Empson.* Ed. John Haffenden. Oxford University Press, 2006.

———. *Seven Types of Ambiguity.* 1930. New York: New Directions, 1966.

Evans, T. F., ed. *Shaw: The Critical Heritage.* London: Routledge, 1976.

Fink, Howard. "Newspeak: The Epitome of Parody Techniques in *Nineteen Eighty-Four.*"

Critical Survey 5.2 (1971): 155–73.

Florence, P. Sargant. "The Cambridge Heretics, 1909–1932." *The Humanist Outlook.* Ed. A. J. Ayer. London: Pemberton, 1968. 224–39.

———. "Cambridge 1909–1919 and its Aftermath." *C .K. Ogden: A Collective Memoir.* Ed. P. Sargant Florence and J. R. L. Anderson. London: Elek Pemberton, 1977. 13–55.

Forster, E. M. *Arctic Summer and Other Fiction.* Abinger Edition. Vol. 9. Ed. Elizabeth Heine and Oliver Stallybrass. New York: Holmes and Meier, 1981.

———. *Aspects of the Novel.* New York: Harcourt, 1927.

———. *Goldsworthy Lowes Dickinson.* 1934. Abinger Edition. Vol. 13. London: Edward Arnold, 1973.

———. *The Longest Journey.* 1907. New York: Vintage, 1993.

———. *A Passage to India.* 1924. New York: Harcourt, 1984.

———. *Selected Letters of E. M. Forster.* 2 Vols. Ed. Mary Lago and P. N. Furbank. Cambridge, MA: Harvard University Press, 1983–85.

Foucault, Michel. *Discipline and Punish: The Birth of the Prison.* 1975. Trans. Alan Sheridan. New York: Vintage, 1979.

———. *The Order of Things.* 1966. New York: Vintage, 1994.

Fowler, Roger. *The Language of George Orwell.* New York: St. Martin's Press, 1995.

Fox, G. F. "The Heretics." *A Newnham Anthology.* Ed. Ann Phillips. Cambridge University Press, 1979. 87–89.

Franks, Gabriel. "Virginia Woolf and the Philosophy of G. E. Moore." *Personalist* 50.2 (Spring 1969): 222–40.

Frazer, Sir James. *The Golden Bough: A Study in Comparative Religion.* 2 vols. London: Macmillan, 1890.

———. *The Golden Bough: A Study in Magic and Religion.* Abr. ed. 1922. New York: Macmillan, 1951.

Fry, Paul. "Empson's Satan: an ambiguous character of the seventh type." *William Empson: The Critical Achievement.* Ed. Christopher Norris and Nigel Mapp. Cambridge: Cambridge University Press, 1993. 156–69.

Furlong, William B. *Shaw and Chesterton: The Metaphysical Jesters.* University Park: Pennsylvania State University Press, 1970.

Gallagher, Catherine. "*Tess of the d'Urbervilles*: Hardy's Anthropology of the Novel." *Tess of the d'Urbervilles.* Ed. John Paul Riquelme. Boston: Bedford, 1998. 422–40.

Garvie, Rev. Alfred Ernest. "Heresy." *Encyclopaedia Britannica.* 11th ed. 1910.

Gibbs, A. M., ed. *Bernard Shaw: Man and Superman and Saint Joan.* London: Macmillan Education Ltd., 1992.

———. *Shaw: Interviews and Recollections.* Iowa City: University of Iowa Press, 1990.

Girard, René. "Dionysus versus the Crucified." *MLN* 99.4 (September 1984): 816–35.

Gladstone, William. "The Place of Heresy and Schism in the Modern Christian Church." *Nineteenth Century* 36.210 (August 1894): 157–74.

Gordon, W. Terrence. *C. K. Ogden: A Bio-bibliographical Study.* Metuchen, NJ: Scarecrow Press, 1990.

Gosse, Edmund. *Father and Son.* 1907. London: Penguin, 1989.

Green, V. H. H. *Religion at Oxford and Cambridge.* London: SCM Press, 1964.

Hanson, Ellis. *Decadence and Catholicism.* Cambridge, MA: Harvard University Press, 1997.

Hardy, Florence Emily. *The Early Years of Thomas Hardy.* London: Macmillan, 1928.

Hardy, Thomas. "Candour in English Fiction." 1890. *Thomas Hardy's Personal Writings.* Ed. H. Orel. London: Macmillan, 1967. 125–33.

———. *The Collected Letters of Thomas Hardy.* Vol. 1. Ed. Richard Purdy and Michael Millgate. Oxford: Clarendon Press, 1978.

———. *Jude the Obscure*. 1895. Ed. Norman Page. New York: Norton, 1999.

———. *The Life and Work of Thomas Hardy*. Ed. Michael Millgate. Athens: University of Georgia Press, 1985.

———. *The Literary Notebooks of Thomas Hardy*. Vol. 2. Ed. Lennart A. Björk. New York: New York University Press, 1985.

———. *The Thomas Hardy Archive: 1. Tess of the d'Urbervilles: A Facsimile of the Manuscript*. Vol. 1. Ed. Simon Gatrell. New York: Garland, 1986.

———. *Tess of the d'Urbervilles*. 1891. Ed. Juliet Grindle and Simon Gatrell. Oxford: Clarendon Press, 1983.

Harrison, Jane. *Epilegomena to the Study of Greek Religion, and Themis*. New York: University Books, 1962.

———. "Heresy and Humanity." *Alpha and Omega*. London: Sidgwick and Jackson, 1915. 27–41.

Hassall, Christopher. *Rupert Brooke*. London: Faber and Faber, 1964.

H. D. *Notes on Thought and Vision & The Wise Sappho*. San Francisco: City Lights, 1982.

Heilbroner, Robert L. *The Worldly Philosophers*. 1953. New York: Touchstone, 1980.

Hennig, John. "The Meaning of All the Saints." *Medieval Studies* 10 (1948): 147–61.

Herbert, George. *The Complete English Poems*. London: Penguin, 2005.

Hill, Holly. *Playing Joan*. New York: Theatre Communications Group, 1987.

Holdcroft, David. "From the One to the Many: Philosophy 1900–30." *The Context of English Literature 1900–1930*. Ed. Michael Bell. New York: Holmes and Meier, 1980. 126–59.

Hollander, John. "Dallying nicely with words." *The Linguistics of Writing: Arguments between Literature and Language*. Ed. Nigel Fabb et al. New York: Methuen, 1987. 123–34.

Holroyd, Michael. *Bernard Shaw*. Vol. 3. New York: Random House, 1991.

Huxley, Aldous. *Brave New World*. 1932. New York: Perennial, 1969.

Hynes, Samuel. "The Whole Contention between Mr Bennett and Mrs Woolf." *Edwardian Occasions*. New York: Oxford University Press, 1972. 24–38.

Imerti, Arthur D. "Editor's Introduction." *The Expulsion of the Triumphant Beast*. New Brunswick, NJ: Rutgers University Press, 1964. 3–65.

Iser, Wolfgang. *The Act of Reading*. Baltimore: Johns Hopkins University Press, 1978.

———. *Walter Pater: The Aesthetic Moment*. Cambridge University Press, 1987.

Jacobus, Mary. "Hardy's Tess: The Making of a Pure Woman." *Tearing the Veil: Essays on Femininity*. Ed. Susan Lipshitz. London: Routledge & Kegan Paul, 1978. 77–92.

James, William. *The Varieties of Religious Experience*. 1902. New York: Modern Library, 1999.

Jauss, Hans Robert. "Literary History as a Challenge to Literary Theory." *New Literary History* 2.1 (Autumn 1970): 7–38.

———. *Toward an Aesthetic of Reception*. Trans. Timothy Bahti. Minneapolis: University of Minnesota Press, 1982.

Joan the Woman [film]. Dir. Cecil B. DeMille. Kino International, 1917.

Johnson, Bruce. "'The Perfection of Species' and Hardy's Tess." *Nature and the Victorian Imagination*. Ed. U. C. Knoepflmacher and G. B. Tennyson. Berkeley: University of California Press, 1977. 259–77.

Joyce, James. "The Bruno Philosophy." *The Critical Writings of James Joyce*. Ed. Ellsworth Mason and Richard Ellmann. New York: Viking, 1959. 132–34.

———. "The Day of the Rabblement." *The Critical Writings of James Joyce*. Ed. Ellsworth Mason and Richard Ellmann. New York: Viking, 1959. 68–72.

——. *Dubliners.* 1914. Ed. Margot Norris. New York: Norton, 2006.

——. *Finnegans Wake.* 1939. New York: Penguin, 1988.

——. "The Holy Office." 1904. *The Critical Writings of James Joyce.* Ed. Ellsworth Mason and Richard Ellmann. New York: Viking Press, 1959. 149–52.

——. *Letters of James Joyce.* Vol. 1. Ed. Stuart Gilbert. New York: Viking, 1957; reissued with corrections 1966. Vols. 2 and 3. Ed. Richard Ellmann. New York: Viking, 1966.

——. *A Portrait of the Artist as a Young Man.* 1916. New York: Viking, 1964.

——. *Stephen Hero.* Ed. John J. Slocum and Herbert Cahoon. New York: New Directions, 1944.

——. *Ulysses.* 1922. Ed. Hans Walter Gabler et al. New York and London: Garland, 1984.

Jordan-Smith, Paul. *On Strange Altars.* New York: Albert & Charles Boni, 1924.

Kant, Immanuel. *Critique of Judgment.* 1;'790. Trans. J. H. Bernard. New York: Hafner, 1951.

Kaplan, Carola M. and Anne B. Simpson, eds. *Seeing Double: Revisioning Edwardian and Modernist Literature.* New York: St. Martin's Press, 1996.

Kelley, Rev. Bennet, C.P. *The New Saint Joseph Baltimore Catechism.* New York: Catholic Book Publishing Co., 1969.

Kenner, Hugh. *A Sinking Island.* London: Barrie & Jenkins, 1987.

Keynes, John Maynard. *The Collected Writings of John Maynard Keynes.* 30 vols. London: Macmillan, 1971–89.

Kinkead-Weekes, Mark. "The Marriage of Opposites in *The Rainbow*." *D. H. Lawrence: Centenary Essays.* Ed. Mara Kalnins. Bristol: Bristol Classic Press, 1986. 21–39.

Kranidis, Rita. *Subversive Discourse.* New York: St. Martin's Press, 1995.

Kurtz, Lester R. *The Politics of Heresy: The Modernist Crisis in Roman Catholicism.* Berkeley: University of California Press, 1986.

Lafourcade, Georges. *Swinburne: A Literary Biography.* New York: William Morrow, 1932.

Laird, J. T. *The Shaping of Tess of the d'Urbervilles.* Oxford: Clarendon Press, 1975.

Laroque, François. "Hallowe'en Customs in 'Clay': A Study of James Joyce's Use of Folklore in *Dubliners.*" *Cahiers Victoriens et Edouardiens* 14 (October 1981): 47–56.

Lawrence, D. H. *The Letters of D. H. Lawrence.* 8 Vols. Ed. James T. Boulton. Cambridge: Cambridge University Press, 1979–2000.

——. "Morality and the Novel." *Phoenix: The Posthumous Papers of D. H. Lawrence.* Ed. Edward D. McDonald. New York: Viking, 1936. 527–32.

——. *The Rainbow.* 1915. New York: Penguin, 1995.

——. *Study of Thomas Hardy and Other Essays.* Ed. Bruce Steele. Cambridge University Press, 1985.

——. "Surgery for the Novel—or a Bomb." 1923. *Phoenix: The Posthumous Papers of D. H. Lawrence.* Ed. Edward D. McDonald. New York: Viking, 1936. 517–20.

——. *Women in Love.* 1920. New York: Penguin, 1983.

Leavis, Q. D. *Fiction and the Reading Public.* 1932. London: Chatto and Windus, 1965.

Lerner, Laurence and John Holmstrom, eds. *Thomas Hardy and His Readers.* New York: Barnes and Noble, 1968.

Levenson, Michael. *A Genealogy of Modernism: A Study of English Literary Doctrine 1908–1922.* Cambridge: Cambridge University Press, 1984.

Levy, Paul. *Moore: G. E. Moore and the Cambridge Apostles.* New York: Holt, Rinehart and Winston, 1979.

Lubenow, W. C. *The Cambridge Apostles, 1820–1914: Liberalism, Imagination, and Friendship in British Intellectual and Professional Life.* Cambridge: Cambridge University Press, 1998.

Lynch, Denis, Rev. *St. Joan: The Life-Story of the Maid of Orleans*. New York: Benzinger Brothers, 1919.

MacCarthy, Desmond. "The Post-Impressionists." *A Bloomsbury Group Reader*. Ed. S. P. Rosenbaum. Oxford: Blackwell, 1993. 97–101.

Magalaner, Marvin and Richard M. Kain. "Virgin and Witch." *James Joyce's Dubliners: A Critical Handbook*. Ed. James R. Baker and Thomas F. Staley. Belmont, CA: Wadsworth Publishing, 1969. 124–29.

Marinetti, Filippo Tommaso. *Marinetti; Selected Writings*. Ed. R. W. Flint. Trans. R. W. Flint and Arthur A. Coppotelli. New York: Farrar, Straus and Giroux, 1972.

Marsh, Joss. *Word Crimes: Blasphemy, Culture, and Literature in Nineteenth-Century England*. University of Chicago Press, 1998.

McHugh, Roland. *Annotations to Finnegans Wake*. Rev. ed. Baltimore and London: Johns Hopkins University Press, 1991.

McNeillie, Andrew. "Bloomsbury." *The Cambridge Companion to Virginia Woolf*. Ed. Sue Roe and Susan Sellers. Cambridge University Press, 2000. 1–28.

McTaggart, John. *Dare To Be Wise*. London: Watts, 1910.

Miller, J. Hillis. *Fiction and Repetition*. Cambridge: Harvard University Press, 1982.

Moore, G. E. *Principia Ethica*. 1903. Cambridge: Cambridge University Press, 1960.

More, Adelyne [C. K. Ogden]. *Fecundity versus Civilisation*. London: George Allen & Unwin, 1917.

Newman, Robert D. "Bloom and the Beast: Joyce's Use of Bruno's Astrological Allegory." *New Alliances in Joyce Studies: "When it's aped to foul a Delfian."* Ed. Bonnie Kime Scott. Newark, DE: University of Delaware Press, 1988. 210–16.

Nietzsche, Friedrich. *The Birth of Tragedy*. 1872. Trans. Clifton P. Fadiman. New York: Dover Publications, 1995.

Norris, Christopher. "Introduction: Empson as literary theorist: from Ambiguity to Complex Words and beyond." *William Empson: The Critical Achievement*. Ed. Christopher Norris and Nigel Mapp. Cambridge: Cambridge University Press, 1993. 1–120.

——. *William Empson and the Philosophy of Literary Criticism*. London: Athlone Press, 1978.

O'Donnell, R. M. *Keynes: Philosophy, Economics, and Politics*. New York: St. Martin's Press, 1989.

Ogden, C. K., trans. "Anna Livia Plurabelle." By James Joyce. *Psyche* 12.2 (October 1931): 92–96.

Odgen, C. K. *Basic English: International Second Language*. New York: Harcourt, 1968.

——. "Can Basic English Be a World Language?" *Picture Post* 23 (October 1943): 23–25.

——. Editorial. *Psyche* 10.2 (October 1929): 1–38.

——. "G. K. Chesterton—An Impression." *Gownsman* 3.55 (November 25, 1911): 195–96.

——. *Jeremy Bentham, 1832–2032; being the Bentham centenary lecture*. London: Kegan Paul, Trench, Trubner & Co., 1932.

——. "Mr. Bernard Shaw as Heretic." *Gownsman* 2.47 (June 3, 1911): 669–70.

——. "Penultimata." *Psyche* 10.3 (Spring 1930): 1–28.

——. Preface. *Tales Told of Shem and Shaun*. By James Joyce. Paris: Black Sun Press, 1929. i–xv.

——. *The System of Basic English*. New York: Harcourt, 1934.

——. "The Universal Language." *Psyche* 9.3 (January 1929): 1–9.

Orwell, George. *The Complete Works of George Orwell*. 20 vols. London: Secker & Warburg, 1997.

——. *Nineteen Eighty-Four.* 1949. New York: Signet, 1984.

Owens, Cóilín. "'Clay' (1): Irish Folklore." *James Joyce Quarterly.* 27.2 (Winter 1990): 337–52.

The Oxford Study Bible. Ed. M. Jack Suggs, Katharine Doob Sakenfield, and James R. Mueller. New York: Oxford University Press, 1992.

Parkes, Adam. *Modernism and the Theater of Censorship.* New York: Oxford University Press, 1996.

Pater, Walter. *Gaston de Latour: The Revised Text.* 1896. Ed. Gerald Monsman. Greensboro, NC: ELT Press, 1995.

——. "Poems by William Morris." *Westminster Review* 34 (October 1868): 300–312.

——. *The Renaissance: Studies in Art and Poetry.* 4th ed. 1893. Ed. Donald L. Hill. Berkeley: University of California Press, 1980.

Pearce, Joseph. *Wisdom and Innocence: A Life of G. K. Chesterton.* London: Hodder and Stoughton, 1996.

Perloff, Marjorie. "Modernist Studies." *Redrawing the Boundaries.* Ed. Stephen Greenblatt and Giles Gunn. New York: MLA, 1992. 154–78.

Peterson, Carla. "*Jude the Obscure:* The Return of the Pagan." *Jude the Obscure.* Ed. Penny Boumelha. New York: St. Martin's Press, 2000. 75–94.

Picciotto, Cyril M. *St. Paul's School.* London: Blackie and Son, 1939.

——. "Via Mystica." Cambridge: Heffer and Sons, 1910.

Pound, Ezra. "The Teacher's Mission." *Literary Essays.* Ed. T. S. Eliot. New York: New Directions, 1968.

Raven, Charles. *A Wanderer's Way.* New York: Henry Holt, 1929.

Richards, I. A. "Co-Author of the 'Meaning of Meaning.'" *C. K. Ogden: A Collective Memoir.* Ed. P. Sargant Florence and J. R. L. Anderson. London: Elek Pemberton, 1977. 96–109.

——. *Principles of Literary Criticism.* 1925. New York: Harcourt, 1961.

——. *Science and Poetry.* London: Kegan Paul, 1926.

Richards, I. A., C. K. Ogden, and James Woods. *The Foundations of Aesthetics.* 1922. New York: Lear Publishers, 1925.

Riquelme, John Paul. "Echoic Language, Uncertainty, and Freedom in *Tess of the d'Urbervilles.*" *Tess of the d'Urbervilles.* Ed. John Paul Riquelme. Boston: Bedford, 1998. 506–20.

Robertson, J. M. *Mr. Shaw and "The Maid."* London: Cobden-Sanderson, 1926.

Rose, Danis, ed. *Finnegans Wake: A Facsimile of Book I, Chapter 5.* Vol. 34. New York and London: Garland Publishing, 1978.

Rose, Jonathan. *The Edwardian Temperament, 1895–1919.* Athens, OH: Ohio University Press, 1986.

Rosenbaum, S. P., ed. *The Bloomsbury Group: A Collection of Memoirs, Commentary and Criticism.* Toronto: University of Toronto Press, 1975.

——. *Edwardian Bloomsbury.* Vol. 2. New York: St. Martin's Press, 1994.

Russell, Bertrand. *The Autobiography of Bertrand Russell, 1872–1914.* London: Allen and Unwin, 1967.

——. *The Collected Papers of Bertrand Russell.* 16 Vols. to date. Ed. Kenneth Blackwell et al. Boston and London: Allen and Unwin, 1983–.

Russell, Dora. "My Friend Ogden." *C. K. Ogden: A Collective Memoir.* Ed. P. Sargant Florence and J. R. L. Anderson. London: Elek Pemberton, 1977. 82–95.

——. *The Tamarisk Tree.* New York: Putnam, 1975.

Sailer, Susan Shaw. "Universalizing Languages: *Finnegans Wake* Meets Basic English." *James Joyce Quarterly* 36.4 (Summer 1999): 853–68.

Schorer, Mark. "Fiction and the 'Analogical Matrix.'" 1948. *The World We Imagine*. New York: Farrar, Straus and Giroux, 1968. 24–45.

Scott, Nathan A., Jr. *The Poetics of Belief*. Chapel Hill: University of North Carolina Press, 1985.

Seiler, R. M. *Walter Pater: The Critical Heritage*. London: Routledge & Kegan Paul, 1980.

Selwyn, Edward. *Tradition and Reason*. Cambridge: Bowes and Bowes, 1911.

Shakespeare, William. *Hamlet. The Riverside Shakespeare*. Ed. G. Blakemore Evans. Boston: Houghton Mifflin, 1974.

Sharp, William. *The Pagan Review* 1:1 (August 1892).

Shattuck, Sandra D. "The Stage of Scholarship: Crossing the Bridge from Harrison to Woolf." *Virginia Woolf and Bloomsbury*. Ed. Jane Marcus. Bloomington: Indiana University Press, 1987. 278–98.

Shaw, Bernard. "The Chesterbelloc: A Lampoon." 1908. *The Collected Works of Bernard Shaw*. Vol. XXIX. New York: Wise and Company, 1932.

———. *Man and Superman*. 1903. Baltimore, MD: Penguin, 1964.

———. "On Miracles: A Retort." 1908. *Shaw on Religion*. Ed. Warren Sylvester Smith. New York: Dodd, Mead and Co., 1967.

———. Postscript. *Back to Methuselah*. London and New York: Oxford, 1945.

———. *Pygmalion*. 1913. New York: Signet, 1980.

———. "The Religion of the Future." Cambridge: The Heretics, 1911.

———. *Saint Joan*. 1924. London: Penguin, 2003.

Shklovsky, Viktor. "Art as Technique." 1917. *Contemporary Literary Criticism: Literary and Cultural Studies*. Ed. Robert Con Davis and Ronald Schleifer. New York: Longman, 1994. 260–72.

Spirit, Jane. "Nineteenth-Century Responses to Montaigne and Bruno: A Context for Pater." *Pater in the 1990s*. Ed. Laurel Brake and Ian Small. Greensboro, NC: ELT Press, 1991. 217–27.

Stewart, Garrett. "Lawrence, 'Being,' and the Allotropic Style." *Novel* 9.3 (Spring 1976): 217–42.

Stewart, Jessie. *Jane Ellen Harrison: A Portrait from Letters*. London: Merlin Press, 1959.

Strachey, Lytton. "Art and Indecency." *The Really Interesting Question and other papers*. Ed. Paul Levy. New York: Coward, McCann & Geoghegan, 1972. 82–90.

Swinburne, Algernon. *The Complete Works of Algernon Charles Swinburne*. Ed. Edmund Gosse and Thomas James Wise. 20 vols. London: Heinemann, 1925.

"Those in Authority." 1929. *Critical Essays on William Empson*. Ed. John Constable. Hants, England: Scolar Press, 1993. 15–16.

Torchiara, Donald T. *Backgrounds for Joyce's Dubliners*. Boston: Allen & Unwin, 1986.

Trevelyan, G. M. *De Haeretico Comburendo*. Cambridge: Heffer and Sons, 1914.

Trewin, J. C. *Sybil Thorndike*. London: Rockliff, 1955.

Turner, Frank M. *The Greek Heritage in Victorian Britain*. New Haven: Yale University Press, 1981.

Tyson, Brian. *The Story of Shaw's Saint Joan*. Kingston, Ontario: McGill-Queen's University Press, 1982.

Vaihinger, Hans. *The Philosophy of "As If."* 1911. Trans. C. K. Ogden. London: Routledge, 1924.

Weintraub, Stanley, ed. *Saint Joan: Fifty Years After*. Baton Rouge: Louisiana State University Press, 1973.

Wells, H. G. *After Democracy*. London: Watts, 1932.

———. *The Shape of Things to Come*. New York: Macmillan, 1933.

Weston, Jessie L. 1920. *From Ritual to Romance*. New York: Doubleday, 1957.

Wilde, Oscar. *The Picture of Dorian Gray.* 1891. New York: Bantam, 1982.

———. "The Sphinx." 1894. *Poetry of the Victorian Period.* Ed. Jerome Buckley and George Woods. New York: Harper Collins, 1965. 820–24.

Williams, Raymond. *Drama from Ibsen to Eliot.* London: Chatto and Windus, 1952.

Wilson, Edwin H. *The Genesis of a Humanist Manifesto.* Ed. Teresa Maciocha. Amherst, NY: Humanist Press, 1995.

Wittgenstein, Ludwig. "A Lecture on Ethics." *The Philosophical Review* 74.1 (January 1965): 3–16.

Wood, Alan. *Bertrand Russell: The Passionate Skeptic.* London: Allen and Unwin, 1957.

Wood, H. G. and J. M. Robertson. *The Historicity of Jesus: Being a Contribution to the "Christ-Myth" Controversy.* Cambridge Daily News, 1912.

Woodward, Kenneth L. *Making Saints.* New York: Simon and Schuster, 1990.

Woolf, Leonard. *Sowing: An Autobiography of the Years 1880 to 1904.* New York: Harcourt, 1960.

Woolf, Virginia. "Character in Fiction." *The Essays of Virginia Woolf.* Ed. Andrew McNeillie. London: Hogarth Press, 1988. 420–38.

———. "Character in Fiction." *The Essays of Virginia Woolf.* Appendix III. Ed. Andrew McNeillie. London: Hogarth Press, 1988. 502–17.

———. *The Diary of Virginia Woolf.* Ed. Anne Oliver Bell. Vol. 2. New York: Harcourt, 1978.

———. *Jacob's Room.* 1922. New York: Harcourt, 1990.

———. *The Letters of Virginia Woolf.* Ed. Nigel Nicolson and Joanne Trautmann. Vol. 3. New York: Harcourt, 1977.

———. *A Room of One's Own.* 1929. Frogmore, Herts: Granada, 1981.

———. "A Sketch of the Past." *Moments of Being.* Ed. Jeanne Schulkind. New York: Harcourt, 1976. 61–137.

———. *To the Lighthouse.* 1927. New York: Harcourt, 1989.

———. *The Voyage Out.* 1915. New York: Harcourt, 1948.

Index

Titles of individual works are listed under the name of the author.